PHILLIP HELLWEGE

A History of Tontines in Germany

Comparative Studies
in the History of Insurance Law

Studien zur vergleichenden Geschichte
des Versicherungsrechts

Edited by / Herausgegeben von
Prof. Dr. Phillip Hellwege

Volume / Band 3

A History of Tontines in Germany

From a multi-purpose financial product to a single-purpose pension product

By

Phillip Hellwege

Duncker & Humblot · Berlin

The project 'A Comparative History of Insurance Law in Europe'
has received funding from the European Research Council (ERC) under
the European Union's Horizon 2020 research and innovation programme
(grant agreement No. 647019).

European Research Council
Established by the European Commission

Bibliographic information of the German national library

The German national library registers this publication in
the German national bibliography; specified bibliographic data
are retrievable on the Internet about http://dnb.d-nb.de.

Printing: CPI buchbücher.de GmbH, Birkach

Printed in Germany

ISSN 2625-638X (Print) / ISSN 2625-6398 (Online)

ISBN 978-3-428-15616-0 (Print)
ISBN 978-3-428-55616-8 (E-Book)
ISBN 978-3-428-85616-9 (Print & E-Book)

Printed on no aging resistant (non-acid) paper
according to ISO 9706 ♾

Preface

The present volume is the third volume of a research project on a Comparative History of Insurance Law in Europe (CHILE). CHILE has received funding from the European Research Council (ERC) under the European Union's Horizon 2020 research and innovation programme (grant agreement No. 647019). I would like to thank the many archives, which I have consulted and visited, for their cooperation and help. Furthermore, my thanks go to the participants of a conference on tontines in November 2016 in Augsburg for the fruitful discussions and to the participants of discussion groups at Edinburgh Law School, the Institute of European and Comparative Law (University of Oxford), the Max Planck Institute for Comparative and International Private Law (Hamburg), and the Max Planck Institute for European Legal History (Frankfurt) for their comments on different stages of work in progress. Finally, I would like to thank Michael Friedman for his critical comments on an earlier draft of this volume and for correcting the English.

Augsburg, July 2018 *Phillip Hellwege*

Contents

A. Introduction

In 1653, Lorenzo Tonti (1602–1684), an Italian who lived in France, proposed to Cardinal Mazarin (1602–1661) a financial product which was later named after him: tontines.

I. A modern definition of tontines

Tonti's proposal can be described as a pooled life annuity scheme and modern literature defines tontines accordingly:[1]

> A tontine ... is a financial scheme under which a group of people invest in a closed fund. Each contract is based on the life of a person duly named ... At the end of each year, the interest on the principal (the annuities) is paid by the tontine issuer to the investors ... with surviving members sharing the annuities due to deceased members. Thus, surviving members enjoy an increase of their annual income ...

Accordingly, a number of investors (e.g. 100) each pay the same sum (e.g. 100 Euro) to the issuer. The issuer in turn promises to pay interest (e.g. 5% per annum) on the raised capital (10,000 Euro) as annuities in such a way that the total sum of annuities (500 Euro) is each year shared between the surviving annuitants. The heirs of deceased annuitants, thus, have no rights in the tontine. Rather, the rights of deceased annuitants accrue to the surviving annuitants. As long as all annuitants are still alive, each will receive the interest on his or her investment as annuities (5 Euro). The higher the number of annuitants of the pool who have died, the higher the share of each surviving annuitant, until the last surviving annuitant receives the total of all annuities (500 Euro per annum based on an original investment of 100 Euro). With the death of the last annuitant the issuer's obligation to pay annuities terminates, and the issuer is allowed to keep the raised capital. He does not have to repay the capital – neither to the investors nor to the annuitants nor to their heirs. The issuer's only obligation is to pay interest on the raised capital until the last surviving annuitant has died.

However, it has to be stressed right from the outset that this is a modern description of tontines. With a life annuity, the capital is lost to the issuer – in the sense that the issuer does not have to repay the capital – and the obligation to pay annuities terminates once the annuitant dies. Thus, if a tontine is described as a pooled life annuity, it follows that the capital in the tontine is similarly lost to the

[1] *Gallais-Hamonno* and *Rietsch*, Financial Engineering, 50.

issuer and that the obligation to pay annuities terminates once the last annuitant dies. Yet, as will be observed further below, the term tontine has in the past been used more loosely to denominate a number of different financial schemes. Many of them could indeed be described as pooled life annuity schemes. Others were annuity lotteries or even simple lotteries. Others were saving schemes, and with these the capital was not lost to the issuer, it instead being split between the surviving members after a fixed period of time. Finally, many schemes were some kind of a hybrid form falling between these different financial products.

Thus, a tontine could serve different functions. If it took the form of a pooled life annuity, the investor could utilize it as a pension product: the longer he or she lived, the higher were his or her chances to outlive the other annuitants and the higher were his or her chances to an increase in disbursed annuities. Alternatively the investor could utilize a tontine as a means to provide for dependants: the investor and the annuitant did not have to be the same person.[2] The investor could make his or her investment for the benefit of a spouse or children so that they would, with good fortune, receive an increasing pension. If the issuer was under no obligation to repay the capital, i.e. if the capital was lost to him, then he could use a tontine as a means to raise capital. By contrast, if a tontine was a saving scheme, the issuer could not use it as a means to raise capital as he had to repay the capital to the investors.

II. The occurrence of tontines in German-speaking territories

Tonti's original plan of 1653 to issue a tontine in France failed.[3] It is generally thought that the first tontines were successfully issued in Dutch cities starting with the city of Kampen in 1670 and the cities of Amsterdam and Groningen in 1671, with France to follow in 1689 and England in 1692.[4] Modern literature mentions that the Danish state unsuccessfully tried to issue a tontine as early as 1653 – the same year in which Tonti proposed his idea to Mazarin.[5] It is claimed that the Dutch tontines can be attributed to Tonti: he had stayed in Amsterdam

---

[2] In detail see the text corresponding to n. 119, below.

[3] *Rietsch* and *Gallais-Hamonno*, Lorenzo Tonti, 19 ff.

[4] *Krünitz*, Encyclopädie LXXI (1796), 288; *Du Pasquier*, (1910) 46 Zeitschrift für Schweizerische Statistik 490, 497; *von Zedtwitz*, 140; *P. Koch*, Tontinengeschäft, 28; *Directie van de Algemeene Maatschappij van Levensverzekering en Lijfrente*, 264–281; *Laspeyres*, 250 f.; *Gelderblom* and *Jonker*, 90 f.; *Schöpfer*, 130; *Braun*, Geschichte, 64–66. On the developments in the Netherlands, France, and England see *Sirks*, 121 ff.; *Delbrel*, 109 ff.; *Macleod*, 143 ff.; *Gallais-Hamonno* and *Rietsch*, Financial Engineering, 49 ff.

[5] *Du Pasquier*, (1910) 46 Zeitschrift für Schweizerische Statistik 491–493; *Braun*, Geschichte, 152 f., 222. *Falck* (1838), 618 n. 94, suggests that the tontine of 1653 was actually issued. On the developments in Scandinavia see *Sunnqvist*, 153 ff.

prior to the year of 1653.[6] The Danish plan of 1653 was proposed by Poul Klingenberg (1615–1690). While modern literature claims that Tonti and Klingenberg had met in Amsterdam,[7] Martin Sunnqvist convincingly argues that they only had indirect contact.[8]

According to modern literature, Germany saw its first tontine in 1698 in Prussia. Tontines reached their apex in the 18th century. Yet even for the 18th century, modern literature refers to only a small number of tontines, in total around ten. In the early 19th century they are said to have been replaced by modern life insurance products. It is argued that by the end of the 19th century the view was predominant that tontines were not an insurance transaction but a form of gambling. Modern German literature contends that life insurance companies were consequently prohibited from issuing tontines.[9] With the implementation of the Second European Life Insurance Directive of 1990,[10] the German *Versicherungsaufsichtsgesetz* (Insurance Regulation Act) of 1901 was adapted in 1994 and life insurance companies were again allowed to operate tontines.[11] Nevertheless, tontines have failed to again gain prominence in Germany.[12] Thus, in Germany tontines are looked upon as a purely historical phenomenon, and they rarely receive coverage in today's insurance law literature.[13]

III. Tontines and the history of life insurance

Thus, it seems as if the immediate practical importance of tontines was limited to the 18th century. Nevertheless, modern German-language literature stresses

---

[6] See, however, the discussion of *Sirks* 125 f.; *Hellwege*, Comparative Analysis, 385 ff.

[7] *Braun*, Geschichte, 64, 222.

[8] *Sunnqvist*, 158 ff.

[9] *P. Koch*, Tontinengeschäft, 29.

[10] Council Directive 90/619/EEC of 8 November 1990 on the coordination of laws, regulations and administrative provisions relating to direct life assurance, 29 Nov. 1990, 50–61.

[11] *P. Koch*, Tontinengeschäft, 29; *Zetzsche*, 287; *Heidel*, 67.

[12] *Heiss* and *Mönnich*, in: Münchener Kommentar zum VVG II, Vor § 150 para. 17; *Wagner*, 654; *Lux*, 29; *Heidel*, 67.

[13] See the short accounts in: *Heiss* and *Mönnich*, in: Münchener Kommentar zum VVG II, Vor § 150 paras. 4, 17; *P. Koch* and *Weiss*, 836; *von Fürstenwerth* and *Weiß*, 637; *Lux*, 29; *Schneider*, in: Prölss/Martin, Vorbemerkung zu §§ 150–171 para. 13; *Winter*, in: Bruck/Möller, Einf. para. 112–114; *idem*, Versicherungsaufsichtsrecht, 449–451; *Schwintowski*, in: Honsell, Berliner Kommentar, Vorbem. §§ 159–178 para. 14; *Nebel*, in: Honsell, Art. 101 para. 7; *Braumüller*, 62; *Kaulbach*, in: idem, § 1 para. 84; *Präve*, in: Kölschbach, Prölss, § 1 paras. 14–17; *R. Schmidt*, in: idem, Prölss, § 1 paras. 77–78; *Grote*, in: Münchener Kommentar zum Versicherungsvertragsgesetz III, AufsichtsR para. 188; *Ortmann* and *Rubin*, in: Schwintowski and Brömmelmeyer, Vor §§ 150 para. 9.

that tontines had a lasting impact on the development of life insurance. Heinrich Braun (1878–1949) argued that:[14]

> Das Tontinenwesen … hat den Versicherungsgedanken verbreitet und weite Kreise für die Lebensversicherung reif gemacht.
>
> Tontines ... helped spread the idea of insurance and made wider circles receptive for the idea of life insurance.

Others add that tontines were forerunners of pension schemes[15] and that they were important for the further development of mortality tables and actuarial science.[16] With respect to legal developments, Hans-Martin Oberholzer claims:[17]

> Dadurch, dass den Tontinen … ein so grosser Erfolg beschieden war, sahen sich die Staaten schon früh gezwungen, gesetzgebungsmässig gegen die gröbsten Auswüchse vorzugehen und so das Fundament für unser heutiges Versicherungsrecht zu legen. Eine Folge dieser Versicherungsgesetzgebungen war die Herausbildung von vertrauenswürdigen Versicherungsanstalten.
>
> Due to the fact that tontines … were such a great success, national legislators felt impelled at an early stage to intervene with respect to their greatest defects. Thereby they laid the basis for today's insurance law. A consequence of this insurance legislation was the creation of trustworthy insurance companies.

Or in the words of Gunter Kürble, who focuses more on the design of the different insurance products rather than on their legal development:[18]

> Der Weg zu einem funktionierenden Lebens- und Rentenversicherungsmarkt war die Krankengeschichte (Anamnese) der Tontine.
>
> The path towards a functioning life and pension insurance market was the patient history (anamnesis) of the tontine.

And L. Gustav Du Pasquier summarizes:[19]

> Die Tontinen haben in der Entwicklung des Versicherungswesens eine ausserordentlich wichtige Rolle gespielt.
>
> Tontines played an extraordinarily important role for the development of insurance.

---

[14] *Braun*, Urkunden und Materialien, 100. See also *idem*, Geschichte, 69; *Schöpfer*, 142; *von Zedtwitz*, 142 f.; *Roloff*, 293 f.; *Oberholzer*, 91; *Du Pasquier*, (1910) 46 Zeitschrift für Schweizerische Statistik 484; *Fuchs*, 21 f.

[15] *P. Koch* and *Weiss*, 836.

[16] *P. Koch*, Geschichte der Versicherungswissenschaft, 34–36; *von Zedtwitz*, 142; *Braun*, Geschichte, 69; *R. Schmidt*, Versicherungsalphabet, 346; *Roloff*, 294; *Oberholzer*, 91; *Du Pasquier*, (1910) 46 Zeitschrift für Schweizerische Statistik 484; *Schöpfer*, 143.

[17] *Oberholzer*, 91. See also *Du Pasquier*, (1910) 46 Zeitschrift für Schweizerische Statistik 484.

[18] *Kürble*, (1990) 79 Zeitschrift für die gesamte Versicherungswissenschaft 598.

[19] *Du Pasquier*, (1910) 46 Zeitschrift für Schweizerische Statistik 484. See also *Oberholzer*, 91; *Manes*, 5.

Even though the extraordinary importance of tontines for the development of insurance has been stressed, there is relatively little literature covering the history of tontines. Further, this literature asserts rather than proves the importance of tontines. But how could a financial instrument – which seems to have been issued only around ten times in Germany – have been of such great importance? And how can Oberholzer claim that tontines were a 'great success'? There seems to be an inherent tension in the coverage of tontines in modern literature. Moreover, modern literature does not resolve this tension. Many works on the history of insurance simply refer to the fact that tontines existed, assert their importance, claim that they have to be put into the context of the history of life insurance, and describe, in general terms, how tontines technically functioned.[20] A detailed analysis of the occurrence of tontines, their importance, their legal aspects, and their impact on the history of insurance (law) is still missing.

IV. Lorenzo Tonti and the origins of tontines

There are further unresolved questions concerning Lorenzo Tonti (1602–1684) and the origin of tontines. It is generally believed that Tonti made his proposal in 1653; one author, however, claims that it was in 1644.[21] German literature often suggests that Tonti lived from 1630 to 1695,[22] but both dates are contested, and often he is referred to as a banker or a medical doctor. Tonti is frequently named as the inventor of tontines.[23] Yet it is generally acknowledged that Tonti was at least inspired by transactions which were already known in Italy prior to 1653. Some authors even claim that tontines had already been proposed to Louis XIII, who was born in 1601 and reigned from 1610 to 1643.[24] Other authors argue or suspect that tontines were invented by the Venetians or – more generally – that they were already known of in Italy.[25] It is their assertion that Tonti only brought them with him to France. Many authors refer in this context to the institutions of *Montes pietatis*, *Monte delle doti*, and *Monte del matrimonio* as models for tontines.[26] Again others argue that tontines were also known in Germany prior to Tonti's proposal, at least since the 16th century, and, indeed,

[20] See, e.g., *Schug*, 245 f.

[21] *Kürble*, (1990) 79 Zeitschrift für die gesamte Versicherungswissenschaft 592.

[22] See, e.g., *Ogris*, HRG V, 276 f.

[23] See, e.g., *Ogris*, HRG V, 276.

[24] *Marperger* (1715), 259. Similar *Schmitt-Lermann*, 64.

[25] *Zedler*, Universal-Lexicon XLIV (1745), 1250; *Seyberth* (1768), 18 f.; *Bergius* (1771), 149; *Krünitz*, Encyclopädie LXXI (1796), 214; *Danz* (1797), 328.

[26] *Pöhls* (1842), 68; *P. Koch*, Tontinengeschäft, 28; *Roloff*, 294; *Oberholzer*, 84; *von Zedtwitz*, 142. See also *Fortunati*, 205.

Montes pietatis were discussed during that century in Germany.[27] Others argue that tontines are nothing but a variation of the life annuity schemes which had long been known in the Netherlands and Germany.[28] Thus, it is an open question as to just what Tonti's innovation was.[29]

V. The objectives of the present volume

The present state of research on tontines thus leaves us in confusion. A detailed analysis of the origins of tontines, their occurrence, their importance, their legal aspects, and their impact on the history of insurance (law) is still missing. The objective of the present volume is to fill some of these gaps with respect to the developments in Germany.

The present volume is the third volume of a research project on a 'Comparative History of Insurance Law in Europe'. The point of departure of this project is the observation that the history of insurance law in Europe is in need of being re-told:[30] most importantly, there are distinct national narratives of insurance (legal) history, and these narratives create the impression of insurance (law) having developed – with the exception of maritime insurance – differently in the individual European countries. To test the present state of research, the project aims to concentrate on what I have called possible points of interaction between the national developments of insurance law in Europe. The research agenda is fully elaborated in the first volume of the project.[31] One of these possible points of interaction is the financial instrument of tontines. Tontines were issued in basically all European countries and beyond. Yet, with the exception of the Netherlands,[32] they have not received an in-depth historical analysis in any of these countries. And this raises the dual questions of whether they had a similar impact on the history of insurance (law) in each of the different European countries and what this impact exactly was.

A comparative analysis of the history of tontines may serve also another purpose: against the background of the current and continuing low-interest phase, it

---

[27] Compare *Lehr* and *von Heckel* (1901), 128; *Du Pasquier*, (1910) 46 Zeitschrift für Schweizerische Statistik 485, discussing Georg Obrecht (1547–1612) and Berthold Holzschuher (1511–1582).

[28] *Lehner*, 18.

[29] *Du Pasquier*, (1909) 54 Vierteljahresschrift der naturforschenden Gesellschaft in Zürich 217.

[30] *Hellwege*, (2014) 131 Zeitschrift der Savigny-Stiftung für Rechtsgeschichte (Germanistische Abteilung) 226–265; *idem*, (2016) 56 American Journal of Legal History 66–75.

[31] *Hellwege*, Introduction, 17 ff.

[32] See especially, *Wagenvoort*, passim. On the literature and on the developments in the Netherlands see also *Sirks*, 121 ff.

has recently been argued that tontine products should be re-launched as pension products of the future.[33] To fully understand the reasons why tontines went out fashion and why they were banned in some countries is essential in such a debate.

In order to explore the history of tontines from comparative perspectives I organized a conference featuring participants from different European countries and beyond. The results of that conference are published in the second volume of the research project.[34] The present volume developed from my own contribution to that volume.[35] I quickly observed that there is much more to write on tontines in German-speaking territories than the space of a conference volume permits. The present volume develops a detailed analysis of the occurrence of tontines, their importance, their legal aspects, and their impact on the history of insurance (law) in German-speaking territories.

Thus, the focus of the present volume is restricted to the importance and impact which tontines had in German-speaking territories. I will not deal with any details of Tonti's vita. And I will only discuss how the idea of tontines came to Germany, refraining from analysing in general what Tonti's innovation really was. Both aspects have been dealt with by different authors in the aforementioned conference volume.[36] Two further points concerning the focus of the present volume and two further editorial points need to be made explicit right from the beginning:

(1) For reasons of simplification I have chosen as title for the present volume 'A History of Tontines in Germany'. By contrast, in the last paragraphs I have spoken of 'German-speaking territories'. Below, I will discuss, for example, four Gdańsk tontines. Today *Danzig* (Gdańsk) is Polish, and in 1657 when the first Gdańsk tontine was issued it was an autonomous city under the Polish crown.[37] It was not German. The reason why I have, nevertheless, included these tontines in the present study is simply because the materials on the Gdańsk tontines are in the German language and because the city of *Danzig* (Gdańsk) was at the time predominantly German-speaking. To me it seemed, and this is the only reason for including the Gdańsk tontines in the present volume, straightforward to put these tontines into the context of the development of tontines in other German-speaking territories.

---

[33] See the discussions of *Milevsky*, 307 ff.; *Weinert*, 317 ff.; *Forman* and *Sabin*, 329 ff.

[34] Hellwege (ed.), The Past, Present, and Future of Tontines, passim.

[35] *Hellwege*, Tontines in German-speaking Territories, 167 ff.

[36] On Tonti's life see *Rietsch* and *Gallais-Hamonno*, Lorenzo Tonti, 19 ff. On the origins of tontines see *Hellwege*, Comparative Analysis, 383 ff.; *idem*, Tontines in German-speaking Territories, 169 ff.; *McKeever*, Tontines in Portugal, 193 ff.; *Fortunati*, 213.

[37] *Loew*, 112; *Böttcher*, 34–45; 'Danzig', in: Brockhaus Enzyklopädie online (accessed on 12 June 2017).

(2) As the present volume is part of a project on the history of insurance law, my focus is on the legal aspects of tontines and on their impact on insurance law. However, before it is possible to present a legal analysis of tontines (below E), it is necessary to develop an understanding of the origins of tontines in German-speaking territories and in particular their factual occurrence (below B), their designs (below C), and the different purposes they served (below D). Even though the discussion of these questions takes up about two-thirds of the present volume, these questions were not my main focus. Their answer is only the basis for discussing the legal aspects which are my main interest. For that reason, the present volume still leaves room for further research on tontines from the perspectives of social history and financial history.

(3) The present volume focuses on tontines in German-speaking territories. Thus, I assume that the readership will be mostly German. Nevertheless, the book is published in English. As a service to German readers, I have given for all cities, territories, principalities, and regions of the then German-speaking world not only the English names but also the German names as some English translations will be unfamiliar to the German readership and could, thus, lead to confusion. For reasons of coherence I have included the German names in all cases, even for those cities, territories, principalities, and regions where the translation is obvious and even for those cities which are today outside Germany, which are no longer German-speaking, and which hence today have non-German names.

(4) The present volume focuses on the development of tontines. As a service to the reader, I have included for most historical protagonists whom I mention in the main text their dates of birth and death. I have not included these dates for modern authors. Furthermore, I have included for the historical literature, which I refer to in the footnotes, the dates of publication. Again, I have not included these dates for modern literature. Including these dates for the historical protagonists and for the historical literature will better allow readers to assess the chronology of the developments for themselves.

B. The occurrence of tontines in German-speaking territories

I. Tontines mentioned in the modern literature

Modern literature refers only to a small number of tontines which were issued in German-speaking territories:[38] it is generally accepted that the first tontine was created in 1698 in Prussia. Two tontines in *Nürnberg* (Nuremberg) from 1777 and 1783 have gained prominence as Johann Wolfgang von Goethe (1749–1832) showed interest in them.[39] Tontines in Gotha (1752), Mainz (1769), Oldenburg (1782), and Potsdam (1788) are briefly mentioned. Tontines in Hamburg dating from 1708 and 1709 are referred to as curious examples of tontine transactions showing elements of a lottery. Further tontines in Hamburg are said to have been issued in 1762 and 1776. The city of Schweinfurt is said to have developed plans for a tontine in 1735. Finally, German literature refers to an Austrian tontine issued in 1760 and a tontine in the (today Italian, but at the time Habsburg) city of *Bozen* (Bolzano) that was initiated in 1737. German literature asserts that in Germany tontines were nearly exclusively issued by the public hand and that privately launched tontines were, unlike in other European countries, the exception.

The relatively small number of tontines which are mentioned in modern literature seems to suggest that tontines were of marginal practical importance – a suggestion which is supported by the observations of Werner Ogris that tontines were only sporadically issued in Germany.[40] This sharply contrasts to the important role which tontines are thought to have played for the development of insurance.[41] And some authors do indeed claim that tontines were widely employed in 18th-century Germany.[42] Prima facie, this assertion accords with a statement made by Georg Heinrich Ayrer (1702–1774) in 1750 that tontines were

---

[38] See on the remainder of the paragraph *Schöpfer*, 132–143; *Fiedler*, 45–75; *von Zedtwitz*, 141 f.; *Du Pasquier*, (1910) 46 Zeitschrift für Schweizerische Statistik 498 f.; *Wortner*, 111; *Schmitt-Lermann*, 65; *Braun*, Geschichte, 162.

[39] *Fleischmann*, 146; *P. Koch*, Tontinengeschäft, 29; *idem*, Versicherungsgedanke bei Goethe, 80.

[40] *Ogris*, Leibrentenvertrag, 131 f., claims that the percentage of life annuities among those instruments which were used by the states to raise capital was relatively small; he suggests that only for the Netherlands might this have been different; as becomes obvious in the next paragraph, Ogris was including tontines in his observation. See also *idem*, HRG V, 276 f. Similarly *von Fürstenwerth* and *Weiß*, 637; *Perlitz*, 259 f.

[41] See the text corresponding to n. 14–19, above.

[42] *P. Koch* and *Weiss*, 836.

frequently used.[43] Still, Ayrer does not give a specific number, instead mentioning only two examples and it is thus unclear just what a 'usu frequentatae' meant to him. Furthermore, Ayrer does not seem to restrict his observation to tontines in Germany. In conclusion, the literature is simply unhelpful in assessing the practical occurrence of tontines in German-speaking territories.

II. The origins of tontines in German-speaking territories

Furthermore, modern literature does not offer a coherent explanation on how tontines came to Germany. It is claimed that Huguenots brought the idea of tontines with them from France when they settled in Prussia in 1685.[44] At first sight this assertion seems plausible. After all, the preamble to the Prussian tontine regulations of 1698 refers to 'subjects of both the German and the French nation, and especially those who were displaced due to religious reasons and who have been received in our state' and who have lost their foreign investments ('Unterthanen so wol Teutscher als Frantzösischer Nation, und insonderheit denenjenigen, so der Religion halber anderwärtig vertrieben und in Unsern Ländern aufgenommen worden').[45] At first blush, it seems indeed plausible that the preamble refers to the fact that Huguenots had made investments in a French tontine, that they lost their money when escaping France, and that they brought the idea of this investment product with them to Prussia.

When discussing this narrative, two separate questions need to be distinguished. The first question is how the idea of tontines came to Germany. This is the question which the narrative provides an answer for. A second, closely related – but still separate – question asks which foreign tontines the Prussian authorities had knowledge of and which foreign tontines the Prussian authorities might have taken into consideration when designing the Prussian tontine of 1698. The narrative answers only the first question: Huguenots brought the idea of tontines with them to Prussia. Nevertheless, this narrative is, for a number of reasons, problematic.

First, the chronology of events does not align with this narrative. It was in 1685 that 50,000 Huguenots came from France to Germany, 20,000 of which settled in Brandenburg.[46] Yet it was only in 1689 that the first tontine was issued

---

[43] *Ayrer* (1750), 25.

[44] *P. Koch*, Tontinengeschäft, 29; *von Zedtwitz*, 141; *Schmitt-Lermann*, 64 f.

[45] Patent wegen der einzurichtenden Leib-Renten d.d. den 30. Decembr. 1698, (1736) 6/1 Corpus Constitutionum Marchicarum 653–658. The regulation is reproduced in: *Schöpfer*, 235–238, and, with a slightly different spelling, in: *Krünitz*, Encyclopädie LXXI (1796), 289–293.

[46] *Schoeps*, 37; *Wienfort*, 28.

in France. It is simply unlikely that the Huguenots invested money in a French tontine after having fled France. Secondly, the purpose of the French tontine of 1689 was to finance the Nine Years War, also known as the War of the League of Augsburg, the War of the Grand Alliance or the War of the Palatine Succession (1688–1697).[47] This war was fought between France and the League of Augsburg; Prussia-Brandenburg had joined the League in 1688. Again, it is unlikely that the Huguenots financed a French war against Prussia after having fled from France to Prussia. Thirdly, the Huguenots coming to Prussia formed less than 0.1% of the French population.[48] The French tontine of 1689 had less than 6,000 subscribers.[49] Statistically, it is, thus, unlikely that the number of Huguenots involved in the French tontine of 1689 was high. Fourthly, the French tontine of 1689 was open only to French investors having residence in France.[50] Thus, the Huguenots were simply not able to invest in the French tontine after having fled France. Finally, there was an English tontine of 1692, and there were tontines in the Netherlands since 1670 and also a proposal for a tontine in Denmark in 1653. Brandenburg-Prussia had ties with both the Netherlands and Denmark: in the Franco-Dutch War (1672–1678) it was, together with Denmark, part of the alliance supporting the Netherlands fighting against France,[51] and in the Nine Years War it was, together with the Netherlands, part of the League of Augsburg. Thus, the idea of tontines might have been imported from countries other than France, too.[52]

Furthermore, in his study on life annuity contracts Ogris briefly refers to the aforementioned tontine of the city of *Danzig* (Gdańsk) of 1657, with further tontines to follow in 1688, 1775, and 1792.[53] *Danzig* (Gdańsk) was at the time an autonomous city under the Polish crown with a German-speaking population.[54] Even though the monograph by Ogris is the central study on the history of life

---

[47] *Clark*, 225; 'Pfälzischer Erbfolgekrieg', in: Brockhaus Enzyklopädie online (accessed on 12 June 2017).

[48] According to *Dölemeyer*, 26, 30, the total number of 160,000 to 170,000 Huguenots fleeing France were about 0.8% of the French population.

[49] *Wyler*, 117; *Gallais-Hamonno* and *Rietsch*, Financial Engineering, 75.

[50] *Gallais-Hamonno* and *Rietsch*, Financial Engineering, 62.

[51] *Zeller*, 215–219; 'Holländischer Krieg', in: Brockhaus Enzyklopädie online (accessed on 12 June 2017).

[52] The Hessisches Staatsarchiv (Marburg), 340 von Dörnberg No. 4311, holds, e.g., a number of letters dated between 1694 and 1722 that were sent by Baron Siegismund von Hayden zu Wesel from London to his family in Wesel, in which he reports of lotteries and tontines and in which he also writes about a London tontine of 1693.

[53] *Ogris*, Leibrentenvertrag, 132.

[54] *Loew*, 112; *Böttcher*, 34–45; 'Danzig', in: Brockhaus Enzyklopädie online (accessed on 12 June 2017).

annuity contracts, his mentioning of that tontine has gone unnoticed by the literature on tontines. The tontine was launched only four years after Tonti's proposal to Mazarin. It predates what is thought to be the first tontines in Europe: the Dutch tontines of the 1670s. And, even though the tontine of 1698 in Prussia might have been the first tontine in Germany, it was predated by a different tontine in a German-speaking city.[55]

In addition, tontines had predecessors in Germany, as it was possible that life annuity contracts would have more than one annuitant and that the annuity of a deceased annuitant would accrue to the surviving annuitants. Otto Stobbe (1831–1887) gives an example from 14th-century *Breslau* (Wrocław):[56]

> Zu Breslau erhalten a. 1342 … 3 Schwestern eine Leibrente von 6 Mark; beim Tode der ersten erlischt eine Mark, beim Tode der zweiten erlöschen 2 Mark, nach aller drei Tode die ganzen 6 Mark.

> In 1342 in Breslau, three sisters received a life annuity of 6 marks; at the death of the first the life annuity was reduced to 5 marks, at the death of the second to 4 marks, and after the death of all three sisters the life annuity extinguished altogether.

Thus, part of the annuity was passed on to the surviving sisters. Stobbe and also Ogris give further examples which prove that such contracts existed with great variations across Germany. Stobbe explains these contracts in general terms:[57]

> Wir begegnen hier für die Auffassung des Verhältnisses der mehreren Rentengläubiger demselben Gegensatz, welcher in den Quellen des deutschen Rechts auch für die mehreren Schuldner nachgewiesen worden ist: Wenn A. u. B. sich gegenüber C. verpflichtet haben, eine bestimmte Summe zu zahlen, so kann dies so viel bedeuten, als: A. ist die Hälfte und B. die andere Hälfte schuldig …, oder auch so viel, als A. und B. müssen zusammen die Summe zahlen, so dass nach dem Fortfall des Einen der Andere die ganze Schuld zu bezahlen hat … Aehnlich ist es hier bei den Leibrentenberechtigten. Wenn den beiden Ehegatten eine Leibrente versprochen ist, so kommt es auf die besondere Intention der Parteien an, ob … nach dem Fortfall des Einen der Ueberlebende die ganze Forderung geltend machen darf. Diese letztere Form treffen wir nun aber nicht bloss bei Leibrenten für zwei Ehegatten, sondern auch bei solchen für einander fremde und für mehr als 2 Personen. Sie entspricht ganz dem, was die spätere Zeit Tontinengesellschaft genannt hat.

> Here, we observe with respect to the relationship of more than one annuitant the same principle which can be found in the German sources also with respect to more than one debtor: if A and B oblige themselves to pay to C a specific sum of money this can mean two things. Either A is obliged to pay half of the sum and B is obliged to pay half of the sum ... Or A and B have to pay the entire sum jointly, so that at the default of the one the other has to pay the full sum ... The same principles apply to annuitants. If

---

[55] Thus, it is wrong to claim that the Prussian tontine of 1698 was the first tontine in the German-speaking world; this is, however, claimed by *Wortner*, 111.

[56] *Stobbe*, Beiträge (1865), 33; *Ogris*, Leibrentenvertrag, 152–155.

[57] *Stobbe*, Beiträge (1865), 34 f.

spouses receive an annuity it depends on the intention of the parties whether ... after the death of one the surviving spouse shall still be entitled to the full annuity. The design of the latter life annuity contract would benefit not only the spouses but also total strangers and situations involving more than just two annuitants. This design correlates to what has in later times been called a tontine society.

Stobbe refers to two early 15th-century examples from Quedlinburg and Berlin. Furthermore, already in 1651, and thus two years before Tonti allegedly proposed his idea of tontines to Mazarin, the German poet Georg Philipp Harsdörffer (1607–1658) referred to a Venetian tontine-type transaction when discussing the institution of *Montes pietatis*:[58]

> Dergleichen haben jüngsthin die Venetiger [sic] erfunden. Ihrer hundert stehen zusammen / und legt ein jeder hundert Ducaten / daß das Haubtgut hundert tausene [sic] Ducaten machet: Von diesem giebt man 5. von Hundert / jedoch also / daß derjenigen Zinse / welche das erst Jahr sterbe / den andern zuwachse: das andre Jahr ingleichem / und so fort / daß die Abzinssung der hundert tausend Ducaten auff einen allein kommen an / der nemlich die anderen überlebet / und mit seinem Tod ist die Schuld bezahlet …

> The same has recently been invented by Venetians. A hundred of them join together / each one of them gives 100 ducats / so that the main capital amounts to 100,000 [sic] ducats. 5% interest is paid / in such a way / that the interest / of the one investor who dies in the first year / accrues to the others. And the same happens also the other year / and so forth / so that the interest on the main capital of 100,000 ducats will be received by one investor only / that is the one who survives all others / and with his death all obligations to pay cease …

Harsdörffer also observes that the Venetians added a lottery-element to these transactions:[59]

> Dieses haben sie noch auf eine Gewinnsüchtige art gerichtet / und üm die Verzinsung zettel heben lassen … / daß einer 2 der andre 3 der dritte /8/9/10/ bis 20, vom hundert bekommen / iedoch länger nicht / als so lang er lebt. Nicht wenig reiche Leute haben Geld hinein gewagt … Die Zettel sind alle zu gleich heraus gehoben worden / und ist keiner leer gewesen / sondern was einem ist abgegangen / das ist dem andern zugegangen / daß die Obrigkeit mehr nicht als 5 vom hundert zu zahlen gehabt.

> They have designed these transactions in even a more acquisitive way / and they have increased the interest rate with tickets ... / so that the one has received 2%, the other 3%, the third 8%, 9%, 10% up to 20% / however, not longer / than he survives. Many rich people have risked money in such a scheme ... The tickets have been drawn all at the same time / and no ticket lost / yet what one does not receive / is gained by the other / so that authorities did not have to pay more than 5% on the capital.

All of these observations support the proposition that tontine schemes were already known in parts of Europe; moreover, even further evidence may be

---

[58] *Harsdörffer* (1651), 279 f. The calculation error is in the original.

[59] *Harsdörffer* (1651), 280.

added:[60] there was a proposal developed by Nicholas Bourey in 1641 in Portugal.[61] In 1653 Klingenberg proposed the idea of a tontine in Denmark. At the same time a similar project was suggested by Duarte de Lima, and this proposal included a lottery element.[62] de Lima came from Portugal.[63] Similarly, Harsdörffer discussed a Venetian tontine-type transaction which featured a lottery element, too. Furthermore, Maura Fortunati mentions a tontine plan in the Duchy of Savoy in the 1630s or 1640s.[64] And Klingenberg had at least considered initiating a tontine in Hamburg in 1653.[65]

All of these findings put a question mark behind the proposition that Tonti invented tontines. However, as it is the main objective of the present volume to analyse the *impact* which tontines had on the development of insurance (law) in German-speaking territories, further research on the origins of tontines needs to be left to future projects.

Finally, the reference that is made in the preamble of the Prussian tontine regulations of 1698 to subjects who had lost their foreign investments need not necessarily have meant investments in tontines: the contemporary German-speaking literature regarded tontines as a special form of life annuity schemes.[66] And people of the time invested in life annuities not only locally but also nationally and internationally.[67] Thus, the preamble might have simply referred to people who had lost their investments in such schemes.

In conclusion, the mono-causal explanation which links the Prussian tontine of 1698 to the arrival of the Huguenots in Brandenburg in 1685 is flawed. It is clear, however, that the Prussian tontine was associated with Tonti as the preamble to the regulations expressly uses the word tontine.[68] Thus, even if tontine-type transactions were known in Germany before Tonti made his proposal to Mazarin, such transactions were thereafter associated with Tonti.

This brings me to the second question: which foreign tontines did the Prussian authorities know of and which foreign tontines might the Prussian authorities have taken into consideration when designing the Prussian tontine of 1698? This question finds a direct answer in an archival file on the tontine of 1698 in the

[60] *Hellwege*, Comparative Analysis, 383 ff..

[61] *McKeever*, Tontines in Portugal, 193 ff.

[62] *Rietsch* and *Gallais-Hamonno*, Lorenzo Tonti, 36; *Sunnqvist*, 157.

[63] *Sunnqvist*, 157.

[64] *Fortunati*, 213.

[65] *Rietsch* and *Gallais-Hamonno*, Lorenzo Tonti, 37.

[66] See the text corresponding to n. 423–450, below.

[67] See the text corresponding to n. 94, below.

[68] Patent wegen der einzurichtenden Leib-Renten d.d. den 30. Decembr. 1698, (1736) 6/1 Corpus Constitutionum Marchicarum 653–658, 654.

Brandenburgisches Landeshauptarchiv (Brandenburg Main State Archive): an undated document refers to a tontine in Venice, the French tontine of 1689, the English tontine of 1692, and a French tontine of 1698.[69] As will become obvious further below, the numbers given for the Venetian tontine reported by Harsdörffer[70] – 100,000 as raised capital, 1,00(0) shares, each share costing 100, and an interest rate of 5% – correspond to those of the Prussian tontine of 1698.[71] Furthermore, the Prussian tontine of 1698 did not introduce any age-based classes. Such classes were a part of Tonti's proposal – the introduction of such classes may actually have been Tonti's innovation – and they were part of the French tontine of 1689. By contrast, the Venetian tontine as reported by Harsdörffer and Bourey's proposal as well as the Kampen tontine of 1670 did not have any age-based classes. It is thus likely that the Prussian administration took the Venetian tontine as a direct model.

III. The three phases of the development of tontines

Against this background let me return to the practical occurrence of tontines in German-speaking territories. For a number reasons it is difficult to fully assess the number and the dimension of tontine transactions. First, there is the simple problem of finding the relevant archival materials on those tontines which were issued or planned but which are not mentioned in modern or contemporary literature. Secondly, tontines appeared under different names: the first Prussian tontine, for example, was simply called a life annuity (*Leibrente*), and it is only the preamble of the associated regulations that used the word tontine. Indeed, in Germany tontines were looked upon as a special form of life annuities.[72] Thus, in order to identify additional tontines, one would have to analyse all life annuity transactions in German-speaking territories so as to assess whether they can be looked upon as tontines. Thirdly, the two Hamburg tontines of 1708 and 1709, which are mentioned in modern literature, are said to have been a mixture between a tontine and a lottery. Thus, one would also need to include hybrid forms of financial products and all lotteries in order to fully assess the practical importance of tontines. Fourthly, for some forgotten tontines I found the publication of plans but no hints as to whether they received enough subscriptions in order to be actually issued. Finally, according to modern literature tontines reached their apex in the 18th century, and in the course of the 19th century their number was again in decline. However, it seems that this narrative does not represent the

[69] Brandenburgisches Landeshauptarchiv, No. 23A C.2720, fol. 10r.

[70] See the text corresponding to n. 58, above.

[71] See the text corresponding to n. 138, below.

[72] See the text corresponding to n. 423–450, below.

actual development that occurred. Rather, it seems that three phases have to be distinguished in the development of tontines.

What we saw in the 17th and 18th centuries were self-contained tontine transactions which were mostly issued by the public hand in order to raise capital. This is the first phase of the development. From the end of the 18th century onwards, and then foremost in the 19th century, tontines were offered by pension funds and savings banks as one of many investment and pension products. This is the second phase of the development. Thus, it seems problematic to claim that tontines experienced their apex in the 18th century and that their number was in decline in the 19th century. Self-contained tontines issued by the public hand indeed witnessed their highpoint in the 18th century, and they had more or less disappeared at the beginning of the 19th century. However, modern literature does not offer any thorough statistical material on the tontine business of pension funds and savings banks in the 19th century. It is, therefore, impossible to claim that the number of tontines was in decline in the 19th century. In the third phase of the development, tontine life insurance products were offered by U.S. life insurance companies at the end of the 19th century and in the early 20th century.

1. The first phase: self-contained tontines in the 17th and 18th centuries

a) Self-contained tontines in German-speaking territories

Let me turn first to those self-contained tontines which were primarily issued by the public hand in the 17th and 18th centuries. Against the background of the difficulties in fully assessing the number and the dimension of tontine transactions, I do not claim to present a complete list of tontine transactions in German-speaking territories. The following schemes and plans are, however, referred to as tontines either in the modern literature or in the literature of the 17th and 18th centuries; or I was able to find materials on them in the various German archives:

1657: Gdańsk
1688: Gdańsk
1692: Bremen
1698: Prussia
1706: Wrocław
1706: Hamburg
1708: Hamburg
1708: Lübeck
1709: Hamburg
1715: Lübeck
1723: Saxony
1735: Schweinfurt
pre-1736: Vienna
1737: Bolzano
1743: Hesse-Kassel
1747: Berlin
1748: Saxony
1749: Wied
1750: Hesse-Kassel
1750 Merseburg
1752: Gotha
1753/55: Augsburg
1755: East Frisia
pre-1757: Saxe-Weimar
1757: Prussia
1758: Mecklenburg
1760: Austria
1762: Hamburg
1763: Cleves
1764: Halberstadt/Berlin
1764: *Freimaurer*
1765: Saxony
1766: Wrocław
1766: Upper Lusatia
1767: Bremen
1768: Wolfenbüttel
1768: Osnabrück
1768: Regensburg
1769: Mainz
1772: Bremen
1772: Swedish-Pomerania
1775: Gdańsk

1776: Hamburg
1776: Mecklenburg-Strelitz
1777: Upper Lusatia
1777: Stade
1777: Nuremberg
1782: Oldenburg
1783: Nuremberg
1787: Mecklenburg
1788: Rostock
1788: Prussia
1792: Gdańsk
1805: Lippe
1805: Bremen
1807: Hamburg
1811: Westphalia

The list is provisional only: further below it will become apparent that some of the investment schemes which the contemporary or modern literature refers to as tontines were in fact pure lotteries or simple life annuity transactions. An article in the *Leipziger Sammlungen von wirthschafftlichen Policey-, Cammer- und Finantz-Sachen*, which was edited by Georg Heinrich Zincke (1692–1769), mentions a number of further tontines:[73] Glückstadt (1696), Frankfurt an der Oder (1710), Erfurt (1713), Altona (1713), and Bargenhusen (1713). The article refers to Paul Jacob Marperger's (1656–1730) book on *Montes pietatis* of 1715 for further discussion of these tontines. However, Marperger's account of these schemes reveals that they were nothing but simple lotteries. None of the prizes were annuities.[74] Thus, I can disregard them for the purpose of the present volume.

This leaves me with 18 tontines or tontine plans prior to 1750. Is this number high enough so that Ayrer could in that year speak of a frequent use of tontines?[75] Even if I was able to identify more tontines than are mentioned in the modern literature and even if I am not able to claim that the above list is complete, it seems for two reasons likely that tontines were not initiated on a day-to-day basis. First, the interest which von Goethe developed in the two *Nürnberger* (Nuremberg) tontines of 1777 and 1783 and the public attention drawn to these tontines across Germany seem to suggest that tontines were not everyday transactions. However, the attention drawn to these tontines may alternatively be explained on the basis of their novel design, a point to which I will come back further below.[76] Secondly, it seems that it was a lengthy process to initiate a tontine: the planning of the Nuremberg tontine of 1777, for example, started in 1748.[77] The discussions in Bremen started at least as early as 1750, but the first Bremen tontine was issued only in 1767.[78] Finally, Manfred Wortner observes:[79]

> Obwohl aber die Tontinen ein lebhaftes Interesse bei der Bevölkerung hervorriefen, scheint die theoretische Diskussion über diese Form von Versorgungseinrichtungen überwogen zu haben gegenüber der praktischen Errichtung solcher Anstalten. Vieles

[73] *Zincke* (1744), 502.

[74] *Marperger* (1715), 332–334 (Altona), 347–354 (Erfurt), 354–357 (Frankfurt an der Oder), 357–362 (Glückstadt), 335–340 (Bargenhusen).

[75] See the text corresponding to n. 43 and the provided references, above.

[76] See the text corresponding to and following n. 260, below.

[77] *Fiedler*, 47–53. See also Staatsarchiv Nürnberg, Reichsstadt Nürnberg D No. 4816.

[78] Staatsarchiv Bremen, No. 2-R.1.a.10.c.4.I and No. 2-R.1.A.10.c.4.II.b.1.a.

[79] *Wortner*, 111 f.

wurde im zeitgenössischen Schrifttum verbreitet für und wider die Tontine; die Zahl der tatsächlich ins Leben gerufenen, derartigen Einrichtungen blieb hingegen verhältnismäßig klein.

Even though tontines evoked a lively interest in the general public, it seems as if the theoretical discussions exceeded their practical importance. The contemporary literature intensely argued the pros and cons of tontines; the number of tontines which were effectively issued, by contrast, remained relatively small.

Thus, Ayrer himself may have been misled by an intense theoretical discourse and simply inferred that tontines were a wide-spread occurrence.

There is one final notable point about the above list: in the 17th and 18th centuries, tontines were issued or planned in German territories, Austria, and the German-speaking parts of the Habsburg lands. However, I was not able to identify any tontine or tontine plan in 17th- and 18th-century Switzerland, even though it is clear that Swiss persons invested in foreign tontines. There were, for example, a number of Swiss investors in the Bolzano tontine of 1737.[80]

b) Foreign tontines

Even if tontines were not issued on a day-to-day basis in German-speaking territories, there is evidence from the 17th and 18th centuries that German, Austrian, and Swiss persons invested in foreign tontines. Thus, Wortner's observation[81] needs to be qualified: the theoretical discussions in the contemporary literature may have reflected the overall practical importance of tontines as a European investment scheme even if the number of tontines which were issued in the German-speaking territories remained relatively small.

For the late 17th century, the preamble to the regulations of the Prussian tontine of 1698 refers to Prussian subjects who had invested their capital in foreign investments schemes, and I have already pointed out that the preamble might be making reference to traditional life annuities and tontines.[82] The preamble, thus, does not prove that Huguenots brought the idea of tontines with them to Prussia. It rather highlights that there was a European market for life annuities and tontines.

---

[80] See Südtiroler Landesarchiv (Bozen), No. 3.23.1.

[81] See the quote in the text corresponding to n. 79, above.

[82] See the text corresponding to n. 66, above.

As to the mid-18th century, Johann Heinrich Gottlob von Justi (1717–1771) hinted that tontines were investment schemes attracting money from all over Europe. He discussed the importance of a state being creditworthy if it wished to issue a tontine:[83]

> Wenn demnach ein Staat keinen Credit hat; so ist es vergebens, an diese Hülfsmittel zu denken, und einen dergleichen Plan zu Leibrenten oder Tontinen bekannt zu machen. Der schlechte Fortgang der Sache wird dieses verwegene Unternehmen vor den Augen von ganz Europa beschämen.

> If a state is not creditworthy, it is of no purpose to think of life annuities and tontines as a means to raise capital and to advertise respective plans. The poor progress of the plan will embarrass this ambitious undertaking before the eyes of all of Europe.

Furthermore, Joseph von Sonnenfels (1732/34–1817) argued that it is problematic if domestic capital is invested in foreign life annuity schemes (including tontines) as this leads to a capital drain. However, he concedes that a state cannot regulate or prevent such investments in foreign financial markets.[84] Similar concerns applied to other financial schemes such as lotteries and annuity societies, and apparently this was one reason why more and more territories developed plans for such schemes.[85] Finally, Johann Heinrich Ludwig Bergius (1718–1781) claimed that the high interest rates which the French tontines usually paid attracted many Dutch and English investors and that Germans invested in Dutch, English, and French life annuity schemes and tontines.[86]

By way of example, we find in the April issue 1779 of the *Leipziger Intelligenz-Blatt* an announcement in connection with a Spanish life annuity lottery stating that anybody who wished to claim an annuity for 1778 had to present his documents to the Spanish consul in Hamburg by the end of April.[87] The lottery had received some coverage in German publications, and it was often referred to as a tontine.[88] Its purpose was to finance a channel in Murcia for navigation and watering purposes. The government wanted to raise 15,000,000 livres. 250,000 shares of 60 livres each were sold. The interest rate was 6%. The total interest paid out was, thus, 900,000 livres. The right to annuities was determined through

---

[83] *von Justi*, Finanzwesen (1766), 577.

[84] *von Sonnenfels*, Grundsätze der Polizey (1771), 412.

[85] The plan for the Bavarian Life Annuity Society (*Rentengesellschaft*) of 1769 was expressly based on these considerations. The plan for this *Rentengesellschaft*, it was basically a lottery, can be found in the Staatsarchiv Nürnberg, Reichsstadt Nürnberg D No. 4816. The hereditary principle did not apply.

[86] *Bergius* (1771), 150, 175.

[87] (1779) Gnädigst privilegirtes Leipziger Intelligenz-Blatt 153.

[88] For the figures that follow see, with slight differences in the details: (1776) Gnädigst privilegirtes Leipziger Intelligenz-Blatt 300–303; *C.H. Korn*, Neueste Geschichte (1777), 94. See furthermore (1778) 1 Göttingische Anzeigen von gelehrten Sachen 93; *Krünitz*, Encyclopädie LXXI (1796), 147–152.

five lotteries, with the highest annuity payment amounting to 20,000 livres. For the first eight years the annuities were paid even if the nominee had died. Thus, it seems unlikely that it was a true tontine as the hereditary principle, which is characteristic for tontines,[89] was missing.[90] The scheme aimed at the European market as it was possible to purchase shares throughout Europe. And indeed, over 40,000 shares amounting to approximately 2,500,000 livres are said to have been bought by Dutch investors. The announcement in the *Leipziger Intelligenz-Blatt* of 1779 suggests that there were sales in Germany, too. Throughout the entire 18th century we find further advertisements, announcements, and financial reports of foreign tontines in German periodicals.[91] And, of course, the Danish tontines were advertised in Schleswig-Holstein and beyond.[92]

The international character of life annuity and tontine transactions is finally reflected in the private law discourse: Wilhelm August Friedrich Danz (1764–1803), for example, used in his discussion of life annuity contracts both the French (*rentes viagères*) and the English terms (annuities upon lives).[93]

In conclusion, even if German tontine issues in the 17th and 18th centuries were the exception, it seems that tontines were nevertheless a relevant investment scheme, with also a number of foreign actors operating in the German market. What needs to be remembered, however, is that this was not a novelty of the 17th and 18th centuries. Since the Middle Ages, life annuities had been sold not only locally but also nationally and internationally.[94]

2. The second phase: tontines issued by pension funds and savings banks in the 19th century

For the 19th century, present day literature claims that it was the emergence of modern life and pension insurance products which caused the number of tontines

[89] See the text corresponding to n. 117 and to and following n. 529 ff., below.

[90] See also *Illescas*, 229 f.

[91] For example, a tontine from The Hague issued in 1771 published a financial report in: (1776) Gnädigst privilegirtes Leipziger Intelligenz-Blatt 312–313. The same tontine is discussed by *Krünitz*, Encyclopädie LXXI (1796), 136–137. An article published in: (1792) Politisches Journal nebst Anzeige von gelehrten und andern Sachen 444, refers to a Copenhagen tontine. And two articles published in: (1734) Kurz-gefaßte Historische Nachrichten zum Behuf der Neuern Europäischen Begebenheiten 757, 812, refer to a French tontine.

[92] (1801) Chronologische Sammlung der im Jahre 1800 ergangenen Verordnungen und Verfügungen für die Herzogthümer Schleswig und Holstein, die Herrschaft Pinneberg, Graffschaft Ranzau und Stadt Altona 79–84; (1803) 5 Neues Deutsches Magazin 327–349.

[93] *Danz* (1797), 326.

[94] *Ogris*, Leibrentenvertrag, 164–172.

to decline.[95] However, this seems to be an oversimplification. What we do not any longer find are self-contained tontines, which were primarily issued by the different German territories and cities in order to finance public projects. Yet pension funds and savings banks offered tontines or tontine-like products throughout the 19th century.[96] In 1828, Baumann went so far as to say:[97]

> Zeitrenteninstitute, oder Sparcassen, und die aus ihnen hervorgehenden Verträge über das menschliche Leben, nämlich Leibrentencontrakte, Tontinen, Lebensversicherungen, und Wittwen-Cassen gewinnen allmälig in Deutschland ein immer größeres Interesse, …

> Annuity funds, or savings banks, and the products dealing with human lives which they market, such as life annuities, tontines, life insurance and widow assurance, are attracting more and more interest in Germany, ...

By way of example, further below I will discuss the tontines issued by the *Würtembergische Leibrenten-Bank* (Württemberg Life Annuity Bank) of 1822, the *Hamburgische Allgemeine Versorgungs-Tontine* (Hamburg General Pension Tontine) of 1822, the Austrian *Allgemeine Versorgungsanstalt* (General Pension Fund) of 1823, and the *Preußische Renten-Versicherungs-Anstalt* (Prussian Pension Insurance Fund) of 1838.[98] The business which these funds attracted was by no means small. When analyzing the total numbers it has to be kept in mind that Germany was throughout the 19th century a fragmentary market with local and regional market players. In an 1838 publication, Robert von Mohl (1799–1875) claimed that the *Stuttgarter Allgemeine Rentenanstalt* (Stuttgart General Pension Fund) of 1833 had by 1838 around 25,000 members in its tontine schemes.[99] The *Bayerische Hypotheken- und Wechselbank* (Bavarian Mortgage and Exchange Bank) of 1835 established in 1839 a *Renten-Anstalt* (pension fund) which issued each year tontines with seven classes.[100] These tontines had by 1841 close to 2,900 members.[101] For the year of 1892 it is alleged that the pension funds in Berlin, Hannover, Darmstadt, Stuttgart, and Karlsruhe had tontines with 103,861 payees in total, that nine Austrian-Hungarian life insurance companies had in the

---

[95] *P. Koch*, Tontinengeschäft, 29; *von Zedtwitz*, 142; *Kürble*, (1990) 79 Zeitschrift für die gesamte Versicherungswissenschaft 597 (with Kürble more exactly dating this development to the second half of the 19th century).

[96] *Wild* (1862), 134 f.; *Lehr* and *von Heckel* (1901), 129.

[97] *Baumann*, Kurze und faßliche Darstellung (1828), iii; see also 37 f.

[98] See the text corresponding to and following n. 301, below.

[99] *von Mohl*, Erörterungen (1838), 11.

[100] Reglementäre Grundbestimmungen der bayerischen Hypotheken- und Wechselbank für die Renten-Anstalt (1839).

[101] Zweiter Rechenschafts-Bericht der Renten-Anstalt der bayerischen Hypotheken- und Wechselbank für das Jahr 1841 (1842).

same year a total of 15,238 tontine policies, and that two Austrian-Hungarian mutual tontine companies had together 89,249 members.[102]

Furthermore, there were the so-called *Sparkassen Tontinen* (savings bank tontines).[103] Their structure was simple: the members of the tontine invested a certain sum and after a fixed number of years – usually 10, 15, or 20 years – the capital was divided between the surviving members. It thus applied the hereditary principle which is characteristic for tontines.[104] If the payee of a *Sparkassen Tontine* was a young girl, it could function as dowry insurance and, indeed, it simply imitated the design of much older investment products.

German pension funds are said to have stopped issuing tontines in the 1870s, e.g. the pension fund of Karlsruhe in 1872. Of course, those tontines which had already been issued remained in force. Kürble, for example, claims that the tontine of the Karlsruhe pension fund which was issued in 1855 only closed in 1950 when the last nominee died at the age of 94.[105]

3. The third phase: tontine life insurance products in the late 19th century

Finally, in the late 19th century the German insurance market saw, as did the insurance markets of other European countries, tontine life insurance products issued by U.S. life insurance companies, which are said to have been active on the German market between 1868 and 1914/17 – a development which, as we will see later in this volume, raised a number of problems.[106] These tontine life insurance products differed greatly from the tontines offered by German pension funds throughout the 19th century, and these differences justify speaking of a third phase in the development of tontines: a phase where the tontine element was only an add-on to a normal life insurance policy. The surpluses flowing from the invested premiums were not paid out to the insured as dividends. Rather, they were accumulated in a tontine scheme and paid out to the surviving insured and those insured, who had not defaulted, after a fixed period of time, usually between 5 and 20 years. The tontine element was, thus, the same mechanism as applied by the aforementioned *Sparkassen Tontinen*. However, the tontine was, unlike with the tontines issued by pension funds and savings banks, no longer the core element of the product, but only added to a life insurance policy.

---

[102] *Brämer* and *Brämer* (1894), 178 f.

[103] *Wild* (1862), 136–153.

[104] See the text corresponding to n. 117, below.

[105] *Kürble*, (1990) 79 Zeitschrift für die gesamte Versicherungswissenschaft 597.

[106] See the text corresponding to and following n. 316, below.

IV. Comparative observations

The practical importance of tontines differed greatly in Europe and beyond. Tontines of the first phase seem to have been issued, or there were at least plans to issue such tontines, in France, England, Ireland, the Netherlands, Denmark, Portugal, Spain, and the U.S.A.[107] In Spain there is only one traceable scheme which is referred to as a tontine: the aforementioned scheme to finance a channel in Murcia. However, it was not a pooled life annuity.[108] In the U.S.A. there was just one plan for a public tontine in the late 18th century, and this plan was never implemented.[109] It seems that the Netherlands, together with Germany, had the highest number of tontines and tontine plans. The reason why Germany had such a high number of tontines and tontine plans seems to be straight forward: Germany consisted of a large number of principalities which all had the right to issue tontines; within Prussia it seems that the different provinces had the right to issue tontines, too.

The second phase started in the late 18th century and was marked by tontines issued by private entities. These existed in England, France, the Netherlands, Italy, and Scandinavia.[110] They had one purpose only. However, this one purpose varied. It is possible to distinguish three different forms of tontines. In England and in the U.S.A. they were primarily issued for the purpose of property development.[111] In Germany, we find tontines which were issued as a pension insurance product by pension funds. And, there were the *Sparkassen Tontinen* which were savings products issued by savings banks. Looking beyond Germany, it seems that tontines in the form of savings products made some appearance in, for example, Italy, Spain, Latin America, Poland, and Hungary. Yet their importance seems to have differed in these countries.[112]

The third phase saw tontine life insurance products, especially those of U.S. life insurance companies. These products were criticised in most, but apparently not all European countries, and as a consequence in some countries tontines were forbidden. This was, for example, the case in Italy, Russia, and Poland.[113]

---

[107] *Gallais-Hamonno* and *Rietsch*, Financial Engineering, 56 ff.; *Delbrel*, 109 ff.; *Sirks*, 126 ff.; *Sunnqvist*, 160 ff.; *McKeever*, Tontines in Portugal, 193 ff.; *Illescas*, 229 ff.

[108] See the text corresponding to and following n. 87, above.

[109] *McKeever*, Evolution of the Tontine in North America, 240.

[110] *Pearson*, 89 ff.; *Delbrel*, 109 ff.; *Sirks*, 126 ff.; *Hellwege*, 176 ff.; *Fortunati*, 216 ff.

[111] *Pearson*, 89 ff.; *McKeever*, The Evolution of the Tontine in North America, 242 ff.

[112] *Fortunati*, 216 ff.; *Illescas*, 229 ff.; *Nasser*, 265 ff.; *Halberda*, 275 ff.; *Tőkey*, 292 ff.

[113] *Fortunati*, 221 ff.; *Halberda*, 283 ff.; *Korchagina*, 298 ff.

V. Conclusion

The present volume is part of a project on a comparative history of insurance law in Europe. Accordingly, its focus should be on legal questions: the different legal aspects of tontines and their impact on the history of insurance law. Nevertheless, it is necessary to develop first an understanding of the factual occurrence of tontines. That was the purpose of the preceding overview. However, as the focus of the present volume is on legal problems, I am able to give, for the reasons outlined above,[114] nothing more than an overview. Nonetheless, it has become clear that the assertion that 'the number of tontines which were effectively issued remained relatively small'[115] needs to be qualified, and it is possible to distinguish three phase in the development of tontines: the number of tontines which were issued by the different German states as self-contained investment schemes in the 17th and 18th centuries indeed seems to have been small. Nevertheless, there were a number of tontines and tontine plans which are not any longer mentioned in the modern literature. Furthermore, in the 17th and 18th centuries the tontine market was a genuinely European market. The self-contained tontines issued by the public hand in the 17th and 18th centuries constitute the first phase in the development of tontines. The assertion that the number of tontines was in decline in the 19th century due to the emergence of modern life insurance schemes seems to be wrong. Throughout the 19th century pension funds and savings banks offered tontines. This is the second phase in the development of tontines. In the third phase of their development, tontine life insurance products were offered by U.S. life insurance companies in the late 19th century and in the early 20th century.

[114] See the text corresponding to and following n. 72, above.

[115] See the full quotation in the text corresponding to n. 79, above.

C. Tontine designs in German-speaking territories

In order to study the legal problems of tontines and in order to analyse their lasting impact on the development of insurance law, it is not enough to give an overview of the factual occurrence of tontines. It is necessary to develop a clear understanding of tontines as a product: their designs differed greatly.

I. Basic tontine designs

Georges Gallais-Hamonno and Christian Rietsch define tontines as follows:[116]

> A tontine ... is a financial scheme under which a group of people invest in a closed fund. Each contract is based on the life of a person duly named (who can be either the investor himself or someone else). At the end of each year, the interest on the principal (the annuities) is paid by the tontine issuer to the investors whose nominees are still alive, with surviving members sharing the annuities due to deceased members. Thus, surviving members enjoy an increase of their annual income ...

In Germany, tontines are also called *Erbklassenrenten* (literally: hereditary class annuities) because the annuities which were due to deceased members are shared – and thus: inherited – by the surviving members of a tontine.[117] This hereditary principle is characteristic of tontines – but for private lawyers it is important to understand that the term hereditary principle does not, in the present context, mean that the deceased's heirs will have any rights in the tontine. And the term hereditary principle does not mean that the surviving members are the

[116] *Gallais-Hamonno* and *Rietsch*, Financial Engineering, 50.

From modern German literature see *Ogris*, Leibrentenvertrag, 131 f.; *Schöpfer*, 129; *Lehr* and *von Heckel* (1901), 126; *von Zedtwitz*, 138; *Schug*, 245 f.; *Wortner*, 112; *Roloff*, 294; *Schmitt-Lermann*, 64; *Braun*, Geschichte, 63 f.; *Du Pasquier*, (1910) 46 Zeitschrift für Schweizerische Statistik 489; *Kürble*, (1990) 79 Zeitschrift für die gesamte Versicherungswissenschaft 592 f.

From German literature of the 18th and 19th centuries see *Göckel* (1722), 16; *Marperger* (1715), 254–286; *idem* and *von Justi* (1760), 278 note k; *von Justi*, Finanzwesen (1766), 576; *Hübner* (1731), 2055; *Nicolai* (1738), 22; *Kaestner* (1744), 5; *Zedler*, Universal-Lexicon XLIV (1745), 1250; *Süßmilch* (1762), 376; *Berch* (1763), 475 f. (German translation of a Swedish author); *Bergius* (1771), 149; *Fuß* Entwurf (1776), 37; *de Florencourt* (1781), 143; *Michelsen* (1784), 171; *J.H. Jung*, Lehrbuch (1789), 213; *idem*, Grundlehre (1792), 858; *Krünitz*, Encyclopädie LXXI (1796), 2, 213; *Danz* (1797), 328; *Euler* (1806), 262–264; *Klaber* (1832), 39; *L. Jung* (1840), 3 f.

[117] *Braun*, Geschichte, 64.

heirs of the deceased member in the meaning of the law of succession. Further below, I will return to the problem of how to explain the hereditary principle.[118]

Gallais-Hamonno and Rietsch point out that tontines have at least two and up to four groups of participants:[119] (1) the issuer, (2) the investor or contributor who buys shares in a tontine, (3) the payee who receives the annuity, and (4) 'the nominee on whose life the contract is based. As long as the nominee lives, the payee ... receives the annuity'.

The investor, the payee, and the nominee may be one and the same person: here the investor buys shares in order to receive the annuity for the rest of his or her life. If the investor and the payee diverge and if the payee and the nominee are the same person, then the tontine may be used to support family members: here the investor buys shares so that his or her spouse receives the annuity for the rest of his or her life. Finally, if the payee and nominee diverge, then the right to the annuity may be assignable and it may be passed on to the payee's heirs if the nominee survives the original payee. While each tontine has one issuer only, there are a multitude of investors, payees, and nominees.

It is obvious that a tontine can function only if the investors base the payees' rights to receive the annuities on the lives of different nominees. If all investors named the same nominee, the tontine would, from the perspective of the payees, not properly work.[120] Similarly, the investment makes sense only if a minimum number of investors participate: only then will the issuer raise the hoped-for capital; and only then is there on the side of payees the hope for increasing annuities. Often tontines were designed to have a specific number of investors: if too few investors subscribed, then the tontine would not be issued.[121]

It follows that issuing a tontine was a two-step process: in a first step the issuer published a tontine plan and invited the general public to subscribe to it. The tontine was issued only if the plan received enough subscriptions, and subsequently each subscriber had to make his or her investment. This two-step process is the reason why it is so difficult to assess the practical occurrence of tontines: what we usually find in contemporary literature are published tontine plans. It does not always become apparent from the published materials whether the advertised tontine received enough subscriptions in order to be issued.

The investor, the payee, and the nominee were always natural persons. By contrast, a number of different entities were issuers of tontines:[122] in the 17th and

[118] See the text corresponding to and following n. 529, below.

[119] *Gallais-Hamonno* and *Rietsch*, Financial Engineering, 51.

[120] *Kürble*, (1990) 79 Zeitschrift für die gesamte Versicherungswissenschaft 593.

[121] *Krünitz*, Encyclopädie LXXI (1796), 11; *Roloff*, 294; *von Zedtwitz*, 138.

[122] On what follows see *Lehr* and *von Heckel* (1901), 126

18th centuries tontines were predominantly issued by states. In the 19th century, tontines were issued by pension funds, insurance companies, and savings banks. Finally, a tontine could also be formed as a mutual society.

German-speaking literature differentiates between four different tontine designs:[123] the simple tontine (*einfache Tontine*), the class tontine (*Klassentontine*), the compound tontine (*zusammengesetzte Tontine*), and the continuous tontine (*kontinuierliche Tontine*). A simple tontine does not differentiate between the ages of the different nominees. A simple tontine is disadvantageous to most investors: if an identical sum is required of all investors and if all investors receive the same starting annuity, the investor who bases his or her contract on the life of a relatively young nominee will typically receive annuity payments for a longer period of time and have a greater chance of increasing annuity payments than those investors who name a relatively old nominee. By contrast, a class tontine is divided into different classes on the basis of the ages of the nominees. Technically speaking, each class represents in itself a tontine. The interest rate for the different classes can vary in order to reflect the different life expectancies.[124] With a compound tontine, the annuity paid on the life of a deceased nominee is not shared equally by the surviving payees. Rather, one part of the annuity is lost, so that the total sum of annuities is reduced gradually. Thus, compared to a class tontine, the increase in the annuities for the remaining payees is levelled. In a further variance, the annuity for the remaining payees may even be capped.[125] The hereditary principle is, thus, not fully carried through. The reason why this design was called a compound tontine is simple: it combines a simple life annuity contract with a tontine transaction.[126] It is worth observing that the example referred to by Stobbe proves that the mechanism of a compound tontine had a long-standing history within life annuity transactions.[127] Finally, with a continuous tontine the issuer initiates each year a class tontine. The advantage of this design is that it can be joined each year. It is said that it was designed by the Swiss mathematician Leonhard Euler (1707–1783).

---

[123] *Wortner*, 114–116; *von Zedtwitz*, 138 f.; *Lehr* and *von Heckel* (1901), 126; *Oberholzer*, 85; *Braun*, Geschichte, 151–162; *Du Pasquier*, (1910) 46 Zeitschrift für Schweizerische Statistik 489–503. The distinction between a simple and a compound tontine was also drawn by *Krünitz*, Encyclopädie LXXI (1796), 218; yet, his definition of simple tontines also included class tontines. Similarly *Oeltermann* (1805), 95. See also *Bergius* (1771), 155–171; *von Justi*, Finanzwesen (1766), 576 f.; *Seyberth* (1768), 19.

[124] *Schöpfer*, 130; *Braun*, Geschichte, 63; *Du Pasquier*, (1910) 46 Zeitschrift für Schweizerische Statistik 491; *L. Jung* (1840), 4; *von Justi*, Finanzwesen (1766), 574.

[125] Compare *Lehr* and *von Heckel* (1901), 127.

[126] See the explanation offered by *Kritter*, (1786) Leipziger Magazin für reine und angewandte Mathematik 506 f.

[127] See the text corresponding to n. 56, above.

Further variances were introduced with respect to whether there was an obligation to return an amount of money equal to the initially invested capital after the last nominee's death:[128] originally the issuer was under no obligation to reimburse the invested capital as the very purpose of issuing a tontine was to raise capital. However, with some tontines the invested capital was divided after the death of the last surviving nominee between the investors (or their heirs), between the heirs of all payees, or between the last surviving payees. Technically speaking, these tontines were no longer pooled life annuity schemes.

In conclusion, there was a multitude of forms, designs, and variations of tontines, even if one focuses on tontines as pooled life annuity schemes only. By way of example, I will now analyse, in chronological order, the different designs of the different tontines and tontine plans found in German-speaking territories. It will become apparent that there were even further variations in the designs.

II. The first phase: self-contained tontines in the 17th and 18th centuries

1. The Gdańsk tontines of 1657 and 1688

In his study on life annuity contracts, Ogris briefly refers to a tontine of the city of *Danzig* (Gdańsk) from 1657, with further tontines to follow in 1688, 1775, and 1792.[129] Ogris refers to one source only: the early 20th-century monograph by Max Foltz on the history of the city's municipal budget. Foltz reproduces the plan for the 1657-tontine.[130] He assumes that the tontine was issued, but he does not offer further proof for this assumption. Any materials on the history of this scheme, its genesis, its models, its sources of inspiration, or its implementation would be of great interest as the Gdańsk tontine of 1657 seems to have been the first tontine which was planned in German-speaking territories. However, I was not able to identify any materials on the tontine in the *Archivum Państwowe w Gdańsku* (Gdańsk State Archive). Thus, the only surviving source on this tontine seems to be its plan and regulations.

The city wanted to raise 100,000 florins through the offering of 1,000 shares of 100 florins each. Article 2 of the tontine regulations expressly mentioned that the tontine was open to every person regardless of his or her nationality. Thus, Art. 2 again indicated that the tontine market, and more generally the life annuity

[128] *Lehr* and *von Heckel* (1901), 127; *Braun*, Geschichte, 64; *Anonymous*, Der redliche und aufrichtige Wirthschafter (1745), 32 f.

[129] *Ogris*, Leibrentenvertrag, 132. From contemporary literature see *Kaestner* (1744), 5; *Ayrer* (1750), 25; *Willenberg* (1701), 7, 18 f.

[130] *Foltz* (1912), 459–461.

market, was not a purely local market. Article 2 further allowed investors to buy multiple shares and to name themselves, their wives, or their children as payee and nominee or to name any other person as nominee. Finally, Art. 13 allowed payees to sell and assign their rights in the tontine; the nominee remained, of course, the same.

The tontine consisted of 10 classes, each with 100 members. The published tontine plan did not define the classes. Instead, the issuer wanted to have flexibility when forming the different classes. Article 3 stated:

> Jedoch sollen diese tausend Personen in zehen Classes abgeteilet werden, da denn jedwede Classis von hundert Personen bestehen wird. Bei der Einteilunge der Personen wird man das Alter … in … Obacht nehmen, damit also junge Leute beieinander, die mitlern Alters auch absonderlich, und endlich die höheren Alters ebenmäßig zusammen bleiben mögen.

> The one thousand nominees will be divided into ten classes and each class will have one hundred nominees. The age of the nominees … will have to be taken into consideration when forming the different classes so that young nominees will be grouped together, so that middle-aged nominees will be separated from the others and so that finally nominees of a higher age will remain together in one class.

Presumably, the issuer did not want to predefine the classes as he was not able to foresee how many subscribers he would be able to attract. If he had pre-defined the classes he might have had to turn down a potential investor if the respective class had already attracted enough subscribers, whereas other classes might not have received enough subscriptions. However, Art. 3 was not in the interest of a potential investor: for the investor it was essential to predict whether his or her nominee fell within the youngest or the oldest in a class.

The interest rate was 6%, and it was the same for all classes. Article 6 pointed out, probably as some kind of advertisement, that the last payee of each class would receive an annuity of 600 florins per annum for the investment of 100 florins. Article 4 stated that the capital of each class was lost to the city's general public once the last surviving nominee of that class had died ('Nach sämtlicher Tode verfället die Summa jedweder Classis obsonderlich dem Publico'). This statement which reappears in other tontine regulations of the 17th and 18th centuries is misleading. What is meant is that the issuer did not have to repay the capital. However, the issuer did not have to wait until the last nominee had died until he could use the raised capital. The capital was immediately at the issuer's disposal. The published plan did not identify any specific purpose for which the raised capital was to be used. However, the tontine was issued in the middle of the Second Northern War (1655–1660), a war which was costly for *Danzig*

(Gdańsk).[131] In summary, the Gdańsk tontine of 1657 is a prime example of a class tontine that was free of any compound tontine elements.

Apparently, the plan found too few subscribers. For that reason a second plan was published in April of the same year.[132] The price of 100 florins per share was seen as being too high, and the second plan set the price per share at 100 talers, which was according to the plan half of the original price. At the same time the second plan defined the composition of the classes: those below the age of 10 years, those between the ages of 10 and 20, and so on, were to be grouped together. However, the issuer still wanted to retain a certain flexibility in forming the classes.

It is striking that the tontine of 1657 exhibits numbers similar to those of the Venetian tontine which Harsdörffer reports on and to those of the Prussian tontine of 1698: 1,000 shares, each at a cost of 100 in order to raise a total capital of 100,000.[133] However, unlike these two schemes, and in accordance with Tonti's proposal, the tontine of 1657 had age-based classes.

The tontine plan of 1688 was more refined. Foltz does not re-produce the full tontine plan, instead only pointing out some differences with the tontine plan of 1657.[134] This leaves some questions unanswered. According to Foltz, the city wanted to sell 495 shares and to raise 347,625 florins. The tontine was made up of 11 classes with 45 members each. The investment differed according to the nominees' age: those investors who named a nominee between one and 20 years of age had to invest 1,000 florins; those who named a nominee between 75 and 80 years of age had to invest 300 florins. Thus, it seems that the tontine of 1688 had, unlike the first tontine plan of 1657, predefined classes.

2. The Bremen loan of 1692

In 1692, the city of Bremen entered into a loan agreement with ten lenders:[135] Gerard von Mastricht was named as the prime contracting partner; the others were referred to as *Consorten* (members of a consortium) or *Mitinteressenten* without being specifically named in the loan agreement. The sum lent was 1,000 talers. The city of Bremen promised to pay interest at a rate of 4% and to repay the full sum of 1,000 talers at the termination of the loan.

---

[131] *Loew*, 109–111.

[132] Notification Von Der zu Dantzig Revidirten Leib-Rente im Monat Aprilis 1657 (Gdańsk 1657).

[133] See the text corresponding to n. 58, above, and to n. 138, below.

[134] *Foltz* (1912), 459–461. See also the discussion of *Willenberg* (1701), 18 f.

[135] Staatsarchiv Bremen, No. 2-R.1.a.10.c.4.I.

Prima facie, the contract was a simple loan. However, the loan agreement was accompanied by a second agreement, and this second agreement added a tontine element to the transaction without using the word tontine. Both agreements appear in one single document, but they follow one another and are kept separate.

The second agreement was formed between the ten lenders, and it names all of them: Gerhard von Mastricht, Hermannus Meyer, Henricus von Aschen, Johannes Alers, Conradus Iken, Bruno Heilman, Diedrich Ter Hellen, Balthasar Baltsers, Johannes von Rheden, and Helena Meinertzhagen. Each contracting partner was to give 100 talers towards the total sum lent of 1,000 talers. Additionally, each of the lenders named a nominee. Apparently, the nominees were the children of the lenders, and the nominees were between three and nine years of age. The paid interest was to be shared equally between those payees and their heirs whose nominees survived. When only two surviving nominees remained, the respective payees had two options. First, they could split equally between them the remainder of all paid interest and, at the termination of the loan agreement, the capital. Thus, the last two payees had the possibility to terminate the tontine element of their agreement. The last two payees would have chosen this option if they did not want to run the risk that their nominee would die first. Alternatively, they had the option to stick to the original agreement. In that case, the payee whose rights were based on the second-to-last surviving nominee would, nevertheless, receive back the original investment of 100 talers.

The document does not use the word tontine. Moreover, it was not a pooled life annuity scheme but a loan agreement. However, the hereditary principle which is characteristic of tontines was applied to the loan agreement of 1692. The 1692 loan agreement's connection to a tontine was also noted in Bremen: the loan agreement survived in a file on tontines in the *Staatsarchiv Bremen* (Bremen State Archive). Furthermore, the Bremen loan agreement of 1692 suggests that the hereditary principle was widespread in the 17th century and not restricted to life annuity contracts; rather it was applied to a variety of contracts. And indeed, Moshe A. Milevsky discusses the application of the hereditary principle to a will in the late 16th century,[136] and John MacLeod suggests that such clauses were widely known and applied to different kinds of transactions.[137] The Bremen loan agreement of 1692, thus, again raises the question as to how innovative Tonti's proposal really was.

---

[136] *Moshe A Milevsky*, King Williams Tontine, 37–39.

[137] *MacLeod*, 144 f., 150 f.

3. The Prussian tontine of 1698

Friedrich III issued a tontine-bond of 100,000 talers featuring 1,000 shares of 100 talers, each at an interest rate of 5%. Thus, the annuities amounted to 5,000 talers in total. It is again striking that these numbers: the costs per share, the raised capital, and the interest rate, reflect the numbers found in the Venetian tontine-type transaction which was discussed by Harsdörffer in 1651.[138] And indeed, an undated document in a file on the Prussian tontine in the *Brandenburgisches Landeshauptarchiv* (Brandenburg Main State Archive) refers to a tontine in Venice, the French tontine of 1689, the English tontine of 1692, and a French tontine of 1698.[139]

Modern literature refers to the 1698-tontine as an example of a simple tontine.[140] However, the tontine did not mix nominees of all ages. Rather, Art. 3 of the tontine regulations made clear that only children were permitted as nominees.[141] The permissible age was not specified in the tontine plan. However, the file in the *Brandenburgisches Landeshauptarchiv* (Brandenburg Main State Archive) suggests that nobody above the age of 18 was permitted as nominee.[142] Thus, it is more exact to refer to the Prussian tontine as a class tontine with one class only. Children having or not having their residence in Prussia could be named as nominees. Furthermore, Art. 3 allowed contributors to name either themselves or any other person as payee. Pursuant to Art. 1, the capital benefitted the military budget.

4. A Wrocław tontine lottery of 1706?

Michael Christoph Hanov (1695–1773) refers to a tontine which was secured by Silesian salt rights (*Salzregal*); although he does not give an exact date, he refers to it as being initiated under the reign of Emperor Joseph, who was Emperor of the Holy Roman Empire from 1705 to 1711.[143] A *Breslauer* (Wrocław) tontine-lottery of 1706 is mentioned by Zincke.[144] Marperger discussed two lotteries of 1706 which had some connection with *Breslau* (Wrocław). The first was initiated by the city of *Breslau* (Wrocław).[145] It was a simple lottery. None of the

---

[138] See the text corresponding to n. 58, above.

[139] Brandenburgisches Landeshauptarchiv, No. 23A C.2720, fol. 10^r.

[140] *von Zedtwitz*, 140; *Du Pasquier*, (1910) 46 Zeitschrift für Schweizerische Statistik 490.

[141] Patent wegen der einzurichtenden Leib-Renten d.d. den 30. Decembr. 1698, (1736) 6/1 Corpus Constitutionum Marchicarum 655.

[142] Brandenburgisches Landeshauptarchiv, No. 23A C.2720, fol. 54^r–74^r, 81^r–91^r.

[143] *Hanov* (1761), 270

[144] *Zincke* (1744), 502.

[145] The regulations are reproduced in: *Marperger* (1715), 340–347.

prizes were annuities. It was, thus, not a tontine. The second lottery was a Hamburg lottery, which is discussed below. This lottery was authorized by Emperor Joseph, and it was secured by Silesian salt rights. The Silesian salt department was based in *Breslau* (Wrocław).

5. Hamburg tontine lotteries of 1706, 1708, and 1709?

Thus, the tontine of 1706 was not a Wrocław tontine, but rather a Hamburg scheme.[146] However, the 1706-scheme was a simple life annuity lottery. It did not feature the hereditary principle which is characteristic of tontines. It is also worth noting that it was not the first life annuity lottery which was conducted in Hamburg. As early as 1701, Samuel Friedrich Willenberg (1663–1748) mentioned a Hamburg life annuity lottery and referred to it as a *revised* lottery, thus suggesting that there were earlier examples of it[147] – and indeed, the first Hamburg lottery which is said to have involved annuities as prizes dates from 1612 with further lotteries to follow.[148]

Two further lotteries were advertised in 1708 and 1709. The 1708 scheme had four classes of prizes:[149] two classes with cash-prizes, one class with simple life annuities as prizes, and the last class with life annuities on the basis of a tontine as prizes. The last class adopted the hereditary principle, and the published plan explicitly spoke of a tontine.[150] It thus seems that this is the scheme which modern literature refers to as a curious example of tontine transactions showing elements of a lottery. However, it was not the first tontine lottery. It became apparent above that Harsdörffer had mentioned a Venetian tontine lottery already in 1651, and Harsdörffer's book was published in Hamburg.[151]

The Hamburg tontine lottery featured 3,000 tickets, each ticket cost 60 marks, and all tickets were divided into 10 to 12 classes with 250 to 300 shares per class. The interest rate was 5%, so that the annuities totalled 9,000 marks. In order to open the lottery also to poorer individuals, it was planned that it was preceded by another lottery: here each ticket cost 12 marks, 10,000 tickets were sold, and 2,000 winners were, as their prize, admitted to the main lottery. Finally, the 1709-

---

[146] The regulations are reproduced in: *Marperger* (1715), 320–331. See also *von Mensi* (1890), 425 referring to it as a lottery of 1707.

[147] *Willenberg* (1701), 7.

[148] *Nordwestdeutsche Klassenlotterie*, 350 Jahre Staatslotterie, passim.

[149] The regulations are reproduced in: *Marperger* (1715), 362–377.

[150] See also *Nordwestdeutsche Klassenlotterie*, 350 Jahre Staatslotterie, passim.

[151] See the text corresponding to n. 59, above.

lottery was not a new lottery plan:[152] it simply modified and improved the plan of 1708. The plan of 1708 had not attracted enough subscriptions.[153]

In conclusion, what at first appeared to be evidence of four separate tontine-plans – *Breslau* (Wrocław) (1706), Hamburg (1706), Hamburg (1708), and Hamburg (1709) – reflects in fact only a single tontine lottery of 1709 alongside the simple lottery embodied by the Hamburg scheme of 1706.

Above I have identified four groups of tontine-participants: the issuer, the investors, the payees, and the nominees. The example of the 1706-lottery introduces a further actor: whereas the city of Hamburg conducted the lottery, it most likely did so in the interest and on account of the Empire. Otherwise it would not be explicable why the payments for the 1706-lottery were secured by Silesian salt rights.[154] Something very similar happened later with the Bolzano tontine.[155]

Finally, the tontine lottery of 1709 suggests again a Venetian influence rather than an influence by Tonti: Tonti had proposed in 1653 a tontine. Of course, Tonti had also proposed in 1656 a lottery plan, and consequently lotteries, and even games,[156] were referred to as tontines.[157] However, Tonti apparently had not mixed the two in order to create a tontine lottery. However, Harsdörffer had reported in 1651 of a Venetian tontine lottery.[158]

6. The Lübeck tontine plans of 1708 and 1715

The city of Lübeck published a short tontine plan in 1708.[159] It was a plan for a simple tontine without any classes. Nevertheless, the plan made explicit that only young people should be allowed as nominees. The plan stated that it would benefit the town treasury (*Stadt-Cassa*) without further pointing out a specific purpose of the tontine. The plan spoke of a *Tondine* and, thus, misspelled the term of art. The tontine was to raise 10,000 talers by selling 100 shares each at a cost of 100 talers. Again, even though the plan spoke of a *Tondine*, the resemblance to the numbers of the Venetian scheme as reported by Harsdörffer in 1651

---

152 The regulations are reproduced in: *Marperger* (1715), 377–393.

153 *Nordwestdeutsche Klassenlotterie*, 350 Jahre Staatslotterie, passim.

154 However, it has also been suggested that the Hamburg lotteries of the early 18th century were planned to pay Hamburg soldiers: *Nordwestdeutsche Klassenlotterie*, 350 Jahre Staatslotterie, passim.

155 See the text corresponding to and following n. 169, below.

156 *Delbrel*, 112.

157 *Rietsch* and *Gallais-Hamonno*, Lorenzo Tonti, 33 ff.

158 See the text corresponding to n. 59, above.

159 Archiv der Hansestadt Lübeck, 3.4-2 Stadt-Cassa No. 483.

is striking.[160] The document which the investor received was called a *Brief*. The interest rate was 3%. And the tontine plan pointed out that, thus, the last payee would receive an annual payment of 300 talers for his or her original investment of 100 talers. The published plan was very short and was much less refined compared to other plans of the time and, even more so, compared to later plans. It is unclear whether the tontine received enough subscriptions in order to be issued.

It is, however, clear that the discussion on whether a tontine or a life annuity scheme should be issued or whether a lottery should be run continued until 1715.[161] Furthermore, the *Archiv der Hansestadt Lübeck* (Archive of the Hanse City Lübeck) contains accounts of a scheme called a *Tondiene* which was issued in 1715 and ran from 1716 to 1748.[162] It had 96 shares, each at a cost of 300 marks. For 33 years, 18 marks were paid out per share and per annum. The annuities did not increase over the 33 years. These numbers correspond to a handwritten plan of 1715 which spoke of a *Tondine*, and the plan makes clear that the capital was not to be repaid upon the termination of the 33 years.[163] Thus, it was not a tontine in the modern sense. It did not apply the hereditary principle which is characteristic of tontines.[164] Presumably, the scheme spoke of a tontine because the capital was non-recoverable. And the scheme proves that the term tontine was used rather loosely to name a variety of different financial schemes.

7. The Saxon tontine lottery plan of 1723

The *Sächsisches Staatsarchiv, Hauptstaatsarchiv Dresden* (Saxon State Archive, Main State Archive Dresden) holds a file with the title: *Lotterie oder Tontine zur Erweiterung des Steuerhauses in Dresden* (Lottery or Tontine for the Purpose of Extending the Tax Administration Building in Dresden).[165] Two documents from the year 1722 drafted in preparation of the scheme indeed speak of a tontine. However, these seem to be the only two references to a tontine in the file. The published scheme from the year 1723 was nothing but a lottery. It had different classes of prizes, some of which were simple money prizes. Some prizes were life annuities. However, the life annuities terminated as soon as the nominee

---

[160] See the text corresponding to n. 58, above.

[161] Archiv der Hansestadt Lübeck, 3.4-2 Stadt-Cassa No. 482 and 5.1-1/08 Krämerkompanie No. 1552.

[162] Archiv der Hansestadt Lübeck, 05.4-4 Tontine-078 No. 01,

[163] Archiv der Hansestadt Lübeck, 3.4-2 Stadt-Cassa No. 482.

[164] See the text corresponding to n. 117, above.

[165] Sächsisches Staatsarchiv (Hauptstaatsarchiv Dresden), 10036 Finanzarchiv Loc. 41493 Rep. 59 Lit. D No. 1282.

died. Thus, the hereditary principle did not apply. It seems that the term tontine was used as a synonym for a simple life annuity lottery.

8. The Schweinfurt tontine plan of 1735

In 1735 the city of Schweinfurt published a plan for a *Leib-Renthen-Societät* (Life Annuity Society).[166] It was a simple tontine. Its 1,000 shares were not divided into classes. Each share was sold for 30 gulden. Thus, the society raised 30,000 gulden. The society paid 4% interest on the capital and, thus, annuities amounting to 1,200 gulden were paid out. The hereditary principle applied. The regulations clearly set out the costs of administration: 1% or 300 gulden were used each year for the administration of the scheme. After the death of the first 400 members the annuity paid out was reduced by 10%, again in order to cover the costs of administration. Furthermore, in the first year no annuities were paid out, and the saved money was used for the costs of issuing the tontine. It is unclear whether the tontine was ultimately issued.

9. A Viennese tontine plan prior to 1736

In his study on Austrian public finance, Franz Mensi von Klarbach (1854–1935) referred to an undated Viennese tontine plan.[167] He suggests that it was drafted prior to 1736 and that the plan was initiated by merchants from Hamburg. According to Mensi the plan had some curious details: the annuity of a deceased member was not shared between the surviving members but was instead offered in an auction to the surviving members. The bid had to be at least for half of the nominal value of the share. The auction proceeds were then split between all investors. According to Mensi, the tontine was never issued. I was not able to identify the file which Mensi refers to in the *Österreichisches Staatsarchiv* (Austrian State Archive).

10. The Bolzano tontine of 1737

A 1738 report in the newspaper *Wöchentlich-kurzgefaßte Historische Nachrichten* on the Bolzano tontine of 1737 documents again the European dimension of tontines as an investment scheme.[168] The tontine was initiated because people

---

[166] The plan can be found in: Staatsarchiv Nürnberg, Reichsstadt Nürnberg D No. 4814. See also *Fiedler*, 54.

[167] *von Mensi* (1890), 429 f.

[168] Nachtrag zu denen wöchentlich-kurzgefaßten Historischen Nachrichten der Neuern Europäischen Begebenheiten, 1stes Stück (Regensburg 1738), 16. The tontine regulations

of the Habsburg territories had up to that time been forced to invest their money in foreign schemes, and the preamble to the tontine regulations refers to foreign tontines as models. The preamble to the tontine regulations also made clear that it was not a tontine of the city of *Bozen* (Bolzano). It was a tontine initiated by the Austrian Archduke:

> Und geben Euch hiermit zu vernemmen / … nachdeme Uns ganz verläßlich zu vernemmen kommen / was für besonderer Nutzen dem gemeinen Weesen durch die in verschiedenen auswärtigen Königreich / und Landen errichtete Tontinen / oder so-genannte Leib-Gedingen zugegangen seye / auch was grosses Verlangen von verschiedenen / sowohl frembden als Unseren Lands-Unterthanen zu Einführung einer gleichen Tontina, oder Leib-Geding in Unseren Erb-Königreich / Fürstenthumb / und Landen geheget: … Wir auß Landes-Vätterlicher / dem Publico zu prospicieren beständig-tragenden Neygung / solch-inständigen Ansinnen zu willfahren / und diesemnach gleichfals in Unseren Oesterreichischen Erb-Landen / und zwar in Unserer / mit allen vornemmen Handels-Städten in Europa in guter Correspondenz-stehenden / auch bey Fried- und Kriegs-Zeiten von jedermann sicher besuchet werden-mögende Stadt Botzen / ein dergleichen Tontina, oder Leib-Geding aufrichten zu lassen / uns genädigist entschlossen haben.

> And We give you to hear / ... after We have reliably found out / what special benefit these tontines / or so-called life annuities which were issued by different foreign kingdoms / and countries / are to the common people / also what great demand of different subjects / both foreign and domestic, there is to introduce a similar tontine or life annuity in Our Kingdom / Duchy / and lands: ... We decided / out of our inclination as father of the nation / that the common people may prosper / and in order to comply with the request, to introduce also in our Austrian hereditary lands / such a tontine or life annuity / in our city of Bolzano / which is well connected with all noble trading towns in Europe / and which may safely be visited both in times of peace and war.

The preamble to the tontine confirms the observation I made above when discussing the Hamburg lottery of 1706.[169] Alongside the issuer, the investors, the payees, and the nominees, there may be another actor when issuing a tontine: here the city of *Bozen* (Bolzano) presumably issued the tontine in the interest and on account of the Austrian Archduke. The regulations made explicit that the tontine of 1737 was open to foreigners. Attached to the regulations, there was a list of representatives from whom shares could be purchased. They were based, among other cities, in Amsterdam, Antwerp, Augsburg, Ancona, Basel, Bern,

are reproduced at 16–19. The regulations are also reproduced in: (1738) 40 Europäischer Staats-Secretarius Welcher die neuesten Begebenheiten unpartheyisch erzehlet, und vernünftig beurtheilet 328–334; (1736/1738) Die Neue Europäische Fama, Welche den gegenwärtigen Zustand der vornehmsten Höfe entdecket 842–850. In addition, the tontine regulations can be found in: Österreichisches Staatsarchiv, AT-OeStA/FHKA SUS Patente 70.5; Südtiroler Landesarchiv (Bozen), No. 3.23.2 Merkantilmagistrat Bozen. Finally, the tontine is mentioned in: *Zedler*, Universal-Lexicon XLIV (1745), 1250; (1752) 2 Neue Europäische Staats- und Reisegeographie 595.

[169] See the text corresponding to n. 155, above.

Breslau (Wrocław), *Köln* (Cologne), Florence, *Danzig* (Gdańsk), Genoa, Hamburg, Leipzig, London, Lyon, Milan, Namur, Nantes, *Nürnberg* (Nuremberg), Paris, Prague, Regensburg, Rome, Strasbourg, and Venice. The tontine plan was published at least in German, Italian, and French.[170] And indeed, it attracted international investors.[171]

The tontine consisted of four classes. Each class had 1,000 shares of 500 florins each:

1st class: age below 25; raised capital 500,000 florins; number of shares 1,000; price per share 500 florins; interest rate 7%; initial annuity per share 35 florins; total amount of annuities 35,000 florins;

2nd class: ages 25–40; raised capital 500,000 florins; number of shares 1,000; price per share 500 florins; interest rate 8%; initial annuity per share 40 florins; total amount of annuities 40,000 florins;

3rd class: ages 41–55; raised capital 500,000 florins; number of shares 1,000; price per share 500 florins; interest rate 9%; initial annuity per share 45 florins; total amount of annuities 45,000 florins;

4th class: age 55 and above; raised capital 500,000 florins; number of shares 1,000; price per share 500 florins; interest rate 10%; initial annuity per share 50 florins; total amount of annuities 50,000 florins.

The tontine thus raised a capital of 2,000,000 florins and initially paid out annuities worth 170,000 florins. It was a compound tontine. The tontine regulations stated that upon the death of a payee, half of his annuity was lost to the issuer and the other half was divided between the surviving payees of that class. If one class died out, half of the annuity which the last payee of that class had received was divided between the surviving classes; the other half was again lost to the issuer. Finally, the raised capital of 2,000,000 florins was lost to the issuer once the tontine came to an end. Apparently, the plan and its resulting figures raised questions among the general public. The plan expressed the calculation plainly: it simply stated that half of every deceased's annuity was split between the surviving payees. In the 4th class, for example, the initial annuity a_1 amounted to 50 florins. After the death of the first nominee the annuity for the surviving 999 annuitants would have been calculated as follows:

$$a_2 = a_1 + \frac{a_1}{2 \times 999}$$

And after the death of the second nominee the annuity for the surviving 998 annuitants would then have been calculated as follows:

[170] Südtiroler Landesarchiv (Bozen), No. 3.23.2 Merkantilmagistrat Bozen.

[171] See the subscriptions collected in: Südtiroler Landesarchiv (Bozen), No. 3.23.1 Merkantilmagistrat Bozen.

$$a_3 = a_2 + \frac{a_2}{2 \times 998}$$

Each time anew, only half of the annuity of the deceased payee was to be split between the surviving payees. The last surviving payee of the 4th class would have thus received only 1,783.90 florins. The original plan was published in January 1736. In November of the same year a clarification was published.[172] The issuer specified the annuity which was to be received by the last payee in each class. In the 4th class it amounted to 25,025 florins. Thus, the original plan expressed the calculation unclearly. For a_2 the calculation remained the same:

$$a_2 = a_1 + \frac{a_1}{2 \times 999}$$

After the death of the second nominee, however, the annuity was to be calculated as follows:

$$a_3 = a_1 + \frac{2 \times a_1}{2 \times 998}$$

After the death of the second-to-last nominee the annuity for the last surviving annuitant was finally to be calculated as follows:

$$a_{1000} = a_1 + \frac{999 \times a_1}{2 \times 1} = 50 + \frac{49{,}950}{2} = 25{,}025$$

11. The Hesse-Kassel tontine lottery plan of 1743

From 1743 on, plans to issue a tontine were discussed in the *Landgrafschaft Hessen-Kassel* (Landgraviate of Hesse-Kassel).[173] The first tontine plan of 1743 consisted of seven classes. The 1st class was for those aged 1 to 7. It was planned to raise a capital of 2,000 talers with 1,000 shares at a price of 2 talers per share. The interest rate was 4%. However, for the first 14 years no annuities were to be paid out. Instead, the interest was added to the raised capital. According to the plan, the accumulated capital amounted to 3,120 talers in 1757. Thereafter, apparently the normal hereditary principle applied.

The 2nd class was for those aged 8 to 14; the 3rd class for those aged 15 to 30. Both classes were designed identically: each class was planned to raise a capital of 10,000 talers with 1,000 shares at the price of 10 talers each. The interest rate

[172] Nachtrag zu denen wöchentlich-kurzgefaßten Historischen Nachrichten der Neuern Europäischen Begebenheiten, 1stes Stück (Regensburg 1738), 20.

[173] Hessisches Staatsarchiv (Marburg), 17 II No. 383.

on the capital of 10,000 talers was 4%. Thus, the paid out annuities amounted to 400 talers. However, it was not planned that each payee would receive the same initial annuity. Rather, the plan involved a lottery element.

The plan explains this lottery element much more clearly for the next two classes. The 4th class was for those aged 30 to 40; the 5th class for those aged 40 to 50. With respect to the price per share, it is unclear whether it was 10 or 25 talers. However, the further calculation seems to be based on the prize of 10 talers per share. Accordingly, both classes were planned to raise a capital of 10,000 talers with 1,000 shares at the price of 10 talers each. The total amount of annuities amounted in both classes to 400 talers. The right to the annuities was determined in a lottery. The first prize was an annuity of 15 talers; 2 persons received an annuity of 10 talers each; 7 persons an annuity of 5 talers; 10 persons an annuity of 4 talers; 30 persons an annuity of 3 talers; 50 persons an annuity of 2 talers; and 100 persons an annuity of 1 taler.

The 6th class was for those aged 50 to 60; and the 7th class for those aged 60 to 70. The price per share was 25 talers, and there were 1,000 shares in each class. Thus, each class was intended to raise 25,000 talers. The interest rate on the raised capital was again 4%. Thus, in each class a total amount of 1,000 talers was to be paid out. Apparently, these last two classes did not involve a lottery element; and the annuities were paid out on the basis of the hereditary principle.

The file at *Hessisches Staatsarchiv* (Hessian State Archive) in Marburg reveals that the drafters of the tontine plan took notice of other projects. The file contains a copy of the printed plan of the Bolzano tontine of 1737, references to French tontines of 1696, 1724, 1734, 1742, and 1745, and references to a Dutch tontine in Frisia.[174]

12. The Berlin tontine plan of 1747

A printed tontine plan of the *Königlich Preußische Dohm-Kirchen Directorium* (Royal Prussian Governing Board of the Cathedral) dating from 10 October 1747 has survived in the *Brandenburgisches Landeshauptarchiv* (Brandenburg Main State Archive).[175] The plan does not make explicit the purpose of the tontine. However, it seems clear – and this purpose is also reflected in the title under which the Brandenburg archive holds the file – that the raised capital was to be used for the reconstruction of the Berlin cathedral. The original cathedral was inaugurated in 1536 and later demolished in 1747. Between 1747 and 1750

174 To my knowledge there was no French public tontine in 1724. See also *Gallais-Hamonno* and *Rietsch*, Financial Engineering, 55 ff.; *Delbrel*, 109 ff.

175 Brandenburgisches Landeshauptarchiv, No. 23A C.2720, fol. 79r–80v.

a new cathedral was built.[176] The tontine planned to raise 30,000 talers. 300 shares were to be sold, each at a price of 100 talers. The interest rate was 5%. Thus, the initial annuity per share amounted to 5 talers, and the last payee received an annuity of 1,500 talers. It was a simple tontine, not a class tontine. And unlike the Prussian tontine of 1698, the plan did not only allow children to be named as nominees. The plan was authorized by Frederic II (the Great) and was published in 1747. However, it is unclear whether the tontine received enough subscriptions in order to be issued.

13. Two Saxon tontine lotteries of 1748

In 1748, Heinrich von Brühl (1700–1763) initiated a tontine for *Sachsen* (Saxony).[177] von Brühl was the powerful first minister to the Saxon elector Friedrich August II, who was at the same time the Polish King and Lithuanian Grand Duke August III. In the late 1740s Saxony was in great financial need.[178] And the 1740s were the time of the first two Silesian Wars. A man by the name of Alexander Mackphaill Baron de Bishopsfield, allegedly of Scottish origin, who supposedly had worked in the financial sector in the Netherlands and who was later imprisoned and convicted,[179] proposed to von Brühl a *Leib-, auch Familien-Renten-Negotiation* (Life and also Family Annuity Negotiation). It was a tontine lottery. However, it had a unique feature which is already reflected in the name: it was a family annuity scheme in the sense that certain payees were able to change the nominee to pass on the right to annuities to future generations in the family. The plan was published in 1748 in both German and French.[180] The plan indicated already in its title that the tontine was to be administered in Leipzig.

The scheme had 5,250 shares divided into 5 classes. Each share cost 200 talers, so that the scheme was to raise 1,050,000 talers in total. Each class was further divided into 20 subclasses. These subclasses were consecutively numbered throughout all 5 classes. The 1st class was, for example, designed as follows:

---

[176] *Demps*, 23–25; *Klingenburg*, 43.

[177] *von Justi*, Leben und Character (1760), 168 f.; *O.F. Schmidt*, Minister Graf Brühl, 82; *Gretschel* (1853), 65 f.

[178] *Groß*, 148 f.

[179] *Liscow* (1844), 66.

[180] Ihrer Königl. Majestät in Pohlen und Churfürstl. Durchl. zu Sachsen Edict wegen der im Monath Januario 1748 zu Leipzig eröffneten Leib- auch Familien-Renten-Negotiation (Dresden 1748); Edit de sa Majesté le Roi de Pologne, Electeur de Saxe concernant la negociation de rentes viageres et de famille ouverte a Leipsig au mois de Janvier 1748 (Dresde 1748). See also Sächsisches Staatsarchiv (Hauptstaatsarchiv Dresden), 10015 Landtag No. 328 (H 108) and 10026 Geheimes Kabinett No. 530/02–04.

subclass	number of shares	cost per share	interest rate	initial annuity per share
1st	5	200 talers	20%	40 talers
2nd	5	200 talers	15%	30 talers
3rd	10	200 talers	10%	20 talers
4th	10	200 talers	9%	18 talers
5th	15	200 talers	8%	16 talers
6th	20	200 talers	7%	14 talers
7th	25	200 talers	6%	12 talers
8th	25	200 talers	6%	12 talers
9th	30	200 talers	5.5%	11 talers
10th	30	200 talers	5.5%	11 talers
11th	40	200 talers	5%	10 talers
12th	40	200 talers	5%	10 talers
13th	50	200 talers	5%	10 talers
14th	50	200 talers	5%	10 talers
15th	55	200 talers	5%	10 talers
16th	60	200 talers	5%	10 talers
17th	80	200 talers	5%	10 talers
18th	100	200 talers	5%	10 talers
19th	150	200 talers	5%	10 talers
20th	200	200 talers	5%	10 talers

In the 2nd class the interest rate of 5% did not start until the 35th subclass; in the 3rd class the interest rate of 5.5% started in the 51th subclass and the interest rate of 5% in the 55th class; and the 4th class was designed identical to the 3rd class. The 5th class had 1,250 shares.

The relatively high interest rates of the plan are best explained by the financial difficulties which *Sachsen* (Saxony) experienced at that time. The allocation of a subscriber to one of the subclasses was presumably determined in a lottery. However, the published plan is unclear as to the exact function of the lottery element as it does not specify the details of that lottery.

It is clear that the subscribers had to name the nominee only after the lottery had been conducted. Thus, the subclasses were not organized according to the nominees' age. Yet it seems likely that subscribers named only young nominees in order to increase the chance of receiving high annuity payments. When subscribing to the scheme, the buyer received a *Loos-Zeddel* (lottery ticket). Once the lottery was conducted, the winner received a *Leib-Renten-Schein* (life annuity bond) after he had named his nominee, and the certificate exhibited the nominee's name.

The lower-numbered subclasses profited from higher initial annuities: 40 talers in the 1st subclass as compared to 10 talers in the 20th subclass. However, higher increases were possible in the higher-numbered subclasses: 200 talers for the last payee of the 1st subclass as compared to 2,000 talers for the last payee of the 20th subclass. The 100th subclass of the 5th class had 300 members and the interest rate was 5%, so that the last payee received an annuity of 3,000 talers. It was only within subclasses that the hereditary principle applied. Thus, strictly speaking each subclass formed its own tontine.

At a certain point in time, the scheme changed its nature to what the plan called a family annuity. However, the published plan is unclear on a number of details. Most importantly, it seems that the last payee of each class was able to replace, within certain time limits, the original nominee and name his or her son or grandson as new nominee and last payee. Thus, the payment of the annuities was prolonged and it would now benefit a family. Nevertheless, the details were complicated: if the last payee named his son as the new nominee, then the grandson became nominee only if the son died before the original nominee. However, it was also possible to name only the grandson as new nominee. Furthermore, the published plan explicitly referred to the option that a payee could adopt somebody in order to name this adopted person as nominee.

Furthermore, it is unclear *when* the scheme changed its nature: according to § 17 of the plan, it seems that the change occurred once there were only 100 payees left – one payee per subclass. In effect, that should have meant that the change only occurred when there was only one payee left in the last subclass: it is unlikely that the second-to-last nominee died in all 100 subclasses in the same year. By contrast, § 18 focused on each subclass: each subclass changed to a family annuity once there was, in that specific class, only one payee left.

In addition, the annuities were re-calculated once the scheme had changed its nature to a family annuity: each payee was to receive 5% of the invested capital in his or her subclass. However, it seems that the annuities did not change, as the published plan simply ordered that, for the calculation of the annuity, a fictitious invested sum was to be used. The last payee of the 1st subclass, for example, was still to receive 200 talers. The sum was, however, to be calculated based on a fictitious investment of 4,000 talers instead of the invested sum of 1,000 talers. It is unclear why the published plan ordered this re-calculation.

Against these nebulous provisions of the published plan, it does not come as a surprise that it proved possible only to fill the subclasses of the 1st class, even though the plan was advertised also in the Netherlands – and it seems that 79 shares of the 1st class were sold in the Netherlands.[181] Furthermore, it was only after the first class was initiated that the payments of the annuities were guaranteed by the Saxon estates. At the same time the estates decided to advertise a

---

[181] Sächsisches Staatsarchiv (Hauptstaatsarchiv Dresden), 10026 Geheimes Kabinett No. 530/02, fol. 328.

second plan for a lottery, similarly consisting of different classes. However, once again only the first class attracted the necessary number of subscriptions.

14. The Wied tontine plan of 1749

In 1749 the shire of Wied advertised a plan for a tontine. It is unclear whether the tontine was issued. At the time, Wied was a sovereign shire which was promoted to a principality in 1784/85 and which lost its sovereignty in 1806.[182] Today the territory is part of *Rheinland-Pfalz* (Rhineland-Palatinate). The tontine was supposed to raise 200,000 talers, with 9,930 shares divided into seven classes:[183]

1st class: ages 60–70; raised capital 8,000 talers; number of shares 80; price per share 100 talers; interest rate 15%; initial annuity per share 15 talers; total amount of annuities 1,200 talers;

2nd class: ages 50–60; raised capital 12,000 talers; number of shares 150; price per share 80 talers; interest rate 10%; initial annuity per share 8 talers; total amount of annuities 1,200 talers;

3rd class: ages 40–50; raised capital 15,000 talers; number of shares 300; price per share 50 talers; interest rate 8%; initial annuity per share 4 talers; total amount of annuities 1,200 talers;

4th class: ages 30–40; raised capital 20,000 talers; number of shares 500; price per share 40 talers; interest rate 6%; initial annuity per share 2.4 talers; total amount of annuities 1,200 talers;

5th class: ages 20–30; raised capital 24,000 talers; number of shares 800; price per share 30 talers; interest rate 5%; initial annuity per share 1.5 talers; total amount of annuities 1,200 talers;

6th class: ages 10–20; raised capital 80,000 talers; number of shares 4,000; price per share 20 talers; interest rate 1.5%;[184] initial annuity per share 0.3 taler; total amount of annuities 1,200 talers;

7th class: ages 1–10; raised capital 41,000 talers; number of shares 4,100; price per share 10 talers; interest rate 2.93%; initial annuity per share 0.29 taler; total amount of annuities 1,200 talers.

The annuity payments for the 6th and 7th classes were postponed. Article 9 explained that the costs of certifying the nominee's life – a certificate which was

[182] 'Wied', in: Brockhaus Enzyklopädie, vol. 30, 40; *Schlüter*, 33 f.; *Troßbach*, 18.

[183] Anschreiben Von Errichtung einer Tontine oder Classen-Leib-Renten-Cassa (Neuwied am Rhein 1749). The Wied tontine of 1749 is mentioned by *Ayrer* (1750), 25.

[184] The interest rates in the 6th and the 7th classes appear relatively odd. The tontine plan explicitly sets out the price per share, the number of shares, and the total amount of annuities paid out per annum. And these numbers correspond to the total amount of shares, the raised capital, and the total amount of annuities paid out per annum for the whole scheme. Thus, a printing error seems unlikely.

needed each year when collecting the annuities[185] – could easily be higher than the initial annuity per share. In the 6th class the total amount of annuity payments, 1,200 talers, was to be collected in a special fund for the first seven years and receive an annual interest rate of 4%. Deducted were the costs of administration. After seven years the capital of the special fund, amounting to 9,971 talers and 18 kreuzers, was to be paid out to the surviving payees of the 6th class, and thereafter the usual payments of annuities commenced. For the 7th class the same procedure was to be applied for ten years. Within the classes the usual hereditary principle applied. When the 1st class died, out half of the total annuity amounting to 600 talers was to be equally divided between the surviving classes. The other 600 talers were split between the surviving members of all classes who had purchased more than one share. An equivalent procedure was to be applied to all other classes. The last surviving payee was to receive a life annuity of 4,000 talers.

According to Art. 30, the investor, the payee, and the nominee did not have to be identical. Finally, Art. 27 clarified that the tontine was not restricted to subjects of the shire: shares were to be sold in Frankfurt, *Köln* (Cologne), Amsterdam, Hamburg, *Nürnberg* (Nuremberg), Augsburg, and other cities, and advertisements were to be published accordingly in newspapers. However, the sale of the shares met with difficulties. In Hanau, for example, it seems to have been forbidden to buy shares in the Wied tontine.[186]

15. The Hesse-Kassel tontine plan of 1750

In 1750, a further tontine was planned in the *Landgrafschaft Hessen-Kassel* (Landgraviate of Hesse-Kassel) to finance and benefit the *Hofhospital St. Elisabeth* in Kassel, a hospital which was founded by the Landgraves of Hesse.[187] The manuscript of the tontine plan is undated. The file holding the manuscript in the *Hessisches Staatsarchiv* (Hessian State Archive) in Marburg is dated to 1750, but a note on the file indicates that the Marburg archivist Gerhard Menk dates it instead to 1780.

The tontine planned to raise 10,000 talers. The annuities totalled 500 talers, so that an interest rate of 5% was to be paid on the capital. It was planned to issue 500 shares each at a price of 20 talers. The 500 shares were to be divided into 5 classes with 100 shares each. The interest rate was in each class the same. Thus, the initial annuity per share amounted to 1 taler. The classes were divided according to the age of the nominees. The 1st class was for those aged 1 to 15; the

---

[185] See the text corresponding to and following n. 561, below.

[186] Hessisches Staatsarchiv (Marburg), 80 No. 6345.

[187] Hessisches Staatsarchiv (Marburg), 40 Rubr. 24 No. 462.

2nd class for those aged 15 to 30; the 3rd class for those aged 30 to 45; the 4th class for those aged 45 to 60; and the 5th class for those of 60 to 75 years of age. The plan applied the hereditary principle. It was, thus, a true class tontine. The last survivor of each class, hence, received an annuity of 100 talers for his or her initial investment of 20 talers.

16. A Merseburg tontine of 1750?

The *Landesarchiv Sachsen-Anhalt* (State Archive for Saxony-Anhalt) in Wernigerode contains accounts of a tontine of the Bishopric Merseburg (*Des Stifts Merseburg Steuer-Cassen-Extract ... zur Tontine*) for the years 1750 to 1755.[188] The Bishopric Merseburg had been secularized in the 16th century and had become part of the *Kurfürstentum Sachsen* (Electorate of Saxony).[189] Between 1657 and 1738 the territories were part of the Duchy of *Sachsen-Merseburg* (Saxe-Merseburg). Until the 18th century, within the Electorate of Saxony and within the Duchy of Saxe-Merseburg, the territories of the former Bishopric were still administered by its own Bishopric-government. The accounts do not allow any conclusion as to what kind of financial scheme it was and whether it was a true tontine.

17. The Gotha tontine lottery of 1752

The Gotha tontine of 1752 was a compound tontine with a lottery element.[190] The tontine had five classes, each class with 100 shares of 200 talers. However, the classes were not arranged according to the age of the nominees. Initially, the annuity payment consisted of two parts: the first part was fixed and passed on to the surviving members of the tontine; the second part was allocated through a lottery and it was lost to the issuer if the nominee died. It was the second part of the annuity payment which made it a compound tontine. A curious detail was that the first hereditary part was not divided between all surviving members of a class upon the death of a nominee. Instead, all shares were numbered consecutively for each class. The hereditary part of the annuity was passed on to the payee of the share corresponding to the next higher surviving number of the same

---

188 Landesarchiv Sachsen-Anhalt (Wernigerode), A 30aII II No. 474.

189 *Wolgast*, 237–253; *Schirmer*, 121–132; *Sames*, 133–150.

190 Plan einer unter Assecuration der Landschafft des Fürstenthums Gotha zu entrichtenden Leib-Renten-Negotiation oder Tontine (Gotha 1752). The regulations of the tontine are also reproduced in: *Krünitz*, Encyclopädie LXXI (1796), 295–303; *Gesner* (1752), 226–238. It is analysed by *Bergius* (1771), 167–171. See also *Braun*, Geschichte, 153–155; *Du Pasquier*, (1910) 46 Zeitschrift für Schweizerische Statistik 498 f.; *von Zedtwitz*, 141; *Wortner*, 115.

class or, if the nominees of the higher numbered shares had already died, to the lowest numbered surviving share of the class. If one class died out, the hereditary part of the annuity of that class was divided between the surviving classes and within the surviving classes between their members.

18. The Augsburg tontine of 1753/55

Starting in 1753 there are a number of publications describing an Augsburg tontine that was planned in connection with the *Gesellschaft der freyen Künste* (Society of the Free Arts), which was renamed in 1755 as the *Kaiserliche Franciscischen Akademie der freyen Künste und Wissenschaften* (Academy of the Free Arts and Sciences in Honour of Emperor Francis).[191] The only modern author who mentions the tontine is Felix Freude, this in his early 20th-century study on the Augsburg academy.[192] The founders of the society and the academy were Johann Daniel Herz the Elder (1693–1754) and his son Johann Daniel Herz the Younger (1722–1792). Herz the Elder was a copperplate engraver and a publisher of respective works. Copperplate engraving was, together with gold- and silverworks, an important economic sector in Augsburg with Europe-wide exports.[193] In 1740 the Augsburg copperplate engravers were negatively affected by a Hungarian import ban on foreign copperplate engravings, and in 1746 this ban was extended to Austria.

Herz the Elder and Herz the Younger, among many other activities, founded in 1753 the *Gesellschaft der freyen Künste*. It was basically a scheme to fund Augsburg copperplate engravers through a tontine. The raised capital was apparently used to pay those copperplate engravers who were members of the society. Investors bought not only rights to annuities but also to etchings, and they were formally members of the society, too. The tontine planned to raise 100,000 florins.

After the death of his father, Herz the Younger changed the society into the academy in 1755. It received imperial privileges. The raised capital was increased to 200,000 florins: 8,000 shares were to be sold for 25 florins each. The investor, the payee, and the nominee did not have to be the same person. And it was explicitly allowed to name public persons as nominees. Between 1757 and

---

[191] Die schon längst von vielen eifrigst verlangte Nachricht von der Beschaffenheit, Einrichtung und Vorhaben der Kaiserl. privilegirten Gesellschaft der freien Künste und Wissenschaft (Augsburg 1753), 25 f.; (1757) Das Neueste aus der anmuthigen Gelehrsamkeit 750–758, 827–831; (1755) Die reisende und correspondirende Pallas oder Kunst-Zeitung 22–24.

[192] *Freude*, passim.

[193] 'Kupferstich', in: *Grünsteudel*, 589.

1774, each investor was to receive 1 florin and 30 kreuzers per annum. The tontine was to start in 1774, and 6,000 florins per annum were to be distributed among the surviving members.

In 1758 Herz the Younger developed a further plan. He wanted to initiate the *Allgemeine Cadetten- und hohe Kunst-Schule in dem Heiligen Römischen Reich*, which was to be a school for the arts. For the purpose of funding that school, Herz the Younger initiated a lottery having 100,000 tickets costing 10 florins each.[194] Among the prizes were shares in the tontine. Furthermore, a specified number of subscribers were allowed to send their children to the school.

These schemes were accompanied by numerous disputes and conflicts: (1) Herz the Elder and Herz the Younger alleged that they had founded the society and the academy to promote the arts and sciences. It was, however, criticized that they were rather driven by economic interests. (2) Father and son were not able to unite all Augsburg copperplate engravers and in fact also met with opposition. (3) The Augsburg publishers of copperplate engravings saw the society and the academy as a competitor. (4) An interim list of investors, payees, and nominees was published in 1755.[195] This list was rather nebulous as it was unclear which names corresponded to investors, to payees or to nominees. However, it seems that the tontine attracted attention from all over Europe, with Austrian, Croatian, Danish, Dutch, English, French, Hungarian, Italian, Jordanian, Polish, Russian, and Swiss contributors, payees, and nominees. However, it might be that this international attention is not so much an indication that tontines were an international investment product, but that, in this special case, the subscriptions came from places where Augsburg copperplate engravers, and especially the family Herz, sold their works. A further list with the names of the first 4,000 nominees was published in 1757.[196] And it was this second list which raised criticism as apparently a number of Augsburg citizens were surprised to learn that they had been named as nominees without knowing by whom. The 1758-lottery equally received international attention.[197] (5) When Herz the Elder died he seemingly left debts to his son, who had to apply for a moratorium on servicing the debt. Herz the Younger wanted to convince the city of Augsburg to guarantee the annuities, but the city declined to do so. Thereafter, Herz the Younger claimed that he himself was able to post assets worth 63,000 florins as

[194] The lottery regulations are to be found in: Augsburger Stadtarchiv, 00059 Kaiserliche Franciscische Akademie der freien Künste No. 1, fol. 150.

[195] (1755) Die reisende und correspondirende Pallas oder Kunst-Zeitung, 65–116.

[196] Verzeichnuß Des halben Theils der, Von der Augspurgischen Gliederschaft Der Kayerlich Franzischen Academie freyer Künsten errichteten Tontine Oder Leib-Renten (Augsburg 1757).

[197] Compare the extensive correspondence collected in: Augsburger Stadtarchiv, 00059 Kaiserliche Franciscische Akademie der freien Künste No. 1.

security, but it was alleged that the figure of 63,000 florins was based on a false appraisal within the moratorium proceedings. Further disputes, conflicts, and lawsuits followed. These numerous and intricate conflicts have been analysed by Freude in his aforementioned monograph on the history of the academy. The academy, and with it most probably the tontine, was finally dissolved with the death of Herz the Younger in 1792. The reason why the Augsburg tontine is worthy of mention is that it was not issued by a state; rather, it seems to have been the first private tontine issued in Germany.

19. The East Frisian tontine plan of 1755

In his *Ostfriesische Geschichte* (East Frisian History) of 1798, Tilemann Dothias Wiarda (1746–1826) claimed that Prussia had planned to issue a tontine to finance the impoldering of new lands in the villages of Rheiderland and Bunde in 1755.[198] *Ostfriesland* (East Frisia) had been a part of Prussia since 1744.[199] Although difficulties in financing this project have been documented,[200] Wiarda is the only author who mentioned this tontine plan. The tontine was to raise a capital of 300,000 talers. It consisted of 600 shares divided into three classes:[201]

1st class: below the age of 20; raised capital 150,000 talers; number of shares 300; price per share 500 talers; interest rate 3.5%; initial annuity per share 17.5 talers; total amount of annuities 5,250 talers;

2nd class: ages 20–40; raised capital 100,000 talers; number of shares 200; price per share 500 talers; interest rate 4%; initial annuity per share 20 talers; total amount of annuities 4,000 talers;

3rd class: above the age of 40; raised capital 50,000 talers; number of shares 100; price per share 500 talers; interest rate 5%; initial annuity per share 25 talers; total amount of annuities 2,500 talers.

The hereditary principle applied. The tontine plan had some curious details: the impoldered land was to be divided between the last surviving members of each class, and they were to be ennobled and to receive jurisdiction over the lands. According to Wiarda the plan was not carried out. And, indeed, the respective file in the *Niedersächsisches Landesarchiv* (State Archive of Lower Saxony) in Aurich does not contain any published tontine plan.

---

198 See *Wiarda* (1798), 379 f.

199 *Deeters*, 64; *Scott*, 165; 'Ostfriesland', in: Brockhaus Enzyklopädie online (accessed on 12 June 2017).

200 Compare *von Schmoller* and *Hintze*, Behördenorganisation X (1910), 219 f.

201 Niedersächsisches Landesarchiv (Aurich), Dep. I No. 3071, fol. 9r–12r.

20. The plan for a Prussian tontine lottery of 1757 and the Saxe-Weimar tontine lottery prior to 1757

Otto Warschauer (1853–1916) in his study on lotteries mentions that Prussia had planned to issue a tontine lottery in 1757 but that this plan was never carried out. The plan was apparently based on another tontine lottery which had been issued by the Duchy of *Sachsen-Weimar* (Saxe-Weimar).[202] I was not able to find further information on these two schemes.

21. The Mecklenburg tontine plan of 1758

In 1758, a tontine plan was, apparently for the first time, discussed in the Duchy of Mecklenburg,[203] with at least two more plans to follow in 1776 and 1787.[204] According to the plan of 1758, 800 shares were to be issued, each at a cost of 100 talers. Thus, the tontine was to raise 80,000 talers. The 800 shares were to be divided into five classes:

1st class: ages 1–10; raised capital 29,200 talers; number of shares 292; price per share 100 talers; interest rate 4%; initial annuity per share 4 talers; total amount of annuities 1,168 talers;

2nd class: ages 10–20; raised capital 28,800 talers; number of shares 288; price per share 100 talers; interest rate 4%; initial annuity per share 4 talers; total amount of annuities 1,152 talers;

3rd class: ages 20–40; raised capital 13,200 talers; number of shares 132; price per share 100 talers; interest rate 6%; initial annuity per share 6 talers; total amount of annuities 792 talers;

4th class: ages 40–60; raised capital 5,600 talers; number of shares 56; price per share 100 talers, interest rate 9%; initial annuity per share 9 talers; total amount of annuities 504 talers;

5th class: age above 60; raised capital 3,200 talers; number of shares 32; price per share 100 talers; interest rate 12%; initial annuity per share 12 talers; total amount of annuities 384 talers.

Thus, a total of 4,000 talers in annuities were to be paid out. It seems that the plan was never realized.

---

202 *Warschauer* (1912), 15.

203 Landeshauptarchiv Schwerin, 3.1-1 (Mecklenburgische Landstände mit Engeren Ausschuß der Ritter- und Landschaft zu Rostock) No. 20 Anhang 27, fol. 14–24.

204 See the text corresponding to and following n. 246 and n. 266, below.

22. The Austrian life annuity fund of 1760

Modern literature refers to the Austrian life annuity fund of 1760 as an example of a tontine.[205] However, an analysis of its regulations[206] reveals that it was a simple life annuity. Austria wanted to raise 4,000,000 gulden to finance its wars, issuing shares of at least 100 gulden. The interest rate was 10%. With the death of the investor the obligation to pay the annuity extinguished, the issuer was under no obligation to repay the capital, and the annuity was not divided between the surviving payees. Thus, the Austrian fund of 1760 did not follow the hereditary principle which is characteristic of tontines. However, it seems that further schemes involving tontines were discussed in the ministry of finance after 1761.[207]

23. The Cleves tontine of 1763

In 1763, the *Landes-Credit-Commission* (State Loan Commission) of the Duchy of *Kleve* (Cleves) and the County of Mark published a plan for a tontine.[208] The principality had been united with Prussia-Brandenburg in the 17th century.[209] According to the plan, the purpose of the tontine was to cover parts of the debts which *Kleve* (Cleves) had incurred as a result of a recent war. The

---

[205] *Fiedler*, 51; *von Zedtwitz*, 142.

[206] The regulations are reproduced in: *Krünitz*, Encyclopädie LXXI (1796), 131–135.

[207] See Österreichisches Staatsarchiv, AT-OeStA/HHStA AKA 8-48: Vortrag Ludwig Graf von Zinzendorf betreffend den Vorschlag einer Tontine (Rentenversicherung). See also Österreichisches Staatsarchiv, AT-OeStA/HHStA AKA 3-69 (perhaps a reply to Zinzendorf's proposal).

[208] Plan zu einer Geld-Negotiation, in Form einer Tontine, zum Besten des Herzogthums Cleve und der Graffschaft Marck; vertheilet in vier Classen, ausmachen eine Summe von 300,000 Reichsthalern (Cleve 1763). In the catalogue of the Staatsbibliothek zu Berlin, the plan is to be found under the entry: 'An Gesamte Land-Gerichter, Königliche und Jurisdictions-Richtere, Magisträte u. Steuer-Receptores in Cleve und Marck, wegen der zu errichtenden Tontine. Es ist unter andern Hülfs-Mitteln, wodurch die in dem glücklich geendigten Kriege, denen Clev- und Märckischen Landen zugezogene Schulden, ... getilget werden können, ... beschlossen worden, eine Tontine von 300000 Rthlr. Capital errichten zu lassen'. The first part of the entry refers to the addressees to whom the commission had sent the plan: all judges, magistrates and tax officers of the duchy. The second part of the entry is the introduction of the letter sent to these officials of the duchy. The plan can also be found in: Brandenburgisches Landeshauptarchiv, No. 23B 1295. Finally, the tontine is mentioned in: (1765) Fortgesetzte Neue Genealogisch-Historische Nachrichten von den Vornehmsten Begebenheiten, welche sich an den Europäischen Höfen zutragen 830.

[209] 'Kleve', in: Brockhaus Enzyklopädie online (accessed on 12 June 2017).

recent war to which the plan refers was the Seven Years War (1754–1763), during which *Kleve* (Cleves) was occupied by the French.[210] It was planned that the tontine would have 4 classes:

1st class: ages 10–20; raised capital 120,000 talers; number of shares 2,400; price per share 50 talers; interest rate 2.5%; initial annuity per share 1.25 talers; total amount of annuities 3,000 talers;

2nd class: ages 20–35; raised capital 90,000 talers; number of shares 1,800; price per share 50 talers; interest rate 3%; initial annuity per share 1.5 talers; total amount of annuities 2,700 talers;

3rd class: ages 35–50; raised capital 60,000 talers; number of shares 1,200; price per share 50 talers; interest rate 3.5%; initial annuity per share 1.75 talers; total amount of annuities 2,100 talers;

4th class: age above 50; raised capital 30,000 talers; number of shares 600; price per share 50 talers; interest rate 4%; initial annuity per share 2 talers; total amount of annuities 1,200 talers.

Thus, the Duchy intended to pay out 9,000 talers in annuities on the raised capital of 300,000 talers. A number of points support the assumption that the tontine did not aim at a European market. First, the plan was sent to judges, magistrates, and tax officials of the Duchy, who were ordered to promote the tontine and to collect subscriptions. The plan does not hint at any international marketing and distribution scheme. Secondly, the interest rate was, compared to other tontines, very low. International investors would have sought out more attractive investment products. Thirdly, the tontine plan makes clear that it was possible to pay for the shares with state bonds which the Duchy had issued during the war. It thus seems that the tontine was a scheme to refinance and consolidate the war debts which the Duchy had incurred. This assumption is reaffirmed by a report to the King by Ludwig Philipp vom Hagen (1724–1771), who was a civil servant in the *General-Ober-Finanz-Kriegs- und Domainen-Directorium*.[211]

Some further points are worth noting. First, the Duchy had been united with Prussia-Brandenburg in the 17th century, and Prussia-Brandenburg had seen other tontine plans: the tontines of 1698 and of 1788. And *Ostfriesland* (East Frisia) had also been part of Prussia since 1744. Secondly, Wiarda claims that the East Frisian tontine plan of 1755 was drafted by a civil servant named du Buis, who was based in the city of *Kleve* (Cleves).[212] Thirdly, it will become clear further below that the *General-Ober-Finanz-Kriegs- und Domainen-Directorium* in Berlin actively recommended to the Prussian provinces and territories that they issue tontines in order to refinance war debts.[213] However, it is unclear

210 *Clark*, 225.

211 Reproduced in: *Posner*, Behördenorganisation XIII (1932), 319.

212 *Wiarda* (1798), 379.

213 See the text corresponding to n. 216, below.

whether the tontine received enough subscriptions to be issued.[214] Attempts to refinance the war debts of *Kleve* (Cleves) through a lottery were similarly unsuccessful: the Prussian government had hoped that a lottery would be able to sell its tickets in Holland, but it did not receive the needed concession.[215]

24. The Halberstadt tontine plan of 1764 and the Wrocław tontine plan of 1766

The two tontine plans for Halberstadt/Berlin of 1764 and for *Breslau* (Wrocław) of 1766 are mentioned only in materials edited by Ernst Posner (1892–1980).[216] These materials suggest that the *General-Ober-Finanz-Kriegs- und Domainen-Directorium* in Berlin recommended to the different Prussian provinces and territories that they refinance their debts resulting from the Seven Years War through either lotteries or tontines. With respect to the introduction of lotteries Prussia had recruited an Italian who had gained experience in lotteries in England.[217] The recommendation to *Breslau* (Wrocław) mentioned the Cleves tontine of 1763 as a model. Both plans were never carried out. Posner cites from Johann Friedrich Ludovici's reply to a report by Ernst Wilhelm von Schlabrendorff (1719–1769), stating that it does not make sense to issue a tontine in *Schlesien* (Silesia): the province was economically weakened by the war and further economic strains were put on the Silesian people by recent monetary reforms. Consequently, the Silesian people would not be able to subscribe to a tontine. In the negotiations over the Halberstadt/Berlin tontine the Swiss mathematician Euler was consulted,[218] a fact that highlights the interaction between those involved in theoretical discussions on tontines, on the one hand, and the administrative figures planning to issue tontines, on the other hand.

---

[214] See the note in: *Posner*, Behördenorganisation XIII (1932), 320.

[215] Compare the note in: *Posner*, Behördenorganisation XIII (1932), 204–208. See also *Warschauer* (1912), 18. There is a printed plan for a lottery of 1765 contained in: Brandenburgisches Landeshauptarchiv, No. 23B 1295. The plan makes explicit that it had modified an earlier plan for a lottery from the year 1763. A published lottery plan for Cleves is also contained in: Sächsisches Staatsarchiv (Hauptstaatsarchiv Dresden), 10025 Geheimes Konsilium Loc. 5350/08.

[216] *Posner*, Behördenorganisation XIII (1932), 30 f., 344–348.

[217] *Warschauer* (1912), 11 f.

[218] *Posner*, Behördenorganisation XIII (1932), 347.

25. A tontine by the Freimaurer after 1764

Two sources mention that sometime after 1764 the *Freimaurer* (Freemasonry) initiated an internal tontine for its members. Apparently it was financially unsound.[219] I was not able to identify further information on this tontine scheme.

26. Saxon tontine plans of 1765

The *Sächsisches Staatsarchiv, Hauptstaatsarchiv Dresden* (Saxon State Archive, Main State Archive Dresden) holds a file with the title: *Die zum Nutzen hiesiger Lande in Vorschlag gebrachte Anlegung [von] Lotterien und Tontine* (Proposition to create lotteries and tontines to the advantage of the local territory).[220] The file contains discussions on a number of French tontines and the Cleves tontine as well as the plans for a number of lotteries. However, it seems that the plans did not materialize and did not result in a published tontine plan.

27. Upper Lusatian tontine lottery plans of 1766

Since 1635/36, the *Markgrafschaft Oberlausitz* (Margraviate of Upper Lusatia) had been tied to the *Kurfürstentum Sachsen* (Electorate of Saxony) without merging with the Electorate. The estates of Upper Lusatia maintained their autonomy.[221] At least since 1714, plans to initiate lotteries were regularly discussed by the Upper Lusatian estates.[222] Since 1765, the purpose of these lottery plans had been made explicit: the generated income was to be used to pay and refinance Upper Lusatian debts. In 1766, the Upper Lusatian estates discussed different proposals for a tontine lottery. One of these proposals planned to have a capital of 15,000 talers and 300 shares, each worth 50 talers. The interest rate was 2%. The hereditary principle applied. However, it seems that the plans for a tontine lottery were never implemented. Instead, the lottery which was initiated in 1770 ran parallel to the 54th *Haager Generalitäts-Lotterie*,[223] the Dutch *Generaliteitsloterij* which was run in The Hague and which, according to the number of references to it in contemporary journals, seems to have been popular in the 18th century throughout Germany. The Upper Lusatian lottery of 1770 did

219 *von Starck* (1781), 147; *Frank* (1875), 31.

220 Sächsisches Staatsarchiv (Hauptstaatsarchiv Dresden), 10025 Geheimes Konsilium Loc. 5350/08.

221 *Schumka*, 143.

222 Sächsisches Staatsarchiv (Staatsfilialarchiv Bautzen), 50001 Landstände der sächsischen Oberlausitz No. 1166.

223 See the published plan in: (1770) Nachlese Oberlausitzischer Nachrichten: sowohl aus neuern als ältern Zeiten 159–161.

not even have its own drawing, instead simply using the drawing lists of the Dutch lottery.

28. Four academic tontine plans of 1766

In 1766 four tontine plans were published in the journal *Neue Beyträge zu der Cameral- und Haushaltungswissenschaft*.[224] The author and the purpose of the publication are not made explicit, but it seems that the publication served purely academic purposes. The first plan resembles a simple tontine. The second plan imitated the Gotha tontine of 1752 with its peculiar lottery element and with its variation of the hereditary principle. The two further plans were a class tontine and a life annuity lottery. The anonymous author called the life annuity lottery a tontine lottery: the issuer would sell 2,000 tickets for 5 talers. The 4% interest on the raised capital of 10,000 talers was then being paid out in the form of two life annuities – awarded by lottery – each worth 200 talers per annum. The hereditary principle which was characteristic of tontines did not apply. For the purpose of the present contribution, the lottery plan is of importance as it proves that the term 'tontine' was not only used by issuers to denote plans which for the modern observer do not count as tontines. Academic discourse, too, used the word tontine rather loosely.

29. The Bremen tontines of 1767 and 1772

The two Bremen tontines are discussed by Christian Nikolaus Roller (1745–1818).[225] Both tontines were issued; moreover, both the printed plan for the 1767-tontine and a list of names of the subscribers and nominees have survived.[226] The 1767-tontine raised 100,000 talers. According to Roller the raised capital was needed for payments which Bremen had to make to its allies in connection with the Seven Years War (1756–1763). The tontine consisted of 1,000 shares in eight classes. The first two classes were designed identically:

1st class: below the age of 10; raised capital 15,000 talers; number of shares 150; price per share 100 talers; interest rate 3.5%; initial annuity per share 3.5 talers; total amount of annuities 525 talers;

2nd class: below the age of 10; raised capital 15,000 talers; number of shares 150; price per share 100 talers; interest rate 3.5%; initial annuity per share 3.5 talers; total amount of annuities 525 talers;

---

224 (1766) 2 Neue Beyträge zu der Cameral- und Haushaltungs-Wissenschaft 156–165.

225 *Roller* (1803), 121, 154, 159, 165.

226 Staatsarchiv Bremen, No. 2-R.1.A.10.c.4.II.b.1.b; Niedersächsisches Landesarchiv (Osnabrück), Depositum 3 b IV No. 5759.

3rd class: ages 10–20; raised capital 20,000 talers; number of shares 200; price per share 100 talers; interest rate 4%; initial annuity per share 4 talers; total amount of annuities 800 talers;

4th class: ages 20–30; raised capital 20,000 talers; number of shares 200; price per share 100 talers; interest rate 4.5%; initial annuity per share 4.5 talers; total amount of annuities 900 talers;

5th class: ages 30–40; raised capital 10,000 talers; number of shares 100; price per share 100 talers; interest rate 5%; initial annuity per share 5 talers; total amount of annuities 500 talers;

6th class: ages 40–50; raised capital 10,000 talers; number of shares 100; price per share 100 talers; interest rate 5.5%; initial annuity per share 5.5 talers; total amount of annuities 550 talers;

7th class: ages 50–60; raised capital 6,000 talers; number of shares 60; price per share 100 talers; interest rate 6.5%; initial annuity per share 6.5 talers; total amount of annuities 390 talers;

8th class: above the age of 60; raised capital 4,000 talers; number of shares 40; price per share 100 talers; interest rate 8%; initial annuity per share 8 talers; total amount of annuities 320 talers.

Thus a total annuities amount of 4,510 talers was paid out. The Bremen tontine of 1767 was a class tontine without any lottery element. The tontine of 1772 was issued to refinance various public debts.[227] It raised 50,000 talers and had 500 shares, each at a cost of 100 talers. The shares were divided into six classes:

1st class: below the age of 10; raised capital 15,000 talers; number of shares 150; price per share 100 talers; interest rate 3.5%; initial annuity per share 3.5 talers; total amount of annuities 525 talers;

2nd class: ages 10–20; raised capital 10,000 talers; number of shares 100; price per share 100 talers; interest rate 4%; initial annuity per share 4 talers; total amount of annuities 400 talers;

3rd class: ages 20–30; raised capital 10,000 talers; number of shares 100; price per share 100 talers; interest rate 4.5%; initial annuity per share 4.5 talers; total amount of annuities 450 talers;

4th class: ages 30–40; raised capital 7,000 talers; number of shares 70; price per share 100 talers; interest rate 5%; initial annuity per share 5 talers; total amount of annuities 350 talers;

5th class: ages 40–50; raised capital 5,000 talers; number of shares 50; price per share 100 talers; interest rate 5.5%; initial annuity per share 5.5 talers; total amount of annuities 275 talers;

6th class: above the age of 50; raised capital 3,000 talers; number of shares 30; price per share 100 talers; interest rate 6.5%; initial annuity per share 6.5 talers; total amount of annuities 195 talers.

---

227 The statutes of the tontine can be found in: Staatsarchiv Bremen, No. 2-R.1.A.10.c.4.II.c.1.b. See also *Roller* (1803), 165.

After the tontine was issued each subscriber received a *Police* (policy) which he had to present when collecting his annuity. This seems to be an important shift in terminology. The Lübeck tontine of 1708, for example, spoke of a *Brief* which the investor was to receive.[228] The word *Brief* can, in the present context, be translated as a 'bond' or 'obligation'. And the Saxon tontine of 1748 spoke of a *Leib-Renten-Schein*, which may be translated as a 'life annuity bond' or 'life annuity obligation'.[229] The Bremen tontine now used the word *Police*, a term which is usually used in the context of insurance.

30. The Wolfenbüttel tontine of 1768

The records of the Duchies of Wolfenbüttel and Blankenburg – the County of Blankenburg had been elevated to a Duchy in 1707 and subsequent to 1737 it was united with the Duchy of *Braunschweig-Wolfenbüttel* (Brunswick-Wolfenbüttel) – in the *Niedersächsische Landesarchiv* (State Archive of Lower Saxony) in Wolfenbüttel contain a file on a tontine plan of 1768.[230] It seems that the tontine was never issued. The tontine was planned to raise 1,000,000 talers, with 10,000 shares divided into 13 classes.

31. The Osnabrück tontine of 1768

Between 1760 and 1768, the city of Osnabrück developed plans to issue a tontine.[231] According to Rhotert a printed tontine plan was published in 1768,[232] but it seems that the plan was never successfully carried through and that no tontine was ever issued in Osnabrück.[233]

The tontine was planned to cover the debts which the city incurred in consequence of the Seven Years War. Following the Peace of Westphalia in 1648, the position of the bishop of Osnabrück had been alternately held by Catholics and Protestants. From 1728 to 1761, Clemens August von Bayern, Archbishop of *Köln* (Cologne), was prince bishop of Osnabrück. Thus, the prince-bishopric and the city of Osnabrück were, as was the Archbishop of Cologne, allies of the

[228] See the text following n. 160, above.

[229] See the text following n. 180, above.

[230] Niedersächsisches Landesarchiv (Wolfenbüttel), 4 Alt 1 No. 2668.

[231] Niedersächsisches Landesarchiv (Osnabrück), Depositum 3 b IV No. 5759.

[232] *Rhotert*, (1908) 33 Mitteilungen des Vereins für Geschichte und Landeskunde von Osnabrück 325.

[233] See also *Rhotert*, (1908) 33 Mitteilungen des Vereins für Geschichte und Landeskunde von Osnabrück 328.

French King. After the death of Clemens August, a member of the House *Braunschweig-Lüneburg* (Brunswick-Lüneburg) had to be elected to the position of the prince bishop of Osnabrück, and in 1764 the second son of King George III of England, Prince Friedrich August (Frederick, Duke of York and Albany), who had been born only in 1763, was elected. As a consequence, both the prince-bishopric and the city of Osnabrück joined the alliance of England and Prussia against France.[234]

The file at the *Niedersächsisches Landesarchiv* (State Archive of Lower Saxony) in Osnabrück concerning the 1768-tontine contains a number of different drafts and, in addition, a printed plan of the Bremen tontine of 1767 as well as two lists with the names of the subscribers and nominees in that latter tontine.[235] Thus, Rhotert's proposition that the city of Osnabrück took the Bremen tontine of 1767 as a model[236] seems prima facie plausible. The printed plan of the Osnabrück tontine is not contained in the file, but Rhotert claims that a plan dated 5 May 1768 was the one which was eventually published.[237]

According to the plan, the city wanted to raise a total of 25,000 talers. The tontine was planned for 500 subscribers divided into 10 classes. Each share cost 50 talers:

1st class: below the age of 10; raised capital 5,000 talers; number of shares 100; price per share 50 talers; interest rate 3%; initial annuity per share 1.5 talers; total amount of annuities 150 talers;

2nd class: ages 10–20; raised capital 5,000 talers; number of shares 100; price per share 50 talers; interest rate 3.5%; initial annuity per share 1.75 talers; total amount of annuities 175 talers;

3rd class: ages 20–30; raised capital 4,500 talers; number of shares 90; price per share 50 talers; interest rate 4%; initial annuity per share 2 talers; total amount of annuities 180 talers;

4th class: ages 30–35; raised capital 2,000 talers; number of shares 40; price per share 50 talers; interest rate 4.5%; initial annuity per share 2.25 talers; total amount of annuities 90 talers;

5th class: ages 35–40; raised capital 2,000 talers; number of shares 40; price per share 50 talers; interest rate 4.5%; initial annuity per share 2.25 talers; total amount of annuities 90 talers;

---

234 *Asch*, 253–266; *van den Heuvel*, 314–316.

235 Niedersächsisches Landesarchiv (Osnabrück), Depositum 3 b IV No. 5759.

236 *Rhotert*, (1908) 33 Mitteilungen des Vereins für Geschichte und Landeskunde von Osnabrück 327.

237 I was not able to identify a plan dated 5 May 1768, but there is a plan dated 3 May 1768 which corresponds to Rhotert's summary of the plan.

6th class: ages 40–45; raised capital 1,500 talers; number of shares 30; price per share 50 talers; interest rate 5%; initial annuity per share 2.5 talers; total amount of annuities 75 talers;

7th class: ages 45–50; raised capital 1,500 talers; number of shares 30; price per share 50 talers; interest rate 5%; initial annuity per share 2.5 talers; total amount of annuities 75 talers;

8th class: ages 50–55; raised capital 1,250 talers; number of shares 25; price per share 50 talers; interest rate 6%; initial annuity per share 3 talers; total amount of annuities 75 talers;

9th class: ages 55–60; raised capital 1,250 talers; number of shares 25; price per share 50 talers; interest rate 7%; initial annuity per share 3.5 talers; total amount of annuities 87,5 talers;

10th class: above the age of 60; raised capital 1,000 talers; number of shares 20; price per share 50 talers; interest rate 8%; initial annuity per share 4 talers; total amount of annuities 80 talers.

Thus, the Osnabrück tontine did not imitate the Bremen tontine design. This stands to reason given that the discussions to issue a tontine in Osnabrück had already started in 1760, a number of draft plans had been worked out, and it was only in July 1767 that Bremen published its plan. Furthermore, the draft regulations for the Osnabrück tontine differ from the regulations for the Bremen tontine. It thus seems more likely that while the drafters of the Osnabrück plan took notice of the Bremen tontine, its actual influence on the drafting process was limited. Furthermore, the documents in the file at the *Niedersächsisches Landesarchiv* (State Archive of Lower Saxony) in Osnabrück concerning the 1768-tontine also refer to a Danish tontine without specifying it further.

32. The Regensburg tontine lottery of 1768

In 1768 the city of Regensburg published a lottery plan.[238] It was published both in German and French. The German version simply referred to a *Geld- und Renten-Lotterie* (Money and Annuity Lottery). However, the French version spoke of a tontine: *Plan de la Lotterie & Tontine*. The lottery awarded annuities which were paid out between 1770 and 1780. However, the plan did not adopt the hereditary principle. If an annuitant died, his or her heirs had a right to the annuities for the remainder of the period. Thus, the word 'tontine' was used to simply refer to an annuity lottery.

[238] It can be found in: Staatsarchiv Nürnberg, Reichsstadt Nürnberg D No. 4816.

33. The Mainzer Life Annuity Society of 1769

Modern literature asserts that the *Kurmaynzer Leibrenten-Gesellschaft* (Mainz Life Annuity Society) of 1769 issued a tontine.[239] Its regulations[240] reveal that it was not a tontine but a simple life annuity combined with a life annuity lottery: it did not adopt the hereditary principle. The society was planned for 40,430 members. The society was open to people of all ages, yet the society was not divided into different classes. Each member had to pay 10 florins when joining the society and then quarterly 45 kreuzers. The right to a life annuity could be acquired via two different tiers which were planned to operate consecutively. The first tier was a lottery: for the first ten years, 708 life annuities were awarded annually; the annuities were paid out for eleven years. The second tier followed in the eleventh year of the society, and it benefited widows: if a widow had been a member of the society for eight years and if she had made her full contribution, she acquired a right to annuity payments for the rest of her life; for that purpose the society formed a fund of 150,000 florins. Finally, in the eleventh year of the society, a number of prizes were awarded by the lottery.

34. The Swedish-Pomeranian tontine lottery of 1772

In 1772 a tontine was initiated in *Schwedisch-Pommern* (Swedish-Pomerania).[241] Swedish-Pomerania was the western part of the former Duchy of *Pommern* (Pomerania). In 1648, at the Peace of Westphalia, it was given as an imperial fiefdom to the Swedish Crown after the last Pomeranian duke had died in 1637 without leaving successors. As an imperial fiefdom it remained part of the Holy Roman Empire of German Nations. At the Congress of Vienna in 1815 it was conveyed to Prussia.[242] Today it forms part of *Mecklenburg-Vorpommern* (Mecklenburg-Western Pomerania). The title of the file in the *Landesarchiv Mecklenburg-Vorpommern* (State Archive of Mecklenburg-Western Pomerania) in Greifswald already suggests that the tontine was in fact a lottery: *Jahrmarkt Acta wegen Errichtung einer Fayance Tontine in den Landes-Jahrmärkten* (File concerning the institution of a faience tontine at the annual state fairs). Moreover, no annuities were awarded as prizes. It was a simple lottery.

---

239 *Braun*, Geschichte, 162.

240 An excerpt from the regulations of the Kurmainzer Leibrenten-Gesellschaft of 1769 are reproduced in: *Krünitz*, Encyclopädie LXXI (1796), 135 f.

241 Landesarchiv Mecklenburg-Vorpommern (Greifswald), No. 2145.

242 *Buchholz*, 238, 303.

35. The Gdańsk tontines of 1775 and 1792

The city of *Danzig* (Gdańsk) published in 1775 and 1792 two further tontine plans.[243] Both tontines consisted of 1,000 shares. The 1775-tontine divided them into three classes:

1st class: below the age of 20; raised capital 120,000 florins; number of shares 400; price per share 300 florins; interest rate 4%; initial annuity per share 12 florins; total amount of annuities 4,800 florins;

2nd class: ages 20–40; raised capital 120,000 florins; number of shares 400; price per share 300 florins; interest rate 5%; initial annuity per share 15 florins; total amount of annuities 6,000 florins;

3rd class: above the age of 40; raised capital 60,000 florins; number of shares 200; price per share 300 florins; interest rate 6%; initial annuity per share 18 florins; total amount of annuities 3,600 florins.

The raised capital, thus, amounted to 300,000 florins and the annuities to 14,800 florins.

By contrast, the 1792-tontine divided the 1,000 shares into four classes:

1st class: below the age of 20; raised capital 120,000 florins; number of shares 400; price per share 300 florins; interest rate 6%; initial annuity per share 18 florins; total amount of annuities 7,200 florins;

2nd class: ages 20–40; raised capital 75,000 florins; number of shares 250; price per share 300 florins; interest rate 7%; initial annuity per share 21 florins; total amount of annuities 5,250 florins;

3rd class: ages 40–60; raised capital 75,000 florins; number of shares 250; price per share 300 florins; interest rate 8%; initial annuity per share 24 florins; total amount of annuities 6,000 florins;

4th class: above the age of 60; raised capital 30,000 florins; number of shares 100; price per share 300 florins; interest rate 10%; initial annuity per share 30 florins; total amount of annuities 3,000 florins.

The raised capital amounted to 300,000 florins and the total sum of annuities to 21,450 florins. Both tontines were class but not compound tontines.

243 Plan d'une Tontine à etablir ou d'un fond à negocier sur rentes viagères sous la garantie des Ordres de la ville. Publié à Danzig le 13. du Mois de Mars 1775 (Danzig 1775); Plan einer aus Schluß sämmtl. Löbl. OOgen dieser Stadt dem Publico zum Besten zu errichtende Tontine oder Negocirung auf Leibrenten, publicirt in Danzig den 27. Jan. 1792 (Danzig 1792).

36. The Hamburg tontine of 1776

In 1776, two plans for tontines were published in Hamburg. A first plan appeared in July.[244] It was a tontine lottery and had 150 classes with 20 tickets each. In total, the lottery thus had 3,000 tickets. The classes were not formed according to the age of the nominee. Each ticket cost 200 marks. The total amount of annuities per class which were available in the different classes were awarded in a lottery. Within the different classes the hereditary principle applied.

In October 1776 the plan for this first tontine was abandoned and a second plan was published.[245] This second plan did not exhibit elements of a lottery. It offered three different investment schemes: a tontine, a simple life annuity, and an annuity running for 50 years. The tontine was divided into classes. Each share cost 200 marks. 20 shares formed a class. The interest rate was 6%. Each class thus received annuity payments amounting to 240 marks. Each contributor had to name a nominee and indicate the nominee's age, residence, and status. However, for the division of the classes the age of the nominee was irrelevant. The classes were filled consecutively according to the date when the shares were sold. It is probable that in practice each contributor named a nominee of a very young age in order to enhance the chance of receiving high annuities. According to Art. 5 the typical hereditary principle applied within each class. Thus, the last payee received the full 240 marks as an annuity payment.

37. The Mecklenburg-Strelitz tontine plan of 1776

Between 1763 and 1776, the estates of the Duchy of Mecklenburg-Strelitz developed tontine plans which culminated in the publication of a draft statute for a *Tontine und Leibrenten-Gesellschaft* (Tontine and Life Annuity Society) in 1776.[246] The tontine was to consist of 1,300 shares, each at a cost of 50 talers, and was to be divided into 5 classes:

1st class: ages 1–10; raised capital 23,725 talers; number of shares 474.5; price per share 50 talers; interest rate 3.5%; initial annuity per share 1.75 talers; total amount of annuities 830.375 talers;

2nd class: ages 10–20; raised capital 23,400 talers; number of shares 468; price per share 50 talers; interest rate 3.75%; initial annuity per share 1.875 talers; total amount of annuities 877.5 talers;

---

[244] The plan is reproduced in: *Krünitz*, Encyclopädie LXXI (1796), 308–312.

[245] Sammlung Hamburgischer Verordnungen, vol. 1 (Hamburg 1783), 125–136. The plan is also reproduced in: *Krünitz*, Encyclopädie LXXI (1796), 312–319.

[246] Landeshauptarchiv Schwerin, 3.1-1 (Mecklenburgische Landstände mit Engeren Ausschuß der Ritter- und Landschaft zu Rostock) No. 20 Anhang 29, fol. 691–705.

3rd class: ages 20–40; raised capital 10,725 talers; number of shares 214.5; price per share 50 talers; interest rate 6%; initial annuity per share 3 talers; total amount of annuities 643.5 talers;

4th class: ages 40–60; raised capital 4,550 talers; number of shares 91; price per share 50 talers; interest rate 9%; initial annuity per share 4.5 talers; total amount of annuities 409.5 talers;

5th class: above the age of 60; raised capital 2,600 talers; number of shares 52; price per share 50 talers; interest rate 12%; initial annuity per share 6 talers; total amount of annuities 312 talers.

The administration costs were estimated at 177.125 talers per annum. The raised capital of 65,000 talers was to be used to consolidate old debts.

The hereditary principle applied. It was not a compound tontine, so that the last surviving payee of each class received the full amount of annuities. Furthermore, if one class died out, the annuities of that class were to accrue to the other classes. Thus, the last surviving payee of the society would receive in total 3,071.875 talers in annuities per annum. According to Art. 18 it was possible to subscribe to the tontine until 17 January 1777. Apparently, the sales did not go as anticipated and, therefore, the deadline was extended to 29 September 1777.[247] Further plans in the Duchy of Mecklenburg were made between 1785 and 1787.[248]

38. The Stade tontine of 1777

In 1777 the city of Stade published a tontine plan.[249] The plan refers to the scheme both as a *Leibrenten-Societät* (Life Annuity Society) and as a tontine. Beginning in 1715 Stade had belonged to Hannover,[250] and thus the tontine plan was approved of by the English king as the preamble makes clear. The preamble of the plan further specifies the purpose of the tontine. It planned to refinance debts amounting to 10,000 talers. The city had planned to sell 200 shares, each at a cost of 50 talers, and the shares were to be divided into 6 classes:

1st class: ages 1–10; raised capital 2,500 talers; number of shares 50; price per share 50 talers; interest rate 3.5%; initial annuity per share 1.75 talers; total amount of annuities 87.5 talers;

---

247 Landeshauptarchiv Schwerin, 3.1-1 (Mecklenburgische Landstände mit Engeren Ausschuß der Ritter- und Landschaft zu Rostock) No. 20 Anhang 29, fol. 711.

248 Landeshauptarchiv Schwerin, 3.1-1 (Mecklenburgische Landstände mit Engeren Ausschuß der Ritter- und Landschaft zu Rostock) No. 20 Anhang 30.

249 Stadtarchiv Stade, St.H. 51–52 No. 18.

250 'Stade', in: Brockhaus Enzyklopädie, vol. 26, 104.

2nd class: ages 10–20; raised capital 2,250 talers; number of shares 45; price per share 50 talers; interest rate 4%; initial annuity per share 2 talers; total amount of annuities 90 talers;

3rd class: ages 20–30; raised capital 2,000 talers; number of shares 40; price per share 50 talers; interest rate 4.5%; initial annuity per share 2.25 talers; total amount of annuities 90 talers;

4th class: ages 30–40; raised capital 1,500 talers; number of shares 30; price per share 50 talers; interest rate 5%; initial annuity per share 2.5 talers; total amount of annuities 75 talers;

5th class: ages 40–50; raised capital 1,000 talers; number of shares 20; price per share 50 talers, interest rate 6%; initial annuity per share 3 talers; total amount of annuities 60 talers;

6th class: above the age of 50; raised capital 750 talers; number of shares 15; price per share 50 talers; interest rate 7%; initial annuity per share 3.5 talers; total amount of annuities 52.5 talers.

Thus, the city intended to pay annuities amounting to 455 talers in total. Article 2 of the statutes clarified that the administrative costs were covered by the city. The purchase of multiple shares was permitted, and investors were allowed to name another person as nominee. Each investor received a document after the tontine was issued, which the statutes referred to as *Police* (policy). Here again, a term normally applied in the context of insurance was used.[251] According to Art. 5, the usual hereditary principle applied within each class. However, if a class died out the annuities did not accrue to the other classes. Furthermore, the tontine was not planned as a compound tontine. Thus, the last surviving member of, for example, the first class, received the full 87.5 talers as an annuity payment.

It seems that the city aimed primarily at a regional market: the tontine was advertised in Hannover, Hamburg, Altona, and Bremen.[252] By the end of July of 1778 it was decided to issue the tontine even though some shares in the 1st, 2nd, and 3rd classes were still available.[253] It seems that this decision was not approved of by the subscribers to these classes. The subscribers of, for example, the 2nd class had hoped for a chance to receive 90 talers as an annuity payment as last surviving payee. However, if not all shares in that class were sold, the last surviving payee would receive correspondingly less. Nevertheless, the city of Stade

[251] See the text corresponding to n. 228, above.

[252] (1778) 38 Hannoverische Anzeigen, 11 May 1778; (1778) 4 Staats- und Gelehrte Zeitung des Hamburgischen unpartheyischen Correpsondenten, 7 January 1778; (1778) 5 Reichs-Post-Reuter, 9 January 1778; (1778) 25 Bremer Zeitung, 27 March 1778.

[253] See the announcements in: (1778) 63 Hannoverische Anzeigen, 7 August 1778; (1778) 130 Staats- und Gelehrte Zeitung des Hamburgischen unpartheyischen Correpsondenten, 15 August 1778; (1778) 127 Reichs-Post-Reuter, 11 August 1778; (1778) 85 Hannoverische Anzeigen, 23 October 1778; (1778) 172 Staats- und Gelehrte Zeitung des Hamburgischen unpartheyischen Correpsondenten, 28 October 1778; (1778) 172 Reichs-Post-Reuter, 28 October 1778; (1778) 91 Bremer Zeitung, 13 November 1778.

still had an interest in issuing the tontine in order to refinance its debts. For that reason the city decided in 1779 to increase the interest rate in each class: the 1st class was to receive 4.5% instead of 3.5%, the 2nd class 5% instead of the original 4%, the 3rd class 5.5% instead of 4.5%, the 4th class 6% instead of 5%, and the 5th class 6.5% instead of 6%.[254] Thereby the city hoped to secure the outstanding subscribers. However, it was made clear that this increase also benefited those who had already subscribed to the tontine. The new conditions were again advertised.[255] Finally, the city was successful and issued the tontine. The city, indeed, sold the shares regionally: of the 200 shares, 93 were, for example, sold in Bremen, 15 in Stade, however none in Hamburg.

39. The Upper Lusatian tontine plan of 1777

In 1766, the estates of the *Oberlausitz* (Upper Lusatia) had discussed different plans for a tontine lottery, but it seems that none of these plans were implemented.[256] In 1777, a further tontine plan was discussed.[257] This time the tontine was not planned as part of a lottery scheme. Rather, it was planned as a traditional class tontine. 1,200 shares were to be sold at a price of 25 talers each. Thus, the tontine was to raise 30,000 talers. The shares were to be divided into 12 classes:

1st class: below the age of 5; raised capital 3,125 talers; price per share 25 talers, total number of shares 125; interest rate 4%; initial annuity per share 1 taler; total amount of annuities 125 talers;

2nd class: ages 5–10; raised capital 3,125 talers; price per share 25 talers; total number of shares 125; interest rate 4%; initial annuity per share 1 taler, total amount of annuities 125 talers;

3rd class: ages 10–15; raised capital 3,750 talers; price per share 25 talers; total number of shares 150; interest rate 4%; initial annuity per share 1.2 talers; total amount of annuities 150 talers;

4th class: ages 15–20; raised capital 3,750 talers; price per share 25 talers; total number of shares 150; interest rate 4%; initial annuity per share 1.2 talers; total amount of annuities 150 talers;

---

254 Stadtarchiv Stade, St.H. 51–52 No. 18.

255 (1779) 13 Bremer Zeitung, 12 February 1779; (1779) 7 Bremer Wöchentliche Nachrichten, 15 February 1779; (1779) 10 Hannoverische Anzeigen, 1 February 1779; (1779) 22 Altonaischer Mercurius, 8 February 1779; (1779) 22 Staats- und Gelehrte Zeitung des Hamburgischen unpartheyischen Correpsondenten, 6 February 1779; (1779) 21 Reichs-Post-Reuter, 5 February 1779; (1779) 22 Hamburgische Neue Zeitung, 6 February 1779.

256 See the text corresponding to and following n. 221, above.

257 Sächsisches Staatsarchiv (Staatsfilialarchiv Bautzen), 50009 Oberamt des Markgraftums Oberlausitz No. 109.

5th class: ages 20–25; raised capital 3,750 talers; price per share 25 talers; total number of shares 150; interest rate 5%; initial annuity per share 1.25 talers, total amount of annuities 187.5 talers;

6th class: ages 25–30; raised capital 2,500 talers; price per share 25 talers; total number of shares 100; interest rate 5%; initial annuity per share 1.25 talers; total amount of annuities 125 talers;

7th class: ages 30–35; raised capital 2,500 talers; price per share 25 talers; total number of shares 100; interest rate 5%; initial annuity per share 1.25 talers; total amount of annuities 125 talers;

8th class: ages 35–40; raised capital 2,500 talers; price per share 25 talers; total number of shares 100; interest rate 5.5%; initial annuity per share 1.375 talers; total amount of annuities 137.5 talers;

9th class: ages 40–45; raised capital 1,250 talers; price per share 25 talers; total number of shares 50; interest rate 6%; initial annuity per share 1.5 talers; total amount of annuities 75 talers;

10th class: ages 45–50; raised capital 1,250 talers; price per share 25 talers; total number of shares 50; interest rate 7%; initial annuity per share 1.75 talers; total amount of annuities 87.5 talers;

11th class: ages 50–55; raised capital 1,250 talers; price per share 25 talers; total number of shares 50; interest rate 8%; initial annuity per share 2 talers; total amount of annuities 100 talers;

12th class: ages 55–60; raised capital 1,250 talers; price per share 25 talers; total number of shares 50; interest rate 9%; initial annuity per share 2.25 talers; total amount of annuities 112.5 talers.

In each class the usual hereditary principle was to apply. If one class died out, the annuities of this class were to benefit the other classes.

40. The Nuremberg tontines of 1777 and of 1783

The tontine of *Nürnberg* (Nuremberg) of 1777 was a compound class tontine.[258] It was called the *Leib-Renten Gesellschaft* (Life Annuity Society), but the preamble also spoke of a tontine. According to Art. 18 of the tontine regulations,

[258] The tontine regulations are printed as: Gründliche Nachricht von einer neuen sehr vorzüglichen und vortheilhaften Reichs-Stadt Nürnbergischen Leib-Renten Gesellschaft (Nürnberg 1777), 1–32. They are also found in: Stadtarchiv Nürnberg, A 6 No. 2538. See also *Fiedler*, 47–75; *Braun*, Geschichte, 155–157; *Du Pasquier*, (1910) 46 Zeitschrift für Schweizerische Statistik 499 f.; *Zedtwitz*, 141; *Wortner*, 115; *Krünitz*, Encyclopädie LXXI (1796), 319.

the investor, the payee, and the nominee did not have to be the same person. It consisted of seven classes:[259]

1st class: age 60 and above; price per share 50 gulden; total number of shares 64; initial annuity per share 7 gulden;

2nd class: ages 50–59; price per share 75 gulden; total number of shares 127; initial annuity per share 6 gulden;

3rd class: ages 40–49; price per share 80 gulden; total number of shares 146; initial annuity per share 5 gulden;

4th class: ages 30–39; price per share 90 gulden; total number of shares 166; initial annuity per share 4 gulden;

5th class: ages 20–29; price per share 104 gulden; total number of shares 432; initial annuity per share 2 gulden and 15 kreuzers;

6th class: ages 13–19; price per share 106 gulden; total number of shares 504; initial annuity per share 2 gulden;

7th class: ages 6–12; price per share 110 gulden; total number of shares 584; initial annuity per share 1 gulden 45 kreuzers.

When a nominee of the first four classes died, half of his or her annuity was divided between the surviving members of that class. The other half went to a fund. The purpose of the fund was primarily to compensate the heirs of deceased members of the tontine. Specifically, if the total sum of annuity payments, which the deceased member had received, did not amount to his or her invested capital plus 4% interest per annum, then the difference between the two sums was to be paid in instalments to his or her heirs. The last three classes were not compound tontines: the full annuity of a deceased nominee was divided between the surviving members of the same class. If a class died out, part of the capital went to the aforementioned fund; the other part was divided among the surviving classes. There were some further complicated details in the design which are of no interest for the present purpose. The purpose of the fund connected to the tontine is explained in the preamble to the regulations of the tontine of 1777:[260]

> Daß die Menschen ihre und der ihrigen Glücks-Umstände immer mehr zu verbessern suchen, dieser Trieb ist einem jeden schon von Natur in das Herz geleget … Viele tausend Menschen haben in dieser Absicht den Weg der mannichfaltigen Lotterien und Tontinen eingeschlagen und auf solchen ihr Glück zu machen getrachtet: Wie wenige aber auf diesen hierzu gelangen können, ist aus der Einrichtung aller dieser Lotterien selbst schon zu ermessen. Nur sehr wenigen von dem Glück begleiteten Einlegern wird es möglich, in denselben große Summen zu gewinnen; alle übrige unglückliche hingegen müssen ihre Einsäze … einbüssen. Eben so ist es auch mit allen bisher bekannten

[259] The total number of shares per class was not predefined in the tontine regulations. It becomes apparent from the list of members: Staatsarchiv Nürnberg, Reichsstadt Nürnberg D No. 4815.

[260] Gründliche Nachricht von einer neuen sehr vorzüglichen und vortheilhaften Reichs-Stadt Nürnbergischen Leib-Renten Gesellschaft (Nürnberg 1777), 7.

Tontinen beschaffen; Die, so ein hohes Alter zu erreichen das Glück haben, geniessen zwar grosse Vortheile; allein den mehrern frühzeitig versterbenden ist ihr Einkaufs-Quantum völlig für sie und die ihrige verlohren; und sie müssen ihr Geld nur dazu angewendet sehen, um jene wenige glücklich zu machen.

That men and women long for improving their fortune and that of their dependants, this longing is by its very nature part of everyone's heart ... For this purpose thousands of men and women have tried to find their fortune in those diverse lotteries and tontines: Yet, how very few have achieved their ambition in these follows from the very nature of lotteries. Only a very few of the contributors will have the luck to win a great sum; all the other unfortunate will lose their contribution ... The same is true for all hitherto known tontines; those who are fortunate to reach a high age will enjoy great benefits; yet, most will die early and will lose their investment for themselves and for their dependants; and they will see their money to be used to make others fortunate.

Accordingly, the design of the Nuremberg tontine aimed at having only winners and no losers, as everyone was at a minimum reimbursed with his or her original investment plus 4% interest. However, it was for this very reason that the design was criticized as being unsound.[261] It has already been noted above that the Nuremberg tontines received nation-wide attention.[262] A public announcement by the tontine's administrative body (*Reichs Stadt Nürnbergische Leib-Renten-Gesellschaft General-Direction*) from the year 1780 hints that the 1777-tontine attracted a number of foreign investors.[263] However, the term foreign most probably referred to investors who were not based in *Nürnberg* (Nuremberg) itself.

The Nuremberg tontine of 1783 was designed essentially the same way as the 1777-tontine.[264] It had in its 1st class 57 shares, in its 2nd class 92 shares, in its 3rd class 173 shares, in its 4th class 217 shares, in its 5th class 440 shares, in its 6th class 458 shares, and in its 7th class 669 shares.[265]

---

261 *Kritter*, (1779) Gothaisches Magazin der Künste und Wissenschaft 370–384; *Vogel* (1843), 121 f.

262 See the text corresponding to n. 39 and the text following n. 75, above.

263 The announcement can be found in: Stadtarchiv Nürnberg, E 6/125 No. 1.

264 The tontine regulations are printed as: Gründliche Nachricht und Statuten von der sehr vorzüglichen und gemeinnützlichen Reichs-Stadt Nürnbergischen zweiten Leibrenten-Gesellschaft (Nürnberg 1783), 3–50 and in: (1783) 5 Schlözer's Stats-Anzeigen 185–223; *Krünitz*, Encyclopädie LXXI (1796), 342–380. They can also be found in: Stadtarchiv Nürnberg, A 6 No. 2611; Staatsarchiv Nürnberg, Reichsstadt Nürnberg Druckschriften No. 713. See also *Braun*, Geschichte, 157.

265 Staatsarchiv Nürnberg, Reichsstadt Nürnberg Rentkammer No. 1950

41. The Mecklenburg tontine plan of 1787

In 1787 the parliament of the Duchy of Mecklenburg discussed a tontine plan.[266] The plan dates from 1785, but it seems that the efforts to introduce a tontine had continued ever since the failure to implement the Mecklenburg-Strelitz tontine plan of 1776. The new plan was based on the Nuremberg tontine.[267] The Mecklenburg tontine, too, was designed in such a way that the heirs of an investor were reimbursed if the investor died before having received annuities amounting to his or her investment. The tontine consisted of 1,400 shares in seven classes:

1st class: above the age of 60; raised capital 4,000 talers; number of shares 50; price per share 80 talers; interest rate 15%; initial annuity per share 12 talers; total amount of annuities 600 talers;

2nd class: ages 50–60; raised capital 9,000 talers; number of shares 100; price per share 90 talers; interest rate 11.11%; initial annuity per share 10 talers; total amount of annuities 1,000 talers;

3rd class: ages 40–50; raised capital 15,000 talers; number of shares 150; price per share 100 talers; interest rate 8%; initial annuity per share 8 talers; total amount of annuities 1,200 talers;

4th class: ages 30–40; raised capital 22,000 talers; number of shares 200; price per share 110 talers; interest rate 5.45%; initial annuity per share 6 talers; total amount of annuities 1,200 talers;

5th class: ages 20–30; raised capital 30,000 talers; number of shares 250; price per share 120 talers; interest rate 3.33%; initial annuity per share 1.5 talers; total amount of annuities 1,000 talers;

6th class: ages 10–20; raised capital 39,000 talers; number of shares 300; price per share 130 talers; interest rate 2.31%; initial annuity per share 3 talers; total amount of annuities 900 talers;

7th class: ages 1–10; raised capital 49,000 talers; number of shares 350; price per share 140 talers; interest rate 1.43%; initial annuity per share 2 talers; total amount of annuities 1,200 talers.

The total investment was 168,000 talers, and the annuities totalled 6,600 talers. It was a compound tontine: one part of the annuity of a deceased member was lost to the tontine fund; the other part was divided between the surviving

[266] The tontine plan is discussed and reproduced in: (1788) Monatsschrift von und für Mecklenburg 181–192 and in: *Krünitz*, Encyclopädie LXXI (1796), 380–407. The plan was later modified: (1788) Monatsschrift von und für Mecklenburg 373–384. See also Landeshauptarchiv Schwerin, 3.1-1 (Mecklenburgische Landstände mit Engeren Ausschuß der Ritter- und Landschaft zu Rostock) No. 20 Anhang 30.

[267] A comparison of both tontine plans is to be found in: (1788) Monatsschrift von und für Mecklenburg 357–372.

members. The tontine had some further complicated details which are of no interest for the present purpose. It is unclear whether the tontine was ever issued.

42. A Rostock tontine of 1788?

There is one source suggesting that there were plans in Rostock to issue a tontine around 1788.[268] However, I was not able to identify further information on this tontine. It may be that the plan is identical to that of the Duchy of Mecklenburg as Rostock was part of the Duchy.

43. The Prussian tontine of 1788

The Prussian tontine of 1788 is called the *Wachsende Leibrenten-Anstalt* (Accumulative Life Annuity Corporation).[269] Modern literature sometimes refers to it as the Potsdam tontine. Indeed, the tontine regulations were issued and signed in Potsdam. However, the raised capital was to be used for building roads in the areas of Magdeburg and Halberstadt. According to Art. 1 of the tontine regulations, only Prussian nationals of at least 45 years of age were able to join the tontine. Article 2 states that the annuity could rise to the level of 20% of the investment. The minimum investment was 500, the maximum investment 2,000 talers. The tontine consisted of four classes, the 1st comprising the ages of 45–50 years, the 2nd ages 50–55, the 3rd ages 55–60, and the 4th class was for those over 60 years of age. The curious detail of the tontine was that the hereditary principle was implemented in a predetermined manner. According to Art. 6, for the first five years the annuity for the first class was at a rate of 5% of the invested capital; thereafter it increased incrementally, in 16 steps, reaching 20% after 40 years. For the other three classes the starting interest rate was higher (6%, 7%, and 8%, respectively), and the maximum interest rate of 20% was reached quicker (after 35, 30, and 25 years, respectively). This tontine design reflected academic discussions of the time. It was observed that the typical tontine was disadvantageous to investors as they could not predict the increase of their annuities:[270]

> Dagegen hat diese Einrichtung der Tontine das Unangenehme für die Interessenten: 1) Daß sie niemals vorher wissen können, wie viel sie in jedem Jahr ihres Lebens an

[268] Grundgesetzlicher neuer Erb-Vertrag der Durchlauchtigsten regierenden Herzogs und Herrn, Herrn Friederich Franz, Herzogs zu Mecklenburg … mit Ihro Erbunterthänigen Stadt Rostock, vollzogen zu Rostock, den 13ten May, 1788 (1788), 170.

[269] Patent wegen Errichtung einer wachsenden Leibrenten-Anstalt zum Betrieb des Chaussee-Baues im Magdeburgischen und Halberstädtschen, (1788) 8 Novum Corpus Constitutionum Prussico-Brandenburgensium Praecipue Marchicarum 2257–2268. The regulations are also reproduced in: *Krünitz*, Encyclopädie LXXI (1796), 202–210.

[270] *Kritter*, (1786) Leipziger Magazin für reine und angewandte Mathematik 509.

Renten bekommen werden, und es kann sich leicht ein Mißtrauen, wenn es gleich unbegründet ist, bey ihnen einschleichen, als ob die Vermehrung ihrer Rente vielleicht von der Direction der Administratoren abhange, wenn sie etwa nicht genugsame Aufmerksamkeit auf die Richtigkeit der Attestate des Lebens anwenden, die jeder Interessent jährlich einsenden muß, wenn er an der Beurtheilung der Rente Theil nehmen will.

By contrast, a tontine has an unpleasant feature for potential investors: 1) that they are never able to predict how much they will receive in annuities in any year of their lives, and this may give rise to a distrust, even if unfounded, that the increase in the annuities depends on the administration of the tontine, when for example the administration does not take the necessary care when checking the certificates which prove that a nominee is still alive, a certificate that each payee has to present in order to draw his annuity.

The Swiss mathematician Nicolaus Fuß (1755–1826), who lived and worked in Russia, therefore suggested in 1776 that the increase in annuities should be set out in advance, arguing that the advantages of such a scheme were manifold.[271] Johann Augustin Kritter (1721–1798) observed in 1786 that such a tontine will need special care when it is designed because the mortality tables on which it is based need to be correct. Otherwise the tontine is likely to cause financial harm to the issuer.[272] Finally, Art. 24 reveals an organizational detail of importance: the tontine was operated by the General Prussian Widow Assurance (*Allgemeine Wittwen-Verpflegungsanstalt*). Thus, the tontine was no longer operated as a single investment product, instead having become part of an assurance and thereby foreshadowing an important development of the 19th century.

44. The Lippe tontine loan of 1805

In 1805 the principality of Lippe issued a tontine in order to raise the capital needed for the establishment of a mental hospital in Brake.[273] The plan is entitled: 'Plan zu einer 50jährigen Tontine' ('Plan for a tontine running for a fixed term of 50 years').[274] The preamble of the plan indicates that the scheme initiated by Lippe was neither a life annuity nor a tontine:

So sehr auch die freywilligen Beyträge dem Irrenhause zu Statten kommen, so genügen sie zur Erbauung und inneren Einrichtung nicht; weshalb dann, um das noch fehlende Baukosten-Capital von 5000 Rthlr. aufzubringen, eine Tontine beliebt ist, die wesentliche Vortheile vor den sonst gewöhnlichen Einrichtungen dieser Art biethet, in denen man sein Einsatz-Capital verliehret, auf den Tod Anderer und eigenes langes Leben

[271] *Fuß*, Entwurf (1776), 48–59.

[272] *Kritter*, (1786) Leipziger Magazin für reine und angewandte Mathematik 510 f.

[273] (1815) Allgemeine Staats-Korrespondenz 201. See also *Bender*, 102–111, 108.

[274] The plan is to be found in: Landesarchiv Nordrhein-Westfalen, Abt. Ostwestfalen Lippe (Detmold), L 92 A No. 5002 and L 77 A No. 5744, fol. 51r–52r, 62r–63v.

nur rechnet, und der Zuletzbleibende allein den Vortheil der höchsten Verzinsung genießet. Die hier verkündigte Tontine dagegen bringt einem jeden sein Capital mit einem baaren Gewinn wieder, welches bis dahin jährlich mit 3 Procent verzinset wird ...

As much the voluntary contributions benefit the mental hospital, they are not sufficient in order to erect and furnish it. For that reason, in order to raise the missing construction costs of 5,000 talers, a tontine is favoured. It will offer important advantages over usual schemes of this kind. In these the investment is lost; investors calculate on the death of others and hope for a long life of their own; and it is the last survivor only who benefits from the full interest rate. By contrast with the herewith proclaimed tontine, each investor will receive his investment together with a profit, and on the invested capital an annual interest rate of 3% will be paid ...

The tontine was initiated to raise 5,000 talers. 100 shares of 50 talers each were sold. However, the investment was not lost; rather, it was repaid to the investors and an interest rate of 3% was paid. Why, then, did the plan not speak of a simple loan? There was a lottery element involved, and this is most probably the reason why the scheme was called a tontine. Specifically, the year when the repayment was due was drawn in a lottery. Each year only 2 shares were repaid. The last two investors were, thus, repaid after 50 years. In addition to the interest, each investor received a bonus once the invested capital was repaid. The bonus depended on the year when the capital was repaid. In the first five years, the bonus was 5 talers, in the next five years 15 talers, then 20 talers, 25 talers, 30 talers, 35 talers, 40 talers, and 45 talers. In the years 46 to 49 the bonus amounted to 50 talers, and in the last year it was 100 talers. Thus, the actual interest rate differed greatly if one includes the bonus in its calculation.[275] In the first year it was 13%: the bonus of 5 talers corresponded to an interest rate of 10% on the invested capital of 50 talers and there was the additional interest rate of 3%. In the 5th year the bonus was again 5 talers. Thus, the investor received in total 62.96 talers. That amounted to an interest rate of 4.72%. In the 6th year the total interest rate went up again to 6.92%. The last two investors received in the 50th year 319.20 talers in total: 219.20 on the basis of the 3% interest rate and an additional bonus of 100 talers. That correlates to an interest rate of 3.78%.

45. The Bremen tontine of 1805

The city of Bremen issued a third tontine in 1805.[276] The tontine raised 200,000 talers. 2,000 shares were sold, each at a price of 100 talers. The 2,000 shares were divided into eight classes:

---

275 The calculations that follow are my own.

276 The printed plan can be found in: Staatsarchiv Bremen, No. 2-R.1.A.10.c.4.II.d.2 vol. 1. See further Staatsarchiv Bremen, No. 2-R.1.a.10.c.4.I.

1st class: below the age of 10; raised capital 40,000 talers; number of shares 400; price per share 100 talers; interest rate 3%; initial annuity per share 3 talers; total amount of annuities 1,200 talers;

2nd class: below the age of 10; raised capital 40,000 talers; number of shares 400; price per share 100 talers; interest rate 3%; initial annuity per share 3 talers; total amount of annuities 1,200 talers;

3rd class: ages 10–20; raised capital 40,000 talers; number of shares 400; price per share 100 talers; interest rate 3.25%; initial annuity per share 3.25 talers; total amount of annuities 1,300 talers;

4th class: ages 20–30; raised capital 40,000 talers; number of shares 400; price per share 100 talers; interest rate 3.5%; initial annuity per share 3.5 talers; total amount of annuities 1,400 talers;

5th class: ages 30–40; raised capital 16,000 talers; number of shares 160; price per share 100 talers; interest rate 4%; initial annuity per share 4 talers; total amount of annuities 640 talers;

6th class: ages 40–50; raised capital 12,000 talers; number of shares 120; price per share 100 talers; interest rate 4.5%; initial annuity per share 4.5 talers; total amount of annuities 540 talers;

7th class: ages 50–60; raised capital 8,000 talers; number of shares 80; price per share 100 talers; interest rate 5.5%; initial annuity per share 5.5 talers; total amount of annuities 440 talers;

8th class: above the age of 60; raised capital 4,000 talers; number of shares 40; price per share 100 talers; interest rate 6.5%; initial annuity per share 6.5 talers; total amount of annuities 260 talers.

The tontine was issued even though not all shares in the different classes were sold. This was in line with the published tontine plan. According to Art. 16, at least half of the shares of each class had to be sold in order for that class to be issued. The 1st class attracted 300 subscribers, the 3rd class 200, the 4th class 200, the 5th class 100, the 6th class 80, the 7th class 80, and the 8th class 40. The 2nd class was not issued. Thus, instead of 2,000 shares, only 1,000 shares were sold. The city of Bremen published an amended tontine plan which reflected these changes.[277]

The Bremen tontine of 1805 explicitly stated that anyone could be named as nominee, but only once. If an individual had already been named as nominee by a subscriber to the tontine, then the later subscriber who wanted to name this same nominee would not be allowed to do so and had to name another nominee.

277 Staatsarchiv Bremen, No. 2-R.1.A.10.c.4.II.d.2 vol. 3.

46. The Hamburg tontine plan of 1807

In 1807 Hamburg published yet another tontine plan.[278] It is the last German tontine which was planned by the public hand to raise capital. At least, it is the last such tontine which I was able to identify. Nevertheless, tontines were still discussed thereafter as an instrument to raise capital: between 1839 and 1841 the city of Bremen built a new bridge across the river Weser. It was a stone bridge replacing the old wooden bridge which dated from 1738. Apparently, it was discussed whether the bridge should be financed through a tontine, but in the end a state bond was issued to raise 125,000 talers.[279]

The Hamburg plan of 1807 refers to high spending which Hamburg had to incur. It was the time of the French occupation of Hamburg.[280] Hamburg wanted to raise 1,000,000 marks. The tontine was planned to have 2,500 shares, each at a cost of 400 marks. The shares were to be divided into four classes:

1st class: below the age of 15; number of shares 1,000; interest rate 3.5%;

2nd class: ages 15–30; number of shares 800; interest rate 4%;

3rd class: ages 30–45; number of shares 500; interest rate 4.5%;

4th class: above the age of 45; number of shares 200; interest rate 5%.

The first three classes were evenly subdivided into two parts, so that the tontine consisted in fact of seven classes. However, the ages of the subdivisions were not strictly predefined. The 500 youngest subscribers of the 1st class formed a subdivision as did the 500 oldest subscribers of the 1st class. The same rule applied to the 2nd and 3rd class of the tontine. Thus, an investor was not able to foresee into which subdivision he would fall. Within the classes and subdivisions the usual hereditary principle applied. If one subdivision of the 1st class died out, 3,000 marks from the total annuities amount of 7,000 marks passed to the other subdivision of the 1st class. The last payee of the 1st class thus received 10,000 marks in annuities. Similar rules applied to the 2nd and 3rd classes. The plan did not receive enough subscription and was therefore abandoned.[281] Instead the city published a plan for a simple life annuity lottery.[282] However, once again sales of shares in the lottery were slower than anticipated.[283]

---

[278] (1807) 7/3 Sammlung Hamburgischer Verordnungen 157–164. The printed plan can also be found in: Staatsarchiv Bremen, No. 2-R.1.a.10.c.4.I.

[279] Staatsarchiv Bremen, No. 2-R.1.B.4.e.

[280] *Gretzschel*, 78 f.; *Klessmann*, 316.

[281] (1807) 7/3 Sammlung Hamburgischer Verordnungen 189.

[282] (1807) 7/3 Sammlung Hamburgischer Verordnungen 197–202.

[283] See (1807) 7/3 Sammlung Hamburgischer Verordnungen 231; (1808) 7/4 Sammlung Hamburgischer Verordnungen 236 f.

47. The Lübeck Tontine or Life Insurance Company of 1809

In 1809, the terms for a tontine were published in Lübeck.[284] Plans for the tontine seem to have first been made in 1790.[285] The full title of the 1809-publication was *Plan der von Privat-Unternehmern, unter öffentlicher Garantie, errichteten Tontine oder Lebens-Versicherungs-Gesellschaft zu Lübeck* (Plan of the Lübeck Tontine or Life Insurance Company, established by Private Business Men, under the Guarantee of the Public Hand). The preamble clarifies that the company served a number of purposes, including to provide a pension for widows and children and to receive a pension for oneself. Furthermore, the preamble makes clear that the contributions should be small enough so that also the less wealthy will be able to participate. Furthermore, the raised capital was to be used for the *St. Annen Armenhaus* (St. Annen Almshouse). The tontine consisted of 1,500 or 2,000 shares, each at a cost of 50 marks. The shares were divided into 5 classes and each class was subdivided into 2 subclasses:

1st class: below the age of 15; price per share 50 marks; interest rate 3.5%:

1st subdivision: number of shares 100; initial annuity per share 1.75 marks; total amount of annuities 175 marks;

2nd subdivision: number of shares 755; initial annuity per share 1.75 marks; total amount of annuities 1,325 marks;[286]

2nd class: ages 15–30; price per share 50 marks; interest rate 4%:

1st subdivision: number of shares 50; initial annuity per share 2 marks; total amount of annuities 100 marks;

2nd subdivision: number of shares 350; initial annuity per share 2 marks; total amount of annuities 700 marks;

3rd class: ages 30–45; price per share 50 talers; interest rate 5%:

1st subdivision: number of shares 30; initial annuity per share 2.5 marks; total amount of annuities 75 marks;

2nd subdivision: number of shares 90; initial annuity per share 2.5 marks; total amount of annuities 225 marks;

4th class: ages 45–60; price per share 50 talers; interest rate 6%:

1st subdivision: number of shares 20; initial annuity per share 3 marks; total amount of annuities 60 marks;

2nd subdivision: number of shares 55; initial annuity per share 3 marks; total amount of annuities 165 marks;

---

284 Archiv der Hansestadt Lübeck, 05.4-4 Tontine-078 No. 01.

285 Archiv der Hansestadt Lübeck, 5.1-1/04 Bergenfahrerkompanie No. 2896.

286 The terms seem to contain a calculation error; the total amount of annuities should be 1,321.25 marks.

5th class: above the age of 60; price per share 50 talers, interest rate 7%:

1st subdivision: number of shares 10; initial annuity per share 3.5 marks; total amount of annuities 35 marks;

2nd subdivision: number of shares 40; initial annuity per share 3.5 marks; total amount of annuities 140 marks.

The hereditary principle applied within each subdivision. If one subdivision died out, then the annuity of that subdivision accrued to the surviving subdivision of that class. If a class died out, the annuities accrued proportionally to the surviving classes. The last surviving annuitant, thus, received the full amount of the annuities of all classes.

The curious detail about the plan is the system of subdivisions. According to § 5 of the terms, the first subdivision had to be chosen if somebody wanted to buy a share with one nominee only. However, the second subdivision opened the possibility that more than one person bought a share and that all of them were nominees of that share. § 6 explains the plan as follows:

> So würden z.B. zwo Personen von 40 und 59 Jahren, wenn jede für sich allein Antheil nehmen will, in die erste Abtheilung der 3ten und 4ten Classe treten müssen, bey einer Verbindung unter einander aber, in die 2te Abtheilung der 3ten Classe gehören; … Die in Verbindung mit andern Getretenen haben den Vortheil, daß beym Absterben des einen Teilnehmers der volle Genuß der Zinsen nicht mit seinem Tode aufhöret, sondern bis auf den Längstlebenden in der Verbindung fortgeht, so daß dieser die Dividende aller in Gesammtheit genommenen Actien lebenslänglich genießt.

> Thus, if, for example, two persons of the ages 40 and 59 wanted each to buy a share for themselves, they would need to join the first subdivision of the 3rd and 4th classes; but if they wanted to buy a share jointly, they would join the 2nd subdivision of the 3rd class; ... Those who jointly join have the advantage that the enjoyment of the full annuity of that share does not terminate with the death of the one, but the enjoyment of the full annuity will continue for the surviving member so that the surviving member will enjoy the full annuity of all jointly bought shares.

Thus, the hereditary principle applied even within the single shares of the second subdivision of each class. This possibility was probably attractive for spouses, and the statutes make clear that they could buy multiple shares in such a way. By 1810 the tontine had received enough subscriptions in order to be issued. However, the original plan was modified. The tontine was issued with 1,500 shares in 5 classes with 18 subdivisions in total. Each member received a *Police* (policy).[287] Again, a term normally applied in the context of insurance was used.[288] In 1886 the tontine was still in operation. The tontine foreshadowed the second phase of the development of tontines. While the Lübeck tontine was a self-contained tontine for the purpose of raising capital, it was not issued by the

---

[287] Archiv der Hansestadt Lübeck, 05.4-4 Tontine-078 No. 04.

[288] See the text corresponding to n. 228 and n. 251, above.

public hand. Rather, it was the product of a private enterprise and called a life insurance company. With the tontines issued by the public hand, the tontine plans were often published as a piece of legislation. For that reason, I was able to refer to these plans as regulations or statutes. With tontines issued by private entities, these terms have to be avoided. Instead, I will speak of terms, conditions, or articles.

48. The Westphalian tontine of 1811

Finally, Jérôme Bonaparte, Napoleon Bonaparte's youngest brother, initiated in 1811 an association under the name of a tontine while he was king of *Westphalen* (Westphalia). The exact nature of this scheme is, however, unclear.[289]

III. The second phase: tontines issued by pension funds in the 19th century

In the second phase of their development, tontines were offered from the end of the 18th century onwards and then foremost in the 19th century by pension funds and savings banks as one out of many pension and savings products. As the present volume aims at assessing the impact which tontines had on the development of life insurance and life insurance law, I will disregard in this section the so-called *Sparkassen Tontinen* which were savings products offered by savings banks.[290] I will come back to these *Sparkassen Tontinen* in the conclusion of this volume.[291] For the first phase I have discussed a large number of tontines and tontine plans. For the second phase, I will only discuss, by way of example, the tontine-based pension products of a much smaller number of pension funds. The stronger focus on the first phase and the exemplary analysis of only a smaller number of tontine products for the 19th century is based on the following three observations. First, it will become apparent in the remainder of this volume that the reservations which modern literature has expressed against tontines are based on the tontine designs of the 17th and 18th centuries and on the U.S. tontine life insurance products of the third phase rather than on those tontines which were issued by pension funds in the second phase. Secondly, the legal discourse on tontines in the 18th century and also in the 19th century can be understood only against the background of the developments of tontines in their first phase. And thirdly, it seemed important to fully assess the progression from the initial tontines in the second half of the 17th century to the pension products in the early

---

[289] Hessisches Staatsarchiv (Marburg), 7 a No. 1/232/48.

[290] On these see the text corresponding to n. 103, above.

[291] See the text corresponding to n. 579, below.

19th century. By contrast, it did not seem to offer any additional value to the analysis to add further examples of tontine pension products for the 19th century. In their designs they seem to have more or less reflected the tontines of the late 18th century.

1. The Hamburg General Pension Fund of 1778

In 1778 the *Allgemeine Versorgungs-Anstalt* (General Pension Fund) was established in Hamburg.[292] It was founded at the initiative of the *Hamburgische Gesellschaft zur Beförderung der Künste und nützlichen Gewerbe* (Hamburg Society for the Encouragement of the Arts and Useful Commerce, today *Patriotische Gesellschaft* – Patriotic Society).[293] The society was founded in 1765.[294] Its models were the Dublin Society for Improving Husbandry, Manufactures and other Useful Arts of 1731 (today Royal Dublin Society) and the Royal Society for the Encouragement of Arts, Manufactures and Commerce of 1754 in London.[295] The Hamburg society was the first of its kind in Germany.

According to the author of the article on annuities in Johann Georg Krünitz's (1728–1796) *Oekonomisch-technologische Encyclopädie* (Economic Technological Encyclopedia), which appeared in 1796, the pension fund offered numerous products, some of which he claimed to be novel in Germany. In essence, all the products were life annuity schemes with different saving plans and with different conditions for the annuity payments.[296] Some of these products imitated the schemes offered by widow and orphan assurances and by funeral funds. The fund offered, for example, *aufgeschobene Leibrenten* (deferred life annuities): the investor made annual contributions during his professional years, and the annuity payments only commenced at a later date to be fixed in the contract. The deferred life annuity was designed for people who could provide for themselves while they were working, but who nevertheless feared that they would have not enough assets to support themselves after their retirement if they reached a high age. It was possible to advance the date of the commencement of the annuity payments, a possibility which was introduced for those who suffered from a working disability due to an unforeseen event such as an accident. The *verbundene Leibrente* (compound life annuity) was a product designed for two or more

[292] On the following account see *Krünitz*, Encyclopädie LXXI (1796), 152–196.

[293] *Wandel*, 3.

[294] On the society see *Kopitzsch*, Hamburgische Gesellschaft, 71–118; *van Dülmen*, 70–72; *Gretzschel*, 72; 'Patriotische Gesellschaft von 1765', in: *Kopitzsch* and *Tilgner*, Hamburg Lexikon, 368 f.

[295] On these see *Wood*, 2, 8.

[296] The statutes of the fund can be found in: Staatsarchiv Nürnberg, Reichsstadt Nürnberg D No. 4814.

persons who wanted to enter into a life annuity scheme together, for example, spouses or siblings living together: the individuals made one investment and the full annuity was paid until the last surviving annuitant had died. Such life annuities contracts were already known in the 14th century.[297] With another life annuity product it was possible, for example, for a husband or father to provide for his wife and children in case of his own death. The annuity payments to the wife and children commenced once the husband died, and they were paid until the wife or children themselves died. However, it seems that apart from the so-called *verbundene Leibrente* (compound life annuity), the Hamburg *Allgemeine Versorgungs-Anstalt* of 1778 did not offer tontine-like products.

2. The Oldenburg tontine of 1782

Modern literature mentions an Oldenburg tontine of 1782.[298] By ordinance of that year, the *Oldenburgische Wittwen- und Waisen Casse* (Widow and Orphan Assurance of Oldenburg) of 1779 was allowed to expand its life annuity business.[299] The preamble of the ordinance explains the reason for this expansion: the poorer classes were until then not able to participate in the life annuity schemes offered by the assurance. Article 1 accordingly restricted access to the new scheme to certain groups of Oldenburg inhabitants who were looked upon as being in need, e.g. childless widows. It was possible to buy an annuity as little as 1 taler. The scheme was not used to raise capital. The sole purpose of the scheme was to support the poor. And the ordinance hints at the deficiencies of the older widow and orphan insurance schemes. Specifically, when they were introduced they were designed for limited groups of people: widows and orphans of school teachers, university professors, or protestant pastors. For these groups widow and orphan assurances were often mandatory. In later stages of development, many of these assurances could be joined voluntarily. However, to join them was costly. Thus, they left a number of people in need.

The ordinance of 1782 does not explain the design of the life annuity scheme. It does not even use the word tontine. Instead, it refers to the ordinance of 1779 which established the assurance.[300] The ordinance of 1779 makes explicit that the assurance covered the areas of the Duchy of Oldenburg and of the Prince-

[297] See the text corresponding to n. 56 f., above

[298] *Braun*, Geschichte, 162.

[299] Verordnung wegen Erweiterung der Wittwen- und Waisen Casse auf Leibrenten, (1782) 5/2 Schlözer's Stats-Anzeigen 38–43. The ordinance is also reproduced in: *Krünitz*, Encyclopädie LXXI (1796), 196–201.

[300] Verordnung wegen einer errichteten Witwen- und Waysen-Casse für die Hochfürstl. Bischöfl. Lübekschen und Herzogl. Holstein-Oldenburgschen Lande (Eutin 1779); Niedersächsisches Landesarchiv (Oldenburg), Best. 222 No. 41.

Bishopric of Lübeck, the latter of which was based in Eutin. That explains why the ordinances were published in Eutin. Today Eutin is part of Schleswig-Holstein. The administration of the assurance was entrusted to the city of Oldenburg. That explains why modern literature speaks of an Oldenburg tontine. Today Oldenburg is part of *Niedersachsen* (Lower Saxony). An analysis of the ordinance reveals that the assurance offered a mere widow and orphan assurance, not a tontine. For civil servants of the Duchy, the assurance was mandatory. All other subjects of the Duchy could join the assurance voluntarily if they were in good health and if they did not pursue a dangerous profession. Article 1 of the ordinance hints that there were other products:

> Seefahrende, Fischer, Lotsen, Matrosen und welche auf den Herings- und Wallfischfang ausgehen, sind zwar von dieser Casse ausgeschlossen, jedoch soll ihnen von der Direction, wenn sie sich desfalls bei derselben melden, angezeigt werden, auf welche Weise sie den Ihrigen, auf den Fall ihres Absterbens, eine Leibrente versichern können.
>
> Seafarers, fishermen, marine-pilots, sailors, and those who pursue herring-fishing and whaling are excluded from joining this assurance, but its administrators shall, if such persons ask to join the assurance, indicate to them how they can buy a life annuity for their dependants.

However, it seems that the life annuity schemes to which Art. 1 refers were not part of the assurance. Art. 15 of the 1779-ordinance explains that the minimum share which could be purchased when joining the assurance voluntarily was for a pension of 10 talers per annum. The 1782-ordinance lowered the minimum pension which had to be purchased to 1 taler. In conclusion, it seems unlikely that the *Oldenburgische Wittwen- und Waisen Casse* started to offer tontines in 1782.

3. The Württemberg Life Annuity Bank of 1822

By concession of the king of Württemberg the *Würtembergische Leibrenten-Bank* (Württemberg Life Annuity Bank) was founded in 1822.[301] The bank was founded by a society of *Gutsbesitzer* (estate holders). The members of this society provided the *Gesellschaftskapital* (capital) which was necessary to found the bank by purchasing shares in the bank, each share at a cost of 10,000 gulden. In essence, the capital was given to the bank on a tontine scheme: the bank paid interest on the capital to the members of the society. The hereditary principle applied. Some further complex provisions applied which are of no interest for the present purpose.

---

301 Landesarchiv Baden-Württemberg (Hauptstaatsarchiv Stuttgart), E 146 No. 8972. See also Landesarchiv Baden-Württemberg (Hauptstaatsarchiv Stuttgart), E 146 No. 8974. And see (1822) Beilage zur Augsburger Allgemeinen Zeitung 713 f.

The bank offered three different products, and the articles of the bank spoke of different classes. The first product was for those who hoped to reach a high age and who, thus, hoped to see a high annuity increase in a traditional tontine scheme. The second product was for those who were risk averse and who wanted to ensure that their heirs would at least receive the invested capital if they had not received annuities worth the invested capital before their death. The third class was for those who were too poor to invest in the first or second product.

Each of these products was divided into 8 sub-divisions according to the age of the nominee: below the age of 6 years, 6–12, 13–20, 21–30, 31–40, 41–50, 51–60 years of age, and above the age of 60 years. With each product, each age sub-division formed its own association (*Genossenschaft*). Each year the different sub-divisions of the three products were offered anew. It was, thus, a continuous tontine. Each class had a minimum and a maximum number of investors. Each sub-division of the first and the second class had at least 40 and up to 400 members. Each sub-division of the third class had at least 500 and up to 5,000 members. All products, sub-divisions, and years were for accounting purposes treated strictly separate.

For the first class the total amount of annuities differed in the individual sub-divisions. If the total amount of 400 shares was sold, then the annuities amounted to 3,000 gulden in the first sub-division and climbed to 6,000 gulden in the eighth sub-division (respectively, 3,000, 3,500, 4,000, 4,000, 4,500, 5,000, 5,500, and 6,000 gulden). Each share cost 250 gulden. It was possible to pay the investment in five annual instalments. It was also possible to buy only a half or quarter share. Of course, a half or a quarter share received only half or a quarter of the total annuity in the event the investor was the last survivor of his sub-division.

The second class consisted of compound tontines. The annuities differed again in the individual sub-divisions. If the total amount of 400 shares was sold, then the annuities, again, amounted to 3,000 gulden in the first and 6,000 gulden in the eighth sub-division. Once the first investor died, the corresponding annuity was divided into two equal shares; in the first sub-division, for example, into two shares of 1,500 each. One share was divided between the surviving members, the other 1,500 between the heirs of the deceased members. Thus, the annuities of the surviving members increased until the last surviving member received the full 1,500 gulden. The annuities of the heirs, by contrast, decreased. The heirs of the first deceased member received the full 1,500 gulden. After the death of the second member, the 1,500 gulden freed for distribution were shared equally between the heirs of the first two deceased members. When there was only one member left, the 1,500 gulden were shared between 399 heirs. After the death of the last member, all payments – also those to the heirs – terminated. The shares of the second class had the same price as in the first class. There was again the possibility of an investment by instalments. And there was again the possibility of purchasing a half or quarter share.

The third class required an investment of only 10 gulden. If the total amount of 5,000 shares was sold, then the annuities amounted to 1,500 gulden in the first class and rose to 3,000 gulden in the eighth class (respectively, 1,500, 1,750, 2,000, 2,000, 2,250, 2,500, 2,750, and 3,000 gulden). The annuities were determined in annual lotteries. The number of tickets differed in the different sub-divisions. In the first sub-division, 60 tickets were drawn; in the eighth sub-division 120 tickets were drawn (respectively, 60, 70, 80, 80, 90, 100, 110, and 120 tickets). In the sixth sub-division the annuities amounted to 2,500 gulden and 100 tickets were drawn. Each selected ticket received an annuity of 25 gulden. However, the total amount of winnings was divided between the surviving investors. If only one winner had survived, he received the full 2,500 gulden. The annuities were paid out to the winners for only one year. The next year, 100 annuities were again drawn among the remaining tickets. Again, the surviving winners shared the 2,500 gulden. If all drawn winners were still alive, they received 25 gulden each. If only one of the drawn winners had survived, then he would receive in that year a payment of 2,500 gulden. If in a year only the tickets of deceased members were drawn, then a second drawing was to be held. Thus, each investor had the chance of receiving at least 25 gulden and at the most 2,500 gulden.

4. The Hamburg General Pension Tontine of 1822

The *Hamburgische Allgemeine Versorgungs-Tontine* (Hamburg General Pension Tontine) was founded in 1822. Initial plans had been published already in 1817.[302] According to the revised plan of 1822, it was intended that the tontine would have 11,000 shares divided into 6 classes. The members had to pay an annual subscription fee for a number of years: the period ranged from 36 years in the 1st class to 18 years in the 6th class. The subscription fee as well depended on the class. Payments had to be made quarterly, but it was possible to pay for four years in advance:[303]

1st class: ages 6–15; 2,500 shares; subscription period 36 years; subscription for four years 92 marks;

2nd class: ages 15-23; 2,500 shares; subscription period 32 years; subscription for four years 116 marks;

302 *Bertheau* (1817); *Anonymous*, (1817) 2/23 Lesefrüchte vom Felde der neuesten Literatur 353–362. Both publications can be found in: Staatsarchiv Hamburg, No. 613-3/91_I A 5.

303 The plan of 1822 can be found in: Staatsarchiv Hamburg, No. 613-3/91_I A 3.

3rd class: ages 23–32; 2,000 shares; subscription period 28 years; subscription for four years 148 marks;

4th class: ages 32–40; 2,000 shares; subscription period 24 years; subscription for four years 184 marks;

5th class: ages 40–47; 1,000 shares; subscription period 20 years; subscription for four years 270 marks;

6th class: ages 47–54: 1,000 shares; subscription period 18 years; subscription for four years 302 marks.

The reason why children below the age of 6 were not permitted is explained by reference to the introduction of vaccinations: since their introduction, tables on the mortality of children below the age of 6 had become outdated and unreliable. Further, no people above the age of 54 were admitted in light of the subscription period.[304] The rights to annuities were determined by annual lottery drawings. The total amount of annuities differed, as did the number of annuities which were distributed:

1st class: total amount of annuities 27,000 marks; number of annuitants 125;

2nd class: total amount of annuities 30,000 marks; number of annuitants 125;

3rd class: total amount of annuities 30,000 marks; number of annuitants 125;

4th class: total amount of annuities 30,000 marks; number of annuitants 125;

5th class: total amount of annuities 24,000 marks; number of annuitants 80;

6th class: total amount of annuities 24,000 marks; number of annuitants 80.

These amounts were awarded only if all shares in a class were sold. Otherwise they were reduced proportionally. Furthermore, the amount of the annuity payments which were awarded differed. To cover the costs of administration, only 90% of the annuities were paid out. And in the first four years of the tontine the annuities were not fully awarded. If a payee died, his or her right to the annuity was again drawn between those members of the class who had, until then, not received an annuity.

In addition to awarding annuities, there were each year single payment prizes in the different classes. However, the lottery for these single payment prizes commenced only after the subscription period had lapsed, for example, after 36 years in the 1st class:

1st class: 20 prizes of 150 marks each;

2nd class: 20 prizes of 200 marks each;

3rd class: 20 prizes of 200 marks each;

4th class: 20 prizes of 200 marks each;

---

304 *Bertheau* (1817), 12.

5th class: 10 prizes of 200 marks each;

6th class: 10 prizes of 200 marks each.

Furthermore, there were, depending on the capital remaining in the tontine, certain sums paid out annually between those members who had not as yet won a right to an annuity in the tontine.

The tontine adopted the hereditary principle which is characteristic for tontines in an unusual way: the right to annuities was drawn only between the surviving members. And the additional annual payments were made only to surviving members. The main feature of the tontine was an annuity lottery. However, once all surviving members of a class had received an annuity through the lottery, the annuities were levelled: the annuities of members who have died were divided equally between those members who had won the lowest annuity until all surviving members received the same annuity. From that point of time the annuities of the deceased members were split equally between the surviving members.

At a certain point of time each class of the tontine was terminated: with the termination of a class, the remaining capital from that class was to be divided between the last surviving members of that class. The class was terminated when each surviving member's share in the remaining capital amounted to at least 100,000 marks. The remaining capital was then distributed between these last surviving members accordingly. It was estimated that this point of time would be reached when the number of surviving members in each class was as follows: in the 1st class 4, in the 2nd class 12, in the 3rd class 6, in the 4th class 11, in the 5th class 4, and in the 6th class 4. At this point, the calculation was made per heads and not per share: this was an important detail if one of the last surviving members had bought multiple shares.

Thus, the raised capital was not applied for purposes outside the tontine. The capital belonged to the members of the tontine or, more specifically, belonged to the last survivors of the tontine classes. And the dividends which the administration earned with the capital benefited all members through the awarded prizes and the further payments. This was looked upon as the great advantage and innovation of the Hamburg tontine.[305]

Apparently, the sales of shares were not as successful as hoped for. The revised tontine articles of the year 1825 speak only of 9,000 shares in 4 classes.[306] The revised articles of the year 1832 point out that the final number of shares was only 5,701.[307] However, the basic design did not change.

---

305 *Bertheau* (1817), 7.

306 The 1825-statutes can be found in: Staatsarchiv Hamburg, No. 613-3/91_I A 3.

307 The 1832-statutes can be found in: Staatsarchiv Hamburg, No. 613-3/91_I A 3.

The tontine experienced financial difficulties. Because of this, the articles were, again and again, revised: in 1825, 1832, 1838, 1844, 1856, 1859, 1882, 1888, 1896, and 1899.[308] This in itself must have been a nuisance to investors. And the revisions caused legal problems as it was contentiously debated how the articles could be changed. It was argued by some tontine members that the tontine administration had not met the material requirements and had not observed the procedural rules for revising the articles. Furthermore, the tontine, its administration, and its general design were, for decades, heavily criticized. The criticism was put forward not only in rather technical and legal publications,[309] but also in the general discourse. A poem on the Hamburg tontine was, for example, published in an 1868 journal:[310]

Die Versorgungs-Tontine in Hamburg

Achtzehnhundertzweiundzwanzig,
Just vor sechsundvierzig Jahren,
Ward gegründet die 'Tontine
Der Versorgung' und – verfahren:

Der Erfolg war ein immenser:
Fünfundachtzig Mark pro anno
Zahlt den achtzigjähr'gen Greisen
Die Tontine jetzt per Mann – o!

Freilich ist mehr Geld vorhanden:
Doch es sollen erst aussterben
Alle bis auf vier – und diese
Sollen schließlich Alles erben!

Jeder erbt dann Hunderttausend
Mark; wie klug gedacht und weise!
Gott in Frankreich lebt nicht besser
Dann wie diese letzten Greise.

Lange darbten sie mit Andern,
Jetzt sind sie allein im Fette;
Um das Leben zu genießen
Stehn sie auf von ihrem Bette.

Hei! – Mit hundert Jahren tanzen
Cancan noch die letzten Viere,
Trinken Rheinwein und Champagner,
Oder gehen gar zum Biere.

Denn Sie haben's jetzt: sie können
Hunderttausend Mark erheben,
Und es glaubt gewiß ein Jeder,
Daß man damit wohl kann leben.

Wenigstens so lange können
Sie sich ihres Daseins freuen,
Daß ein – Testament sie machen;
Wenn die Kosten sie nicht scheuen.

---

[308] The different versions of the statutes can be found in: Staatsarchiv Hamburg, No. 613-3/91_I A 3. The revised version of the regulations from 1838 is reproduced as: Plan (Statuten) der Hamburgischen allgemeinen Versorgungs-Tontine von 1822, neu revidirt 1832, abermals revidirt, in: *Pöhls* (1842), 348–357.

[309] *Benecke* (1832); *Lohse*, *Boutin* and *Coqui* (1832); *Zimmermann*, Sendschreiben (1832); *Stoltenberg* (1832); *Averdieck* (1837); Insel Rügen. Freihafen für Wahrheit, Recht und offene Rede. Ein Beiblatt zur allgemeinen deutschen Bürgerzeitung, 1 December 1832; *Anonymous*, Kritik und Erläuterung (1871). The last publication is found in: Staatsarchiv Hamburg, No. 613-3/91_I A 5. See from the case law *Ober-Gericht Hamburg*, (1872) 5 Beiblatt zur Hamburgischen Handelsgerichts-Zeitung 105–110; *Ober-Appellations-Gericht der freien Hansestädte zu Lübeck*, (1874) 7 Sammlung der Entscheidungen des Ober-Appellationsgerichts der freien Hansestädte zu Lübeck 321.

[310] Staatsarchiv Hamburg, No. 613-3/91_I A 5. The poem was probably cut out of a newspaper. The file does not make clear which newspaper it was taken from.

Und dafür, daß sie im Leben
Darbten, können sie dann sterben
Ruhig, wenn das Geld gezählt ist,
Das bestimmt für ihre Erben!

Die Tontine der Versorgung
Ist in meisterhaften Händen;
So muß kommen es! – sagt Lehmann;
So muß man das Geld verwenden!

Glücklich, wer an der Tontine
Einen Antheil wird erreichen!
Und zum Schluß homerisch lachen
Die glücklichsten Vier Leichen!

In May 1905, the directors of the tontine proposed to close the 1st class of the tontine early, effective 1 January 1906, by dividing the remaining capital between the surviving members of that class. In May 1905, 13 members of that class were still alive. The proposal estimated the next annuity to be 3,515 marks per share. Furthermore, the proposal estimated that each of the 13 surviving members would receive approximately 34,000 marks. Finally, the proposal clarified that the 2nd and the 3rd classes had been closed early by following a similar procedure. During the negotiations, further members became deceased. In May 1906, the last surviving class of the tontine was dissolved: 11 payees – 2 living in Copenhagen, 1 in Riga, 1 in Brussels, 1 in St. Louis, and the other 6 in Germany – received between 38,772 and 45,234 marks. In total 452,340 marks were paid out.[311]

5. The Austrian General Pension Fund of 1823

In Austria, the *Allgemeine Versorgungsanstalt* (General Pension Fund) of 1823, which merged in 1825 with the *Erste österreichische Spar-Casse* (First Austrian Savings Bank) of 1819, engaged in the tontine business.[312] Each year seven classes were opened for subscription: below the age of 10, 10–20, 20–35, 35–50, 50–60, 60–65, and above the age of 65. In 1825 the tontine had already close to 9,000 subscribers, in 1830 close to 40,000. The tontine was open only to Austrian citizens. A complete contribution amounted to 200 gulden. It was possible to pay the complete contribution in instalments, but the first instalment was set at a minimum of 10 gulden in the first 5 classes, 50 gulden in the 6th class, and 100 gulden in the 7th class. Furthermore, the number of incomplete contributions per class was restricted. In cases of an incomplete contribution, the annuity was also proportionally smaller. The interest rate in the different classes ranged from 4% in the 1st class to 6.5% in the 7th class. If a member died, his or her heirs had a right to the difference between the invested sum and the received annuities. The Austrian General Pension Fund, thus, applied the main innovation of the

---

311 Staatsarchiv Hamburg, No. 613-3/91_I F 1.

312 *Molnar von Müllersheim* (1827); *von Sonnleithner* (1831); *Klaber* (1832), 40; *Haidinger* (1842), 1.

Nuremberg tontine.[313] The same rule applied when a member emigrated from Austria. Otherwise, the typical hereditary principle of tontines applied, with the special feature that 10% of the deceased's annuities were used to cover the costs of administration. It was, thus, a compound tontine.

6. The Prussian Pension Insurance Fund of 1838

The *Preußische Renten-Versicherungs-Anstalt* (Prussian Pension Insurance Fund) was founded in 1838 and existed under that name until 1929 when it was merged with some other funds. The preamble of the articles[314] made clear the purpose of the fund: it should help people to provide for their own pension and to provide for the support of dependants; additionally, it had schemes to allow the poor to participate in the fund. Consequently, the fund was not designed to be an investment scheme for the European financial market. According to Art. 2, the fund was open only to Prussian citizens and citizens of member states of the *Deutscher Bund* (German Confederation). A contributor bought an immediate right to annuities by investing 100 talers. The regulations spoke in Art. 5 of a *vollständige Einlage* (complete contribution). However, in order to open the fund also for the poor, it was possible to invest less than 100 talers. Thus, Art. 5 also spoke of an *unvollständige Einlage* (incomplete contribution). The minimum incomplete contribution was 10 talers. In that case the annuities were, of course, proportionally smaller. What is important is that those who contributed less than 100 talers did not buy an immediate right to have the annuity paid out. Instead, the annuity was each year added to the investment until the full contribution of 100 talers was reached. Only then was the annuity paid out to the contributor. Of course, it was open to the investor of an incomplete contribution to complete the contribution early by making voluntary payments towards the contribution. The tontine consisted of six classes divided on the basis of the age of the nominees: below the age of 12, 12–24, 24–35, 36–45, 45–55, and above the age of 55. The 6th class, for those nominees over the age of 55, did not allow incomplete contributions. And in each class only a limited number of incomplete contributions were permissible, most probably in order to safeguard the financial soundness of the fund. It was possible to join the tontine each year such that the new subscribers of a given year formed an independent tontine according to their class. Thus, the Prussian fund followed the principle of a continuous class tontine. The interest rate was between 3% in the 1st class and slightly over 5% in the 6th class, so

[313] See the text corresponding to and following n. 258, above.

[314] The regulations are published as: Statuten der Preußischen Renten-Versicherungs-Anstalt zu Berlin (1838). See also *L. Jung* (1840), 6 and the short summaries in: (1838) Hallisches patriotisches Wochenblatt 1613–1616; Regensburger Zeitung, 16 February 1839.

that every payee, on the basis of a complete contribution, received a starting annuity between 3 talers and slightly over 5 talers. According to Art. 21, the hereditary principle applied, this including several complex provisions on how, for example, a possible refund affected the amount of the annuity. Furthermore, the annuity was capped at 150 talers for a complete contribution. Any surplus from one class benefited, according to a number of complex provisions, other classes of the fund. If a contributor of an incomplete contribution died or emigrated, his or her heirs (in the case of death) or he himself or she herself (in the case of emigration) had a right to a refund of the contributions. If a contributor of a complete contribution died or emigrated, the same provisions applied for the difference between the contribution and any received annuities. Thus, the Prussian Pension Insurance Fund similarly applied the main innovation of the Nuremberg tontine.[315] The articles had a detailed provision on a reserve fund, and the pension fund invested the raised capital. If the pension scheme received higher returns than it was bound to pay out in annuities, then the excess was paid into the reserve fund. This fund was used to cover the costs of administration of the tontine and to cover losses which might be generated while the tontine was running.

IV. The third phase: tontine life insurance products in the late 19th century

Between 1868 and 1917, U.S. life insurance companies were active on the German insurance market. The Germania Life Assurance Society of New York was the first in 1868, followed by the Equitable Life Assurance Society of New York in 1877, the New York Life Insurance Company in 1882, and the Mutual Life Insurance Company of New York in 1886.[316]

The products of the latter three companies, in particular, combined tontines with life insurance.[317] The insured paid premiums for a life insurance product, the dividends on the premiums were accumulated in a tontine scheme, and the capital of the tontine was to be divided after a fixed period of time – usually 10, 15 or 20 years – between the surviving insured. If an insured had to terminate the tontine before that date, he or she lost all rights in the tontine.

The U.S. life insurance companies were criticized for these products. Yet, it was not so much the product itself which raised concerns. To save money in a

---

315 See the text corresponding to and following n. 258, above.

316 *Gutjahr* (1920), 19.

317 The following account is based on *Taussig* (1885), 1–26; *Cyon* (1892), 9; *Wiese*, Tontinen-Versicherung (1892), 10 f.; *Anonymous*, Berliner Börsen-Zeitung (1888), 11; *Du Pasquier*, (1910) 46 Zeitschrift für Schweizerische Statistik 511; *Gutjahr* (1920), 20, 30–32, 41–46; *Braun*, Geschichte, 304–307, 315 f.; *Kürble*, (1990) 79 Zeitschrift für die gesamte Versicherungswissenschaft 600.

tontine scheme and to divide the proceeds between the surviving members of that scheme was a mechanism which was already known to dowry assurances and one which had also been applied by the so-called *Sparkassen Tontinen* (savings bank tontines) throughout the 19th century.[318]

It was rather the marketing strategies and the lack of transparency which were criticized: the American insurance companies promised much higher interest rates for their tontine products than their European competitors – but without legally binding themselves. At the end of the day, they were not able to fulfil their promises and paid out much smaller dividends than anticipated. In 1891, Prussia ordered these companies to meet specific accounting standards as regards their tontine products. In essence, they had to maintain separate accounts for each class of the tontine. And they had to increase their deposits with the Prussian state. The American insurance companies claimed that these were discriminatory acts, and the intervention of the Prussian government caused diplomatic turmoil. Nevertheless, all insurance companies had to meet the accounting standards, and all foreign insurance companies had to have deposits with the Prussian state.

In 1894 the Equitable Life Assurance Society of New York pulled out of the Prussian market and in 1895 out of the Saxon market. The New York Life Insurance Company and the Mutual Life Insurance Company of New York lost their concessions in Prussia in 1895. In the city of Hamburg, they remained active. By contrast, in *Bayern* (Bavaria), the Equitable Life Assurance Society of New York and the New York Life Insurance Company were never allowed to introduce their tontine products. The New York Life Insurance Company was readmitted in Prussia in 1899 and was also allowed to sell its products even after the introduction of the *Versicherungsaufsichtsgesetz* (Insurance Regulation Act) of 1901. It left the German market only in 1914. Of course, existing policies were still valid, and one can as late as the 1930s still find case law concerning a tontine product of the New York Life Insurance Company.[319] The Germania Life Assurance Society was able to operate its insurance business in Germany even after 1914 and stopped its activities on the German market only in 1917. I will return to the criticism levied against the tontine products of the U.S. life insurance companies later in this volume.[320]

---

318 See the text corresponding to n. 103, above.

319 *Reichsgericht* (Imperial Court), (1930) 129 Entscheidungen des Reichsgerichts in Zivilsachen (RGZ) 134–143.

320 See the text corresponding to n. 511–513 and to n. 579, below.

V. Conclusion and comparative observations

The development of tontines in Germany falls into three phases. In their first phase, tontines were offered primarily by the public hand as self-contained investment schemes for the purpose of raising capital. The first phase covers the 17th and 18th centuries. In their second phase, tontines were offered by pension funds and savings banks for the purpose of offering pension and savings products to the general public. The second phase covers the 19th century. At the end of the 18th century and in the beginning of the 19th century, both phases, of course, overlapped. In their third phase, tontines were offered by U.S. life insurance companies for the purpose of marketing life insurance products. A tontine scheme was only an add-on to a life insurance product. The third phase covers the end of the 19th century and stretches into the beginning of the 20th century.

For a number of reasons, it is difficult to fully assess the practical importance of tontines in their first phase of development. (1) There is the simple problem of finding the relevant archival materials on those tontines which were issued or planned but which are not mentioned in either modern or contemporary literature. (2) Tontines appeared with different names: the first Prussian tontine was simply called a life annuity. It is only the preamble of the regulations that used the word tontine. In order to fully assess the number of tontines which existed in the 17th and 18th centuries, one would need to identify all life annuity schemes and analyse whether they can be looked upon as tontines. (3) For some forgotten tontines I found the publication of plans but no hints whether they received enough subscriptions in order to be actually issued. (4) Today, we define tontines as a pooled life annuity schemes. The characteristic feature is that the annuities of deceased members accrue to the surviving members of the tontine so that the annuities increase over time. This is generally referred to as the hereditary principle. However, in the 17th and 18th century the term was used much more loosely. Foremost, lotteries were called tontines. Some of these were life annuity lotteries which, however, did not apply the hereditary principle. Others were simple lotteries. Loan agreements which included a lottery element were also called tontines. And then there were a number of tontines which included a lottery element. In addition to the above mentioned schemes, a Bavarian lottery may serve as a further example of such lotteries being referred to as tontines: in 1776, *Bayern* (Bavaria) published a plan which envisioned instituting an annuity fund (*Rentengesellschaft*) with 50,000 shares.[321] The plan spoke of a tontine, but it was a simple annuity lottery.[322] Among the prizes of the lottery were annuity payments. According to the plan, the annuities were to be paid out for only ten years. And,

---

[321] Plan von Ihro Churfürstl. Durchleucht genädigst-privilegierten und zum Nutzen des Publici errichteten Renntengesellschaft (München 1776).

[322] On an earlier example of a life annuity lottery see *J.T. Koch*, 61–70.

more importantly, if a payee died, his annuity was not divided between the surviving payees; rather the deceased's heirs had a right to the annuity for the remaining time. (5) However, it is not only in the 17th and 18th centuries that the term tontine was used rather loosely. Some 17th and 18th century investment products that modern literature has labelled tontines were in fact not tontines under the modern definition. This is, for example, the case with the Austrian life annuity fund of 1760.[323]

Nevertheless, it has been possible to identify a larger number of tontines and tontine plans in German-speaking territories than are mentioned in modern literature: a number of tontines and tontine plans have simply been forgotten in modern literature. Furthermore, it has become apparent that tontines were marketed on a European scale; Germans invested in foreign tontines and related schemes, and German tontines were marketed internationally, too. In conclusion, it is safe to say that 17th and 18th century tontines and tontine-like products played a much more important role as an investment product than is generally acknowledged.

The late 18th century saw a number of improvements and novelties in tontine designs. Three improvements seem to have been of importance for the further development of tontines. (1) Foremost, the Nuremberg tontine of 1777 introduced a scheme under which the invested capital was always at least nominally compensated: if the annuities which the payee received did not amount to the invested capital before the investor died, the heirs were reimbursed the balance. (2) The Prussian tontine of 1788 applied the hereditary principle in a particular and pre-specified manner: the increase of the annuities was predetermined and it was capped. (3) Finally, the possibility to pay the investment in instalments opened tontines to poorer individuals.

The developments in the tontine designs did not occur in isolation. The fact that tontines were marketed on an international scale already suggests that tontine designers took notice of the designs of tontines not only in other German territories but also as seen internationally. As pointed out earlier, in designing its tontine of 1698, the Prussian administration took notice of a tontine in Venice, the French tontine of 1689, the English tontine of 1692, and a French tontine of 1698.[324] Walter Fiedler has pointed out that the city of *Nürnberg* (Nuremberg), when planning its tontine of 1777, studied the Schweinfurt tontine of 1735, the Hamburg tontine of 1776, and a Danish tontine of 1775.[325] The corresponding file on the tontine in the *Staatsarchiv Nürnberg* (State Archive of Nuremberg)[326] contains, furthermore, the French tontine plans and regulations from the years

---

[323] See the text corresponding to n. 206, above.

[324] See the text corresponding to n. 69, above.

[325] *Fiedler*, 53–55.

[326] Staatsarchiv Nürnberg, Reichsstadt Nürnberg D No. 4816, D No. 4814.

1689, 1709, 1733, 1734, 1743, 1744, 1745, 1759, the plans for the Bolzano tontine of 1737, the plan of a Hague tontine of 1771, the plan of an Amsterdam scheme of 1771, the statutes of the Hamburg *Allgemeine Versorgungs-Anstalt* (General Pension Fund) of 1778, and the regulations of the Austrian life annuity fund of 1760. The drafters of the Mecklenburg tontine plan of 1787 took notice of the two Nuremberg tontines of 1777 and 1783.[327] The drafters of the Stade tontine of 1777 analysed the Bremen tontine of 1772; the regulations and the policies of both tontines exhibit a number of parallels.[328] The file in the *Staatsarchiv Bremen* (Bremen State Archive) on tontines contains the Bremen loan agreement of 1692, references to the Wied tontine of 1749, and the statutes of the *Kurmaynzer Leibrenten-Gesellschaft* (Mainz Life Annuity Society) of 1769.[329] In designing the Saxon tontine plan of 1765, French tontines and the Cleves tontine of 1763 were consulted.[330] Many more examples could be added. But there are not only direct references in the archival materials which prove that tontine designs largely took notice of other national and international tontines. There are also striking parallels between different tontines: Gallais-Hamonno and Rietsch mention that both the Danish tontine plan of 1653 and the tontine plan of 1667 for the States of Languedoc contained a provision according to which the purchasers of a very high number of shares were to be ennobled.[331] According to the East Frisian tontine plan of 1755, the last three survivors were similarly to be ennobled.[332] A Zeeland tontine of 1755 as reported by Boudewijn Sirks recalls the design of the Gotha tontine of 1752.[333] An Italian tontine of 1793 mentioned by Maura Fortunati seems to have adopted the main innovation introduced by the Nuremberg tontine of 1777.[334] Finally, the tontine designers took note of the national and international literature on tontines and, more importantly, on actuarial questions regarding mortality.[335]

By the end of the 18th century and then in the 19th century, an important shift occurred. The number of self-contained tontines which were issued by the public

[327] Landeshauptarchiv Schwerin, 3.1-1 (Mecklenburgische Landstände mit Engeren Ausschuß der Ritter- und Landschaft zu Rostock) No. 20 Anhang 30.

[328] Stadtarchiv Stade, St.H. 51–52 No. 18.

[329] Staatsarchiv Bremen, No. 2-R.1.a.10.c.4.I.

[330] Sächsisches Staatsarchiv (Hauptstaatsarchiv Dresden), 10025 Geheimes Konsilium Loc. 5350/08.

[331] *Gallais-Hamonno* and *Rietsch*, Financial Engineering, 38.

[332] See the text following n. 201, above.

[333] *Sirks*, 136 and see the text corresponding to and following n. 190, above.

[334] *Fortunati*, 214 f. and see the text corresponding to and following n. 258, above.

[335] See, e.g., Sächsisches Staatsarchiv (Hauptstaatsarchiv Dresden), 10025 Geheimes Konsilium Loc. 5350/08; Staatsarchiv Nürnberg, Reichsstadt Nürnberg D No. 4816, D No. 4814; Landeshauptarchiv Schwerin, 3.1-1 (Mecklenburgische Landstände mit Engeren Ausschuß der Ritter- und Landschaft zu Rostock) No. 20 Anhang 29.

hand declined. Pension funds and savings banks started to offer tontines as one of many investment and insurance products. This marked the beginning of the second phase of the developments of tontines. I have focused on those tontines which were offered by pension funds and, by way of example, I have analysed the products offered by the *Würtembergische Leibrenten-Bank* (Württemberg Life Annuity Bank) of 1822, by the *Hamburgische Allgemeine Versorgungs-Tontine* (Hamburg General Pension Tontine) of 1822, by the Austrian *Allgemeine Versorgungsanstalt* (General Pension Fund) of 1823, and by the *Preußische Renten-Versicherungs-Anstalt* (Prussian Pension Insurance Fund) of 1838. For the late 18th century I have discussed the Hamburg *Allgemeine Versorgungs-Anstalt* (General Pension Fund) of 1778 and the *Oldenburgische Wittwen- und Waisen Casse* (Widow and Orphan Assurance of Oldenburg) of 1779. Not all products offered by these pension funds and assurances were in fact tontine products.

Many more examples could be added for the late 18th century and subsequently the 19th century: A short note published in 1787 refers to tontines issued by the *Württemberg Allgemeine Wittwen- und Waisenkasse* (Württemberg General Widow and Orphan Assurance) of 1756. The assurance had sold 4,000 shares in the tontine, and the author alleges that the assurance paid out excessively high annuities, that in 1786 the annuities had to be reduced, that a number of contributors terminated their membership in the tontine, and that they received back 40% of their investment.[336] In 1770, the *Churbaierische Renten-Gesellschaft* (Electorate-Bavarian Pension Association) advertised in an Augsburg newspaper a scheme which it called a tontine and annuity lottery.[337] In 1791 a Munich newspaper published a short announcement on a planned tontine to be issued by an *Assekuranzgesellschaft auf das Leben* (Assurance Society on Lives) in Leipzig.[338] And there was a scheme imitating the *Hamburgische Allgemeine Versorgungs-Tontine* (Hamburg General Pension Tontine) of 1822 in Rostock: the *Rostocker Versorgungs-Tontine* (Rostock Pension Tontine) of 1831.[339]

In a treatise on the *Allgemeine Versorgungsanstalt im Großherzogthum Baden* (General Pension Fund in the Grand Duchy Baden), which was founded in 1835 in Karlsruhe and which is today part of the *Karlsruher Lebensversicherung AG* (Karlsruhe Life Insurance), Carl Ludwig Beger (1790–1871) explained the purpose and the design of these pension funds:[340]

---

[336] *Röder* (1787), 110 f.

[337] Augspurgische Ordinari Postzeitung, 21 May 1770.

[338] (1792) Münchener Intelligenzblatt 33 f.

[339] Neue Speyerer Zeitung, 25 February 1834; Staats und Gelehrte Zeitung des Hamburgischen unpartheiischen Correpsondenten, 9 September 1831; (1831) Leipziger Zeitung 800, 934, 1328.

[340] *Beger* (1835), 5 f.

Man kann Sicherheit der öconomischen Existenz für sich und die Seinigen suchen und mehr und minder finden: … 4. In einer sogenannten Versorgungsanstalt, welche einzelne Eigenthümlichkeiten der Leibrenten-Anstalt und Tontinen vereinigt. Sie achtet allein auf das Alter des Theilnehmers, sichert, je nach diesem, für eine vorausbestimmte Einlage eine bestimmte Jahresrente alsbald zu und läßt diese durch Erbtheile der Abgehenden bis zu einer gewissen Höhe sich vermehren. Dasjenige, was der Abgehende an seiner Einlage in den jährlichen Renten nicht bereits bezogen hat, erstattet sie an die Erben desselben und was hienach in der Anstalt zurückbleibt überläßt sie den überlebenden Mitgliedern derselben Altersklasse derselben Gesellschaft oder den übrigen Klassen oder nachrückenden Jahresgesellschaften. Sie hebt darauf ab, daß die Theilnehmer selbst, während ihres Lebens, zu entsprechenden Bezügen aus der Anstalt, zur öconomischen Versorgung im einrückenden Alter, gelangen.

One can more or less find means of economic protection for oneself and for one's dependants: ... 4. Through a so-called pension fund, which combines certain features of life annuity societies and tontines. A pension fund is only concerned about the age of those who want to join, and it will promise each member for a certain investment a specified annual return which depends on the age when joining the fund. The promised return will be increased, up to a certain sum, by the hereditary parts of the deceased's annuities. If the deceased had not, before he died, received annuities equalling his investment, the fund will reimburse his or her heirs the balance. The remainder will benefit the surviving members of the same class, the other classes which were founded in the same year or all other classes. A pension fund has the function that its members can, through their own investment, safeguard their economic maintenance when they are old.

According to Beger it was the Austrian *Allgemeine Versorgungsanstalt* (General Pension Fund) of 1823 which served as a model for the General Pension Fund in the Grand Duchy Baden. The Baden fund adopted the refund mechanism of the Nuremberg tontine of 1777. And it capped the increase of the annuities. Beger's account gives the impression that he described in general terms how pension funds of his time functioned. And Beger points out the great advantage of these products compared to life insurance products: no one was excluded from joining a pension fund on the basis of his or her state of health or professional occupation.[341]

In conclusion, the number of tontines in the 19th century was not in decline when modern life insurance schemes emerged. Tontines seem to have remained an important pension product.[342]

In the late 19th and early 20th centuries, U.S. life insurance companies offered tontine life insurance products. This is the third phase of the development of tontines. With these tontine life insurance products, the tontine was only an add-on element to a standard life insurance product: the dividends on the premiums were accumulated in a tontine scheme, and the accumulated capital was divided after

---

341 *Beger* (1835), 7.

342 See the text corresponding to n. 95–105, above.

a fixed period of time between the surviving insured. If an insured had to terminate the tontine before that date, he or she lost all rights in the tontine. The tontine element in these life insurance policies was a simple imitation of the known mechanism applied by dowry assurances and of the mechanism which also formed the basis of the *Sparkassen Tontinen* (savings bank tontines) throughout the 19th century.[343]

---

[343] See the text corresponding to n. 103, above.

D. From a multi-purpose to a single-purpose financial product

The development of tontines in their three phases may also be analysed and summarized from a different perspective by focusing on the functions which tontines served.

I. The first phase: self-contained tontines in the 17th and 18th centuries

In their first phase of development tontines were in the 17th and 18th centuries multi-purpose financial products. They were issued mostly by the public hand as self-contained schemes. For investors, these tontines functioned primarily as a means to generate a pension either for themselves or for a dependant.[344] This purpose is made explicit in many of the 17th- and 18th-century tontine plans and regulations.[345]

For investors tontines could, in addition, function as a simple investment which was used for speculative purposes. It was accepted that a payee could, in principle, sell and transfer his rights in a tontine.[346] Bergius points out that in Holland, England, and France it was common to trade with rights in tontines: contributors invested in tontines in order to subsequently sell their rights at a profit.[347] Article 13 of the regulations of the tontine of the city of *Danzig* (Gdańsk) of 1657 expressly allowed payees to sell and assign their rights in the tontine. A similar provision is contained in the plan for the Schweinfurt tontine of 1735. In a similar vein, Art. 18 of the regulations of the Nuremberg tontine of 1777 allowed the sale and transfer of the payee's rights in the tontine, with the annuity still being dependant on the original nominee's life.

---

[344] *Krünitz*, Encyclopädie LXXI (1796), 213 f.; Gründliche Nachricht von einer neuen sehr vorzüglichen und vortheilhaften Reichs-Stadt Nürnbergischen Leib-Renten Gesellschaft (Nürnberg 1777), 30; (1757) Das Neueste aus der anmuthigen Gelehrsamkeit 757; *Wortner*, 113; *Roloff*, 294; *Schöpfer*, 133; *Braun*, Geschichte, 66 f.; *Du Pasquier*, (1910) 46 Zeitschrift für Schweizerische Statistik 489.

[345] Art. 1 of the regulations of the Prussian tontine of 1698; Art. 9 of the regulations of the tontine plan of the shire of Wied of 1749; preamble to the regulations of the Gotha tontine of 1752.

[346] *Krünitz*, Encyclopädie LXXI (1796), 8.

[347] *Bergius* (1771), 150.

Finally, many, but not all 18th-century tontines exhibited lottery elements, and the rights to the annuities were drawn in a lottery. Thus, for investors these tontines also served a gambling purpose.

For issuers, tontines were a means of raising capital. This was the predominant reason why the public hand planned and issued tontines in the 17th and 18th centuries.[348] In 1657 the city of *Danzig* (Gdańsk) simply wanted to remedy its financial straits,[349] yet it is clear that these financial straits were experienced in connection with the Second Northern War.[350] The Cleves tontine of 1763 was planned to refinance and consolidate the debts following the Seven Years War.[351] Many other tontines were also planned with the intention of covering the costs of a war. However, there were other purposes, too: the planned East Frisian tontine of 1755 was to finance the impoldering of new lands.[352] *Nürnberg* (Nuremberg) had originally planned its tontine in order to raise capital for the University of Altdorf (1622–1809).[353] The title of the Prussian tontine of 1788 makes clear that the raised capital was to be used for building roads in the areas of Magdeburg and Halberstadt. The planned Augsburg tontine of 1753/55 was allegedly initiated in order to support the arts and sciences.[354] Whether life annuities and tontines should be used by the state for raising capital seems to have been matter of controversy among authors of the 18th century: whereas Johann George Leib (1670–1727), without further discussion and without restrictions, preferred such schemes as a means of raising capital,[355] Bergius, von Justi, and Jakob Friedrich von Bielfeld (1717–1770) looked upon tontines as a means of raising extraordinary capital only.[356]

The fact that tontines were multi-purpose financial products combined with, first, the public hand's desire (and frequent need) to raise capital and, second, the contributors' pursuit of an interesting investment may explain a number of points in the observed tontine designs. Gallais-Hamonno and Rietsch recommend that the age-based classes in a tontine should cover only a small age span, 5 years at the most:[357]

---

[348] *Lehner*, 18; *Roloff*, 294; *Schöpfer*, 133; *Zetzsche*, 286; *Oberholzer*, 84; *Wortner*, 113; *Braun*, Geschichte, 64.

[349] *Foltz* (1912), 297.

[350] See the text corresponding to n. 131, above.

[351] See the text following n. 210, above.

[352] See the text corresponding to n. 198, above.

[353] *Fiedler*, 47.

[354] (1757) Das Neueste aus der anmuthigen Gelehrsamkeit 755.

[355] *Leib* (1708), 33–36.

[356] *Bergius* (1771), 149; *von Justi*, Finanzwesen (1766), 574; *idem*, Staatswirthschaft (1758), 456–458; *von Bielfeld* (1761), 532.

[357] *Gallais-Hamonno* and *Rietsch*, Financial Engineering, 53.

> The most important component is the distribution of the nominees among age groups or classes in order to group together nominees having a similar probability of surviving. Thus, the introduction of classes is at the heart of the fairness of a tontine.

However, the tontines and tontine plans in German-speaking territories usually covered a larger age span. An age span of 5 years was the exception. Often we find age spans of 10, sometimes even of 15 or 20 years. In the view of Gallais-Hamonno and Rietsch, the tontines and tontine plans in German-speaking territories were, thus, actuarially unfair. Did issuers in German-speaking territories not understand how to design an actuarially fair tontine product?

I think the larger age span is better explained on different grounds, namely that tontines were often used as a means to raise capital after a war. Here the treasury was in need of money, but the local population did not, as a consequence of the war, have sufficient funds to invest in a tontine. That was the explicit reason why the *Breslau* (Wrocław) tontine plan of 1766 was never implemented.[358] That was most probably the reason why some tontines did not find enough subscribers in order to be issued. And that was perhaps the reason why many tontines aimed at a European market. Accordingly, issuers had to take the possibility into consideration that the tontine would attract only a small number of subscribers. In order to enhance the chances that the tontine would receive enough subscriptions it was advisable to keep the total number of shares small. However, each class needed a minimum number of shares such that each investor had the chance to receive a substantial increase. Thus, the tontines had to have a small number of classes and this resulted in each class covering a larger age span.

The need to raise capital on the side of issuers also explains the diverse designs of the schemes of the 17th and 18th centuries: in order to make investment schemes more attractive to potential contributors, the issuers not only offered pure pension products but added elements of a lottery to the tontine schemes.

Gallais-Hamonno and Rietsch recommend further that the interest rate should increase in the different classes:[359]

> The second fundamental component of a tontine is an increase in the interest rate along with the average age of each class. The underlying idea is that the payee should be reimbursed on the invested principal over time. Otherwise, the tontine is actuarially unfair.

Indeed, with most tontines and tontine plans in German-speaking territories the interest rate increased. However, it seems that the financial needs of treasuries to raise capital made them promise higher interest rates than was advisable. The Stade tontine of 1777 may serve as an example. In that case the city of Stade still had an interest in issuing the tontine in order to refinance its debts when it turned

---

358 See the text corresponding to n. 218, above.

359 *Gallais-Hamonno* and *Rietsch*, Financial Engineering, 54.

out that the original plan did not attract enough subscribers, and for that reason the city decided in 1779 to increase the interest rates in each class.[360]

In addition, there is one feature of many tontines and tontine plans which seems to be explainable only against the background that issuers sought to create an attractive investment even if that meant adopting a feature which was to their own disadvantage. Despite the interest rate increasing along with the average age of each class, in some tontines and tontine plans the obligation to pay the annuities did not terminate when the last survivor of a class had died. Instead, the total amount of annuities was shared by the surviving classes. Thus, the younger classes profited from the higher interest rates of the older classes. And the issuer had to pay the higher interest rates until the last survivor of the youngest class had died.

The preceding paragraphs concern the manifold purposes which tontines served when they were designed as a pooled life annuity scheme. Yet it should be recalled that some schemes were called a tontine even though they were simple lotteries or some other kind of investment product. The word tontine was used rather loosely. These schemes served, of course, their own purposes.

II. The second phase: tontines issued by pension funds in the 19th century

In the late 18th century and then in the 19th century, an important shift occurred. Specifically, when pension funds and savings banks started to issue tontines in the second phase of their development, tontines were transformed into single-purpose financial products: they were only a means to generate a pension or they were utilized as a savings plan. Thus, there were two single-purpose financial products with two distinct purposes.

As early as the 18th century, issuers of state-run tontines tried to exclude the tendency whereby tontines were used as a mere investment. For instance, Art. 31 of the regulations of the planned tontine of the shire of Wied of 1749 and Art. 10 of the regulation of the Prussian tontine of 1698 restricted the possibility to transfer the right to the annuities, and Art. 10 of the Prussian regulations gave an explanation of this restriction: the tontine was initiated primarily for the support of one's children.

In the 17th and 18th century tontines were often marketed internationally in order to attract investors from all over Europe. By contrast, the Austrian *Allgemeine Versorgungsanstalt* (General Pension Fund) of 1823 was open only to

[360] See the text corresponding to n. 254, above.

Austrian citizens,[361] and the *Preußische Renten-Versicherungs-Anstalt* (Prussian Pension Insurance Fund) of 1838 to only Prussian citizens and citizens of member states of the *Deutscher Bund* (German Confederation).[362] Again, this restriction may be interpreted as reflecting the transformation of tontines from a multi-purpose investment product to a single-purpose pension product.

However, it is clear that this transformation was not fully reflected in the tontine designs. One would think that the pension funds of the 19th century did not any longer include a lottery element in their products. Nevertheless, some products offered by the *Würtembergische Leibrenten-Bank* (Württemberg Life Annuity Bank) of 1822 and the tontine offered by *Hamburgische Allgemeine Versorgungs-Tontine* (Hamburg General Pension Tontine) of 1822 still exhibited lottery elements.

There is one final question which is beyond the scope of the present contribution: in how far did the tontines of the first and the second phase fulfil their function as pension products? Answering this question would make it necessary to analyse the purchasing power of the different annuity payments.

III. The third phase: tontine life insurance products in the late 19th century

In the third phase of the development, tontines were reduced to an add-on to a standard life policy for the purpose of marketing it. It was thus a way to distribute the dividends on premiums.

---

[361] See the text following n. 312, above.

[362] See the text following n. 314, above.

E. Tontines and the development life insurance

According to the German-language literature, '[t]ontines played an extraordinary important role for the development of insurance'.[363] Yet, the fact that tontines were multi-purpose products[364] puts them not only into the context of the history of insurance but also into other historical contexts: they belong just as much to the history of public finance, state bonds, and lotteries.[365] Thus, it would be an interesting research question to assess the historical importance of tontines in these contexts, too. However, this is beyond the scope of the present volume. I will concentrate on the role which tontines played for the development of insurance. I have already pointed out that the modern German-language literature identifies three different aspects regarding the importance of tontines in this context.[366]

I. Tontines and the development of actuarial science

First, it is argued that tontines were of utmost importance in further developing mortality tables and actuarial science.[367] Indeed, this was the main focus of German-language 18th-century literature.[368] It was a truly European discourse: German-speaking authors discussed the findings of, for example, Dutch, English, and French authors. Nevertheless, the discussions did not exclusively focus on tontines. Rather, German-language 18th-century literature discussed mortality tables and actuarial problems in connection with tontines, other life annuity schemes, widow and orphan assurances, and funeral funds. Tontines were one

---

363 See the references in n. 19, above.

364 See 106 ff., above.

365 The connection between lotteries and tontines is also stressed by the volume published on the occasion of the 350th anniversary of the Hamburg lotteries in 1962: *Nordwestdeutsche Klassenlotterie*, 350 Jahre Staatslotterie, passim. See also *J.T. Koch*, 61–70. On the history of lotteries in Frankfurt see most recently *Kullick*, passim.

366 See the text corresponding to n. 14–19, above.

367 See the references in n. 16, above.

368 See e.g., *Kritter*, (1786) Leipziger Magazin für reine und angewandte Mathematik 501–531; *idem*, (1781) 2 Göttingisches Magazin der Wissenschaft und Literatur 390–416; *Fuß*, Éclaircissemens (1776) (translated into German by *Kritter* as: Erläuterungen); *Bergius* (1771), 151; *Süßmilch* (1762), 374 f.; *de Florencourt* (1781), 149. From modern literature see e.g., *P. Koch*, Geschichte der Versicherungswissenschaft, 34–36.

out of many relevant products. The second half of the 18th century saw a diversification of pension and insurance-like products, as the Hamburg *Allgemeine Versorgungs-Anstalt* (General Pension Fund) of 1778 proves.[369] This diversification was strongly rooted in the 18th-century Enlightenment. And in 1761, von Bielfeld explicitly highlighted the fact that tontine calculations may be useful for the purpose of designing life insurance products.[370]

II. Spreading the idea of life insurance

Secondly, it is alleged that tontines 'helped spread the idea of insurance and made wider circles receptive for the idea of life insurance'.[371] This assertion sounds plausible. After all, in the late 18th century tontines were transformed into single-purpose pension products. From the late 18th century onwards they were issued by pension funds. At the same time, the issuers became aware of the fact that they had to open their products to poorer populations by introducing, foremost, the possibility of making incomplete contributions.[372]

However, there are other institutions which could have had the same effect of spreading the idea of insurance, e.g., widow and orphan assurances. Indeed, the development that issuers became aware that they had to open their products to poorer individuals was not restricted to tontines.[373] In the 17th century, widow and orphan assurances were introduced in many German territories as a means of the state to provide for civil servants, for example. In the 18th century, widow and orphan assurances were introduced which could be joined by anybody on a voluntary basis. However, joining a widow and orphan assurance required a considerable investment. In the late 18th century, widow and orphan assurances were opened to the poorer, too, as the example of the *Oldenburgische Wittwen- und Waisen Casse* (Widow and Orphan Assurance of Oldenburg) of 1779 proves.[374]

Thus, in order to prove the special importance of tontines, one would need to undertake statistical research on the number of people participating in tontines as compared to widow and orphan assurances. Furthermore, it would be of interest to know which social classes participated in the different schemes and how these numbers and the social standing of participants evolved in the course of the 18th century. Robin Pearson points out that to his 'knowledge, no-one has yet carried out a comprehensive analysis of the social composition of investors in tontines.

---

369 See the text corresponding to n. 292–297, above.

370 *von Bielfeld* (1761), 543.

371 See the references in n. 14, above.

372 See e.g., the text corresponding to and following n. 314, above.

373 On the discussion in the Duchy of Saxe-Weimar see *Ventzke*, 355–359.

374 See the text corresponding to and following n. 299, above.

It may have varied between countries.'[375] And I may add that I am not aware of any such analysis for Germany. However, such analysis is beyond the scope of the present volume.

Nevertheless, it would be feasible to carry out such an analysis. The file on the Prussian tontine of 1698 in the *Brandenburgisches Landeshauptarchiv* (Brandenburg Main State Archive) contains lists of nominees in that tontine.[376] Equally, the files concerning the Bolzano tontine of 1737 at the *Südtiroler Landesarchiv* (Archive of the Province of South Tyrol) in *Bozen* (Bolzano) contain a number of letters of subscription.[377] And the file concerning the Osnabrück tontine of 1768 at the *Niedersächsisches Landesarchiv* (State Archive of Lower Saxony) in Osnabrück contains two lists with the names of the subscribers and nominees in the Bremen tontine of 1767.[378] Similarly, the *Staatsarchiv Bremen* (State Archive of Bremen) holds a complete list of all investors and nominees of the Bremen tontines of 1767, 1772, and 1805.[379] Again, the *Stadtarchiv Stade* (City Archive in Stade) holds a complete list of the 1777-tontine,[380] the *Staatsarchiv Nürnberg* (State Archive Nuremberg) has lists of the members of the 1777-tontine,[381] the *Archiv der Hansestadt Lübeck* (Archive of the Hanse City Lübeck) includes a list of all members of the 1809 tontine,[382] and the *Staatsarchiv Hamburg* (Hamburg State Archive) contains a list of all the members of the *Hamburgische Allgemeine Versorgungs-Tontine* (Hamburg General Pension Tontine) of 1822.[383] The list for the Stade tontine of 1777 suggests that it was mostly people living in towns like Bremen and Stade who subscribed to the tontine; the list also includes the profession of some of the subscribers: civil servants, military officers, ship masters, medical doctors, pastors, and two senators of the city of Bremen.

Above, I pointed out that it is beyond the scope of the present contribution to answer the question in how far the tontines of the first and the second phase did fulfil their function as pension products.[384] The fact that civil servants and pastors subscribed to the Stade tontine of 1777 may, however, suggest that a tontine served only as one component to provide for dependants because civil servants

---

[375] *Pearson*, 97.

[376] Brandenburgisches Landeshauptarchiv, No. 23A C.2720, fol. 54^r–74^r, 81^r–91^r.

[377] Südtiroler Landesarchiv (Bozen), No. 3.23.1 Merkantilmagistrat Bozen.

[378] Niedersächsisches Landesarchiv (Osnabrück), Depositum 3 b IV No. 5759.

[379] Staatsarchiv Bremen, No. 2-R.1.A.10.c.4.II.b.1.d, No. 2-R.1.A.10.c.4.II.c.1.b, and No. 2-R.1.A.10.c.4.II.d.2 vol. 1–3.

[380] Stadtarchiv Stade, St.H. 51–52 No. 18.

[381] Staatsarchiv Nürnberg, Reichsstadt Nürnberg D No. 4815.

[382] Archiv der Hansestadt Lübeck, 05.4-4 Tontine-078 No. 01.

[383] Staatsarchiv Hamburg, No. 613-3/91_I E 1.

[384] See 110, above.

and pastors were usually obliged to participate in a widow and orphan assurance scheme. Yet again, verifying this hypothesis is beyond the scope of the present contribution.

III. The legal aspects of tontines and the development of life insurance law

Turning to the impact which tontines had on the development of insurance law, I have already pointed out that the modern German-language literature asserts the importance of tontines rather than proves it.[385] An analysis of the legal aspects of tontines and their impact on the history of insurance law is hitherto missing. And modern literature is contradictory without discussing these discrepancies. Oberholzer, for example, claims that national legislators, early on, felt impelled to intervene:[386]

> Dadurch, dass den Tontinen … ein so grosser Erfolg beschieden war, sahen sich die Staaten schon früh gezwungen, gesetzgebungsmässig gegen die gröbsten Auswüchse vorzugehen und so das Fundament für unser heutiges Versicherungsrecht zu legen. Eine Folge dieser Versicherungsgesetzgebungen war die Herausbildung von vertrauenswürdigen Versicherungsanstalten.
>
> Due to the fact that tontines … were such a great success, national legislators felt impelled at an early stage to intervene with respect to their greatest defects. Thereby they laid the basis for today's insurance law. A consequence of this insurance legislation was the creation of trustworthy insurance companies.

There is one immediate problem with Oberholzer's claim: in the 17th and 18th centuries tontines were issued by the public hand. Thus, it is not plausible that legislators, at an early stage, had to intervene in order to remedy the greatest defects of tontines. The need for legislative intervention could have arisen only when private entities were allowed to issue tontines. This occurred only in the late 18th century and then primarily in the 19th century. In contrast to Oberholzer, Peter Koch asserts that the first legislation on tontines in Europe was enacted in France as late as 1905:[387]

> Eine gesetzliche Regelung haben die Tontinen erstmals in Frankreich durch das Versicherungsaufsichtsgesetz vom 17.3.1905 gefunden, das die Tontinen ausdrücklich den Lebensversicherungsunternehmen gleichstellte, sie eingehend regelte und der staatlichen Versicherungsaufsicht unterwarf.
>
> The first legislation on tontines was enacted in France: the Insurance Regulation Act of 17 March 1905. It equated tontines with life-insurance companies, it regulated them in detail, and it subjected them to public regulatory control.

---

[385] See the text following n. 19, above.

[386] *Oberholzer*, 91.

[387] *P. Koch*, Tontinengeschäft, 28.

Koch's proposition falls short for one simple reason: with those tontines which were issued by the public hand, the regulations governing the specific tontines were published as legislation even though the relationship between the issuer and the investors were – as will become obvious further below – always analysed in terms of contract law.[388] Furthermore, Part I, Title 12, § 348 of the *Allgemeines Landrecht für die Preußischen Staaten* (General Prussian Territorial Law – ALR) of 1794 at least mentions tontines.

In my analysis, I will first focus on the classification of tontines and their legal permissibility (below 1). In a second step I will analyse the impact of tontines on the law of insurance regulation and insurance supervision (below 2). In the remainder of this subsection, I will discuss the different legal problems which arise with tontines (below 3–10). As tontines were looked upon as a special form of life annuity contracts in the 17th, 18th, and 19th centuries, I will be able to draw on the rules governing life annuity transactions even though not all problems which may arise in the context of life annuity contracts equally arise in the context of tontine transactions.

It will become apparent that the German-language literature of the 17th, 18th, and 19th centuries rarely fully discussed tontines. Nevertheless, there are two different contexts, or genres of literature, in which tontines received at least some coverage. First, there are the authors representing the German and Austrian 18th-century administrative sciences – the so-called *Kameralismus* (cameralism) which is the equivalent of French mercantilism.[389] The *Kameralisten* primarily discussed tontines from the perspectives of public finances and public welfare. These perspectives relate to the legal permissibility of tontines. Secondly, there is the private law discourse. In the 19th century, tontines were not covered at all by the authors of the *Pandektenwissenschaften*, authors who exclusively focused on Roman law. This is again explainable on the basis that tontines were looked upon as a special form of life annuity contracts, and life annuity contracts were seen as an invention of the Middle Ages. Thus, in the 19th-century private law discourse, tontines were only discussed by authors writing on the different local laws and by authors writing not on Roman, but on German law. However, even these authors, as well as the authors of the 18th century, do not offer a full discussion of tontines. Justus Claproth (1728–1805) clarified why the discussion on tontines, as well as on life annuity societies and widow assurances, could be so brief: the rules governing tontines were fully contained in the plans, statutes, or regulations of the different tontines.[390] Thus, these plans, too, are an important source for the following legal analysis.

---

388 See the text corresponding to n. 442, below.

389 See on the distinction between the two concepts *Simon*, 65–82.

390 *Claproth* (1798), 1084.

Nevertheless, I will not discuss all issues which are addressed in these plans. Many of the 17th- and 18th-century plans, for example, stated that it was not possible to execute into the payee's rights in the tontine and that no taxes had to be paid on the received annuities.[391] These details do not seem to be of any relevance for the history of insurance law, and thus I have not taken them into consideration for my analysis.

1. Classifying tontines: life annuity, insurance or gambling?

Modern insurance scholars and legal historians are not in agreement on how to characterize tontines. According to some authors they do count as a form of insurance.[392] Others call them a pre- or transition-form of insurance.[393] Some authors ascribe to them a quasi-insurance character.[394] Again other scholars reject the insurance element in tontines, as they do not involve any form of risk transfer[395] or as the risk is not transferred to the issuer of the tontine, but rather spread among the investors.[396] Many claim that tontines have a speculative character,[397] and that they are rather some kind of gambling or lottery.[398] Some speak of a special form of life annuity[399] or of a hybrid between gambling and insurance[400] or between life annuity and speculation.[401] Hermann and Karl Brämer explained in 1894 why they think that a tontine is of speculative character:[402]

> Die zufällige Beerbung verstorbener Mitglieder einer Tontinenanstalt durch die überlebenden wird von den ernsthaften Lebensversicherern als eine Lotterie verurteilt: die Einen kommen nicht zum richtigen, die Andren zu einem übertrieben hohen Genusse von Leistungen der Anstalt, und nur Wenige erreichen dasjenige Mass, welches ihrer

---

391 See e.g., Art. 20 and Art. 22 of the regulations of the Nuremberg tontine of 1777: Gründliche Nachricht (n. 258), 25 f.; Art. 15 of the regulations of the planned Hamburg tontine of 1776: Sammlung (n. 245), 130; Art. 44 of the regulations of the planned tontine in Wied of 1749: Anschreiben (n. 183), 14.

392 *Schug*, 246, 265; *Lehr* and *von Heckel* (1901), 125.

393 *Roloff*, 293; *Perlitz*, 259.

394 *P. Koch* and *Weiss*, 836.

395 *Nebel*, in: Honsell, Art. 101 para. 7; *Präve*, in: Kölschbach, Prölss, § 1 para. 14; *Brämer* and *Brämer* (1894), 71; *von Zedtwitz*, 142.

396 *Heiss* and *Mönnich*, in: Münchener Kommentar zum VVG II, Vor § 150 para. 17.

397 *Schöpfer*, 129; *Fuchs*, 20–22; *Lehner*, 18; *von Zedtwitz*, 142; *Ogris*, Leibrentenvertrag, 131.

398 *Präve*, in: Kölschbach, Prölss, § 1 para. 14; *Roelli* and *Jaeger* (1933), Art. 73 para. 30; *Ogris*, Leibrentenvertrag, 131 f.; *von Zedtwitz*, 142; *Oberholzer*, 84.

399 *Zetzsche*, 286; *Schug*, 261.

400 *Roloff*, 294; *Fiedler*, 45; *Wortner*, 110; *Lehner*, 18; *Schmitt-Lermann*, 64 f.; *Schmidt*, Versicherungsalphabet, 346.

401 *Lehner*, 18; *Ogris*, Leibrentenvertrag, 131.

402 *Brämer* and *Brämer* (1894), 178. See also *Schöpfer*, 141.

> persönlichen Leistung entspricht. Schon die erste französische Staatstontine … gab dafür das arge Beispiel, dass die 1726 gestorbene letzte Rentnerin zuletzt 73 500 Livres Jahresrente empfing.
>
> Respectable life insurance companies will condemn the accidental transfer of the rights of a deceased member of a tontine to the surviving members as a lottery: some members will not receive a benefit correlating to their contribution; others will receive a benefit that is excessively high; and only with a few will the benefits conform to their personal contribution. Already the first French tontine ... may serve as a negative example in that the last surviving annuitant who died in 1726 received an annuity of 73,500 livres.

The characterization of tontines as a life annuity, an insurance, a manner of gambling or a lottery is of importance for the question whether tontines should be prohibited: according to modern literature their speculative character led to moral reservations against them and to their decline;[403] the view that tontines do not count as insurance but are a form of gambling is said to have been predominant by the end of the 19th century; consequently, it is assumed that life insurance companies were prohibited from issuing tontines from the late 19th century until the implementation, in 1994, of the Second European Life Insurance Directive of 1990 into German law.[404]

The immediate problem with this narrative and with these modern characterizations is, first, that they do not distinguish between the different designs of tontines: with some designs the speculative character was more obvious than with others; and there are means to prevent annuities from becoming excessive, as is the case with compound tontines or when the annuity is capped as was the case with the Prussian tontine of 1788 and the *Preußische Renten-Versicherungs-Anstalt* (Prussian Pension Insurance Fund) of 1838.[405] A modern author captures this notion well:[406]

> Wird eine Tontine auf versicherungsmathematischer Basis berechnet, so kann sie eine Form der Rentenversicherung darstellen, bei der das versicherungstechnische Risiko zwischen Veranstalter (Versicherer) und Teilnehmer aufgeteilt wird. Der Teilnehmer wird seinen Teil des ‚Risikos' als Chance begreifen, im Falle eines überdurchschnittlich langen Lebens eine höhere Rente zu erhalten.
>
> If a tontine is based on sound actuarial calculations, then it will be a form of pension insurance. The insurable risk is split between the issuer and the annuitant. The annuitant will understand his part of the risk as the chance that he will receive a high annuity if he reaches an age which is above the average.

---

403 *Schöpfer*, 141.

404 See the text corresponding to n. 11, above.

405 See the text corresponding to n. 269 and n. 314, above.

406 *Kürble*, (1990) 79 Zeitschrift für die gesamte Versicherungswissenschaft 593.

a) 18th-century Kameralismus

In his *Lehrbuch der Finanz-Wissenschaft* (Treatise on Finances) of 1789, Johann Heinrich Jung-Stilling (1740–1817) rejected tontines as a means for the state to raise capital:[407]

> Wenn aber auch der Staat nichts dabey verliert, so ist deswegen doch die Errichtung einer Tontine nicht erlaubt: denn wie kan ein Hazard-Spiel zwischen zwo Partheyen gerecht seyn, in welchem die eine Parthey immer nothwendig verlieren muß, die andere aber nie verlieren kann und wenn es Grundgesez der Polizey ist, daß sie nie Hazard-Spiele … erlauben darf, wie kan es denn recht seyn, daß sie selbst mitspielt?

> Even if the state does not lose anything, issuing a tontine is nevertheless prohibited: for how can a hazardous game between two parties be just if one party necessarily has to lose and the other will always win; it is a fundamental principle of public administration that it may never allow hazardous games; but how can it then be lawful, if the public hand takes part in such a game?

Jung-Stilling assumed that a tontine could never be issued by a private entity because it is a form of gambling. He argued that the public hand should for the same reason not be allowed to issue tontines. As Fiedler observed, in 1778 the city of Frankfurt took a similar position. Specifically, after the city of *Nürnberg* (Nuremberg) had asked other cities to advertise its tontine of 1777, the city of Frankfurt declined to do so, pointing out that all tontines and comparable hazardous games were illegal and prohibited.[408]

However, one has to be cautious when interpreting rejections of tontines as being a form of illegal gambling. For instance, according to a Prussian act of the year 1817, the *Erneute Verbot des Spielens in auswärtigen Lotterien, des Kollektierens für dieselben und der Privatausspielung* (Renewed Prohibition of Playing in Foreign Lotteries, of Collecting Payments for such Lotteries and of Private Draws),[409] it was forbidden either to participate in foreign lotteries or collect money for foreign lotteries. In 1822 the Prussian *Königliche Regierung zu Berlin* (Royal Government in Berlin) enacted an ordinance clarifying that the 1817 act applied to the *Hamburgische Allgemeine Versorgungs-Tontine* (Hamburg General Pension Tontine) of 1822 because it was, as the ordinance pointed out, nothing but a lottery.[410] Two things are important when interpreting the act and the ordinance. First, the Hamburg tontine indeed had a strong lottery element,[411] and

---

[407] *J.H. Jung*, Lehrbuch (1789), 214. See also *idem*, Grundlehre (1792), 858 f.; *Beckmann* (1804), 323–325 (who discusses tontines only as a form of lottery).

[408] *Fiedler*, 62 cites from the letter of the city of Frankfurt of August 3, 1778. On Frankfurt's position towards lotteries in the 18th century see now *Kullick*, passim.

[409] (1817) Gesetz-Sammlung für die Königlichen-Preußischen Staaten 4.

[410] (1822) Amts-Blatt der Königlich-Preußischen Regierung zu Berlin 166 f.

[411] See the text following n. 303, above.

we do not know whether the Prussian government would have qualified all tontines as a lottery. Secondly, only foreign lotteries were forbidden by the act. Similarly, the *Rostocker Versorgungs-Tontine* (Rostock Pension Tontine) of 1831[412] was prohibited throughout Prussia as being a foreign lottery[413] because Rostock was part of the Grand Duchy of Mecklenburg.

Thus, in order to fully understand Jung-Stilling's rejection of tontines we would need to know what kind of tontine designs he had in mind. However, it is unnecessary to hypothesize on this question because Jung-Stilling's reservations were not widely shared in the German-language literature of the 18th century. Johann Peter Süßmilch (1707–1767), for example, explicitly rejected the view that tontines were a form of gambling.[414] And at a time in which tontines were not issued by private entities but by the public hand and at a time in which the public hand also engaged in lotteries, the question of whether or not tontines should be prohibited because they are a form of gambling simply did not arise. Most authors, as for example Leib, Bergius, and von Justi, looked upon tontines – together with life annuities and lotteries – as lawful means for the state to raise capital.[415]

The discussion for and against tontines did not turn on the classification of tontines as a form of gambling; rather, it was based on general arguments of public welfare. Marperger discussed in 1715 whether it should not be compulsory for parents to invest in a life annuity for the support of their children. von Justi disagreed when he prepared a new, annotated edition of Marperger's work in 1760:[416]

> Ohngeachtet ich selbst davor halte, daß ein Vater seine Kinder nicht besser versorgen kann, als durch Einlegung in eine sichere Tontine …; denn sterben die Kinder, so haben sie ohnedem nichts nöthig, bleiben sie aber leben: so haben sie dadurch die allgewisseste und reichlichste Versorgung; so bin ich doch weit entfernt, den Vorschlag des Verfassers zu billigen, daß die Aeltern und Vormünder zur Einlegung in eine Tontine gezwungen werden könnten. Solche Anstalten müssen auf eine vollkommenen Freyheit und einem guten Zutrauen beruhen …

[412] See the text corresponding to n. 339, above.

[413] (1831) 16 Amtsblatt der Königlichen Regierung zu Köln 222; (1831) Amts-Blatt der Königlich Preussischen Regierung zu Minden 267; (1831) 22 Amts-Blatt der Königlichen Regierung zu Breslau 270 f.; (1831) 21 Amts-Blatt der Königlichen Regierung zu Stettin 375; (1831) 16 Amts-Blatt der Königlichen Oppelnschen Regierung 193; Amts-Blatt der Königlich Preußischen Regierung zu Frankfurth a.d.O. 266; (1831) 21 Amts-Blatt der Königlich Preußischen Regierung zu Marienwerder 345; (1831) 15 Annalen der Preußischen innern Staats-Verwaltung 536.

[414] *Süßmilch* (1762), 397.

[415] *Leib* (1708), 33–36; *Bergius* (1771), 149; *von Justi*, Finanzwesen (1766), 574; *idem*, Staatswirthschaft (1758), 456–458. See also the discussion of *Große*, 67–77.

[416] *von Justi*, in: *Marperger* and *von Justi* (1760), 296 note o. See also *Schöpfer*, 134.

> Notwithstanding that I personally think that a father cannot act more prudently in support of his children than to invest in a safe tontine ...; for if the children die they are not in any event in the need of anything; however, if they stay alive: then they will have the most certain and most plentiful support; nevertheless I am far from in approval with the author's view that parents and guardians should be obliged to invest in a tontine. Such institutions have to be based on complete voluntariness and good trust ...

Others looked upon tontines as being problematic.[417] People who invested all their assets in a tontine and thereby were able to claim high annuities would lose any incentive to work; thus they would no longer contribute to further public welfare by their own labour. These concerns were far from new. Similar reservations had been raised against *Montes pietatis* as means of providing for daughters.[418] Furthermore, if people who invested their assets in a tontine were at that point of time unmarried, they would have problems in founding a family as they would not have any assets left for supporting their surviving spouse and as they would not have any assets to pass on to their potential descendants. As a consequence such individuals would not be able to rely on their spouse or descendants when they were old and in need of nursing. They would have to pay for such services. If married when acquiring shares in a tontine, investors took those assets away from their heirs, who would neither see the invested capital nor benefit from the annuities. In conclusion, tontines disturbed, according to a wide-spread view, the social structure of 18th-century families.

Further financial welfare arguments against tontines were presented by von Sonnenfels. He argued that they negatively affected money circulation and led to a capital drain in a given economy if people invested in foreign life annuity schemes, including tontines.[419]

Süßmilch acknowledged these arguments against tontines but nevertheless claimed that their usefulness in supporting dependants prevailed.[420] And Krünitz concluded in 1796 that only the public hand should issue tontines and that it should issue tontines only after careful consideration of their negative effects.[421]

In conclusion, the 18th-century *Kameralisten* did not focus on the question of whether tontines were a form of gambling or a form of lottery and that they should, therefore, be prohibited. The question simply did not arise in a setting in which tontines were issued by the public hand and in which the public hand also

---

417 *Kritter*, (1786) Leipziger Magazin für reine und angewandte Mathematik 503; *Vogel* (1843), 120; *L. Jung* (1840), 5 f. (but see also 39–41); *von Sonnenfels*, Grundsätze der Polizey (1771), 412, 419. See also *Büsch* (1800), 779 f.

418 See e.g., the discussion by the early 16th-century author *Murmellius* (1623), 63.

419 *von Sonnenfels*, Grundsätze der Polizey (1771), 412, 419.

420 *Süßmilch* (1762), 376 f.

421 *Krünitz*, Encyclopädie LXXI (1796), 8 f.

exercised the right to run lotteries. The discourse, thus, focused on more general issues of public and financial welfare.

b) 19th-century discourse in political economics

The 19th-century discourse on political economics followed the same path:[422] it was still argued that tontines conflicted with family structures, that investors would lose their incentive to work, and that for these reasons the public hand should use tontines only exceptionally in order to raise capital. In fact, the whole discourse was anachronistic. 19th-century Germany saw tontines being issued by pension funds, life insurance companies, and savings banks. The public hand, by contrast, was no longer issuing tontines.

c) The private law discourse of the 18th and 19th centuries

The private law discourse of the 18th and 19th centuries briefly mentioned tontines and discussed them in the context of life annuities:[423] tontines, life annuities, insurance contracts, widow and orphan assurances, and gambling contracts formed the class of aleatory contracts (*gewagte Verträge*). Aleatory contracts were not *per se* forbidden, and tontines were looked upon as being permissible. The definition of aleatory contracts was indeed so broad as to include these different kinds of contracts:[424]

> Aleatorische Verträge (Glücksverträge) sind diejenigen, wodurch ungewisse oder ihrer Quantität oder Qualität nach unbestimmte Vortheile gegen eine bestimmte oder gleichfalls ungewisse Gegenleistung versprochen werden.

---

[422] *Krug* (1808), 218; *Say* (1819), 445; *von Jakob* (1825), 618 f.; *von Soden*, Lehrbuch (1810), 391 f.; *idem*, Die National-Oekonomie (1815), 76 f.; *Lotz* (1822), 425; *Nebenius* (1829), 343; *Baumstark* (1833), 288; *von Mohl*, Polizei-Wissenschaft (1844), 100; *idem*, Erörterungen (1838), 8. Differently *Lueder* (1804), 762–772; *von Struensee* (1800), 181–186, 480–482; *von Malchus* (1830), 437. On what follows see the discussion of *Große*, 103–105, 123–126.

[423] *Willenberg* (1701), 7, 18 f.; *Ayrer* (1750), 25; *Hanov* (1761), 246; *Seyberth* (1768); *Danz* (1797), 305–332, 328; *Rößig* (1797), 319–321; *Claproth* (1798), 1083 f.; *Oeltermann* (1805), 94 f.; *Göde* (1806), 199–201; *Ortloff* (1828), 472; *Pöhls* (1842), 66–70; *Mittermaier* (1843), 83; *Phillips* (1846), 556; *Bluntschli* (1854), 83; *Hiersemenzel* (1855), 356; *Walter* (1855), 426; *Maurenbrecher* (1855), 82 f.; *C.F. Koch*, Recht der Forderungen (1859), 855; *Bierer* (1863), 279 f.; *Sintenis* (1864), 325; *Förster* (1873), 131 f.; *Beseler* (1885), 533; *Stobbe*, Handbuch (1885), 348, 351; *Haberstich* (1885), 327; *Fischer* (1887), 411; *Gengler* (1892), 442; *von Stubenrauch* (1894), 521; *von Gerber* and *Cosack* (1895), 373; *Endemann* (6th edn., 1899), 858; *idem* (8th edn., 1903), 1188; *Oertmann* (1899), Vor § 759 para. 5, § 759 para. 2; *Leske* (1900), 301.

[424] See e.g., the definition of *Mittermaier* (1843), 72.

> Aleatory contracts (contracts for a chance) are those contracts under which an uncertain or, with respect to the quantity or quality, undetermined performance is promised in exchange for a certain, or equally uncertain, counter-performance.

The discussions were, however, by no means uniform, instead reflecting great variety in detail. Julius Hubert Hillebrand (1819–1868), for example, did not put tontines under the heading of aleatory contracts; rather, he discussed life annuity contracts, tontines, and widow and orphan assurances directly after, and as distinct from, lotteries and betting.[425]

Johann Georg Estor (1699–1773) offered a classification which is at first sight distinct. He mentioned tontines when enumerating the different types of sales contracts. He categorized lotteries and tontines as a *Glückskauf* (purchase of a chance to win) and only later in his list did he mention the purchase of a life annuity.[426] Along similar lines, Rudolph Freiherr von Holzschuher (1777–1861) classified life annuity contracts, lottery contracts, and insurance contracts as contracts of sale. However, he did not view life annuity contracts (including tontines[427]) as a *Glückskauf*; he distinguished life annuity contracts from lottery contracts.[428] And Franz Förster (1819–1878) discussed life annuity contracts as contracts for the sale of a right to annuities.[429] Heinrich Dernburg (1829–1907), however, made clear that a life annuity contract could be classified as a contract for sale only if the annuitant had paid for the right to the annuities, and he stressed that this right could also be acquired gratuitously.[430]

Georg Beseler (1809–1888) discussed tontines together with life annuities under the heading 'Life Insurance and Life Annuity Contracts' ('Die Lebensversicherung und der Leibrentenvertrag').[431] Carl Friedrich Wilhelm von Gerber (1823–1891) and Konrad Cosack (1855–1933) argued that, from a legal point of view, insurance contracts and life annuity contracts (including tontines) were related to each other.[432] Wilhelm Karup (1829–1870) argued:[433]

> Die Tontine basirt auf den zwei Hauptprincipien der Lebensversicherung: Association und den Chancen der Mortalität, und deshalb zählt man sie … zur Lebensversicherung … Dass die Rente eine fortwährend steigende ist und zwar ohne dass die Höhe der Steigerung sich im Voraus genau bestimmen lasse, raubt ihr durchaus nicht den Charakter der Lebensversicherung.

---

425 *Hillebrand* (1864), 401.

426 *Estor* (1758), 519.

427 *von Holzschuher* (1864), 758 n. **.

428 *von Holzschuher* (1864), 758–822.

429 *Förster* (1873), 128–132. See similarly *Nicolai* (1738), 8.

430 *Dernburg*, Schuldverhältnisse (1915), 135, 140. See also *Mittermaier* (1843), 80.

431 *Beseler* (1885), 531.

432 *von Gerber* and *Cosack* (1895), 373.

433 *Karup* (1874), 10.

> Tontines are based on the two main principles of life insurance: association and mortality. That is why tontines count as life insurance … The fact that the annuity continuously increases and that this increase is not predictable does not put its character as life insurance into question.

Others treated life annuity and insurance separately,[434] and Heinrich Gottfried Philipp Gengler (1817–1901) argued that life annuity contracts, as well as widow and orphan assurances, were distinct from insurance transactions.[435] The Swiss author Albert Kurz (1806–1864) discussed life annuity contracts as a special form of life insurance contracts, but he argued that a foreign life insurance company which offered life annuities and life insurance contracts without official permission would be in breach of the prohibition against advertising prohibited lotteries.[436] In a similar vein, Ludwig Rückert (1830–1884) proposed that a tontine was a hybrid between a life annuity and gambling.[437] Johann Caspar Bluntschli (1808–1881) had moral reservations against tontines:[438]

> Solche Tontinen geben indessen insofern sittlichen Anstoss, als die Mitglieder der nämlichen Klasse gewissermassen auf den Tod ihrer Genossen speculieren: ein Uebelstand, der dadurch vermieden werden kann, dass die steigende Grösse der Rente durch eine objective Wahrscheinlichkeitsberechnung fixirt und so von den Zufällen des wirklichen Todes möglichst unabhängig gemacht wird.

> Such tontines give insofar rise to moral concerns as the members of the different classes speculate on the death of the other members of that class: a mischief which is avoidable by fixing the increasing annuity to an objective calculation of probabilities and by thereby detaching it from the chances of the actual death of its members.

Christian Friedrich Koch (1798–1872) presented the discussion slightly differently.[439] He asked the question of whether tontines needed to be supervised by public authorities the same way as lotteries, and he referred to an unsuccessful initiative by the Prussian Ministry of Justice asking the Prussian Ministry of the Interior to take corresponding steps. Koch argued that a tontine was as much an aleatory contract as a life annuity, and as life annuities do not raise legal concerns, the same should be true for tontines.

In conclusion, tontines were generally categorized as life annuity contracts and were accordingly regarded as permissible transactions. The private law discourse, thus, seems to have focused on tontines offered by pension funds, as it was not possible to categorize the savings schemes offered by *Sparkassen Tontinen* as life annuity contracts.

---

[434] *Hillebrand* (1864), 401.

[435] *Gengler* (1892), 441. See also *Staudinger*, Lebensversicherungsvertrag (1858), 20.

[436] *Kurz* (1858), 432 (without discussing tontines).

[437] *Rückert* (1857), 11.

[438] *Bluntschli* (1854), 83.

[439] *C.F. Koch*, Recht der Forderungen (1859), 856 n. 4a.

Furthermore, it comes as no surprise that private law discourse in the 19th century discussed whether tontines were a form of insurance: it was already during the 18th century that the tontine regulations adopted a terminology which was traditionally used in the context of insurance. The Lübeck tontine of 1708 still spoke of a *Brief* (bond or obligation) which the investor was to receive and the Saxon tontine of 1748 of a *Leib-Renten-Schein* (life annuity bond or life annuity obligation).[440] Yet the Bremen tontine of 1772, the Stade tontine of 1777 and the Lübeck tontine of 1805 subsequently used the word *Police* (policy).[441]

There is a final point which needs to be stressed. In the 17th and 18th centuries tontines were primarily issued by the public hand on the basis of tontine plans and regulations that were – similar to a piece of legislation – published in the official journals of the respective state. Nevertheless, tontine transactions were discussed as contracts, and thus the relationship between the public hand, as issuer, and the investor was regulated by contract law.[442]

d) The private law discourse of the 20th century

For the 20th century, the position of Swiss law seems to be settled: tontines were classified as a form of gambling, not of insurance, and they were prohibited.[443] Modern German literature on insurance law suggests that in Germany, too, tontine transactions were simply forbidden from the late 19th century until the 1994 implementation of the Second European Life Insurance Directive of 1990 into German law.[444] And Rudolf Müller-Erzbach (1874–1959), for example, indeed claimed in the early 20th century that tontines were prohibited.[445]

Yet the drafters of the *Bürgerliches Gesetzbuch* (German Civil Code) did not call into question the permissibility of tontines, viewing them as one possible design of a life annuity contract.[446] Consequently, the private law discourse continued to discuss tontines as a permitted form of a life annuity contract. A life annuity contract under §§ 759–761 BGB can have more than one annuitant, and it depends on the terms of the life annuity contract whether the annuity of a deceased annuitant is shared by the surviving annuitants.[447] Basically, that was the

---

[440] See the text following n. 160 and n. 180, above.

[441] See the text following n. 228, n. 251, and n. 287, above.

[442] See e.g., *de Florencourt* (1781), 143.

[443] *Roelli* and *Jaeger* (1933), Art. 73 para. 30.

[444] *Schwintowski*, in: Honsell, Berliner Kommentar, Vorbem. §§ 159–178 para. 14.

[445] *Müller-Erzbach* (1928), 710.

[446] Motive zu dem Entwurfe eines Bürgerlichen Gesetzbuches (1896), 639.

[447] *Scherer* (1899), 1065; *Leske* (1900), 301; *Oertmann* (1899), 485; *Crome* (1902), 609; *Goldmann* and *Lilienthal* (1903), 803; *Sepp*, Leibrentenvertrag (1905), 22 f.; *Dernburg*, Schuldverhältnisse (1915), 144; *A. Korn*, Handbuch (1908), 219, 262; *Scherling*, in:

same analysis that had been used already by Stobbe to analyse 14th- and 15th-century life annuity contracts.[448] Nevertheless, most private law authors of the 20th century tended to ignore tontines. This is fully explainable on the basis of their practical unimportance.[449] It seems that new textbooks, as well as commentaries on the BGB which first appeared after 1900, did not bother to mention tontines, whereas those textbooks and commentaries which first appeared at the turn of the century and which have gone through multiple editions continued to cover tontines. The multi-volume commentary on the BGB founded by Julius von Staudinger (1836–1902) exhibits, for example, a remarkable continuity: in the chapter on life annuity contracts, basically the same passage was carried through its different editions, suggesting until today that tontines are simply a permissible variance of life annuity contracts and that it depends on the interpretation of the contract whether the contract implements the hereditary principle in instances where there is more than one annuitant.[450]

How are we to explain the paradox that it is today believed that tontines were prohibited throughout the 20th century whereas the private law discourse of that century presented them as a permissible form of a life annuity contract under §§ 759–761 BGB? One possible answer would be that tontines were generally permitted and that it was insurance companies which were prohibited from issuing tontines under the provisions of the *Versicherungsaufsichtsgesetz* (Insurance Regulation Act – VAG) of 1901. However, there is an immediate problem with this explanation, namely that the VAG of 1901 does not explicitly mention tontines. Furthermore, the private law discourse was fully aware of the connection to insurance. Otto von Gierke (1841–1921) argued that life annuity contracts may be insurance transactions as the investor seeks insurance against the risk that his or her assets will not be sufficient to support him- or herself upon reaching a high age. Legally, he continued, they are, however, treated separately from insurance

---

Soergel (1926), § 759 para. 2; *Oegg*, in: Planck's Kommentar (1928), § 759 para. 2.b)α); *Bovensiepen* (1928), 944; *Warneyer* (1930), § 759 para. II; *Bätge* (1936), 278; *Oegg*, in: Reichsgerichtsräte (1939), 759 para. 3. For the position in Austria see *Krainz* (1907), 291.

[448] See the text corresponding to n. 57, above.

[449] On the practical unimportance see *Dernburg*, Schuldverhältnisse (1915), 144. *Riebesell* (1930), 1572 claims the opposite: 'In Frankreich und Holland wird Tontinenversicherung in erheblichem Umfang betrieben, neuerdings auch in Deutschland …' ('In France and in the Netherlands there is a large volume of tontine insurance business; lately the same is true in Germany …').

[450] *Engelmann*, in: Staudingers Kommentar (1929), § 759 para. 2; *Brändl*, in: Staudingers Kommentar (1939), § 759 para. 3; *idem*, in: Staudingers Kommentar (1975), § 759 para. 3; *Amann*, in: Staudingers Kommentar (1986), § 759 para. 14; *idem*, in: Staudingers Kommentar (1996), § 759 para. 14; *idem*, in: Staudingers Kommentar (2001), § 759 para. 14; *Mayer*, in: Staudingers Kommentar (2008), § 759 para. 25; *idem*, in: Staudingers Kommentar (2015), § 759 para. 25. See also *Keidel*, in: Staudinger Handausgabe (1931), § 759 BGB para. 2.

contracts. von Gierke acknowledged that a life annuity contract could also be sold by a private individual or that it could also be entered into gratuitously. Accordingly, it was not related to insurance contracts.[451] It was acknowledged that life insurers could sell life annuity contracts and tontines, and it was stressed that in this case the contract was covered by both the VAG of 1901 and the *Gesetz über den Versicherungsvertrag* (Insurance Contract Act) of 1908.[452]

Finally, the insurance law discourse is not definite on the classification of tontines: some authors treated tontines as a purely historical institution without any relevance for the present insurance business.[453] Others referred to them without mentioning that they were prohibited.[454] Alfred Manes (1877–1963) argued in 1932 that tontines *should* be forbidden by the insurance regulation authorities.[455] Julius von Gierke (1875–1960), Otto von Gierke's son, explained his concerns in 1937 more thoroughly:[456]

> Schließlich darf der Plan auch nicht so sein, daß der mögliche Zuwachs an Renten infolge des Absterbens der Beteiligten derart hoch ist, daß er den Gedanken eines maßvollen Ausgleichs … völlig beseitigt … So aber ist es bei den reinen Tontinen. Sie sind gemäß unserer heutigen deutschen Volksanschauung als Glücksspiel anzusehen. Die gegenteilige Ansicht des Reichsgerichts ist unbedingt abzulehnen. Gegen eine Anwendung des Tontinensystems auf mäßigen Gewinnausgleich ist selbstverständlich nichts einzuwenden.

> Finally, the possible increase of the annuities should, according to the plan, not be so high that the tontine conflicts with the idea of a measured adjustment ... This was, however, the case with pure tontines. Today they are looked upon as a form of gambling. The opposite view of the Imperial Court should not be followed. Of course, it raises no concerns if the tontine system leads to a moderate adjustment.

Three points are worth noting. First, Julius von Gierke was referring to the well-established definition of insurance which required that it must be operated on the basis of an actuarial plan. von Gierke argued that tontines were lacking such an actuarial plan as the increase of the annuities could be exceedingly high. In the footnote he refers to the first French tontine. For that reason tontines were rather a form of gambling. Secondly, he notes that the *Reichsgericht* (Imperial

---

451 *O. von Gierke* (1917), 799 n. 25, 800, 804 f.

452 *Warneyer* (1930), § 759 para. I; *Brändl*, in: Staudingers Kommentar (1939), Vor § 759 para. 25. See also *Crome* (1902), 608, 827; *Mayer*, in: Staudingers Kommentar (2015), Vor § 759 para. 56. See also *Oberlandesgericht München* (Higher Regional Court), (1924) Zeitschrift für Rechtspflege in Bayern 230 f.; *Reichsgericht* (Imperial Court), (1927) 31 Leipziger Zeitschrift für Deutsches Recht 1389.

453 *Hagen* (1922), 345.

454 *Bruck*, Privatversicherungsrecht (1930), 413; *idem*, Versicherungsvertrag (1932), § 1 para. 6; *Koenige* and *Petersen* (1928), § 6 para. 3.

455 *Manes*, 98. See also *Präve*, in: Kölschbach, Prölss, § 1 para. 14.

456 *J. von Gierke* (1937), 85.

Court) was of a different opinion. Thirdly, he admits that tontines were permissible if the increase in annuities was only moderate.

e) Conclusion

Thus, tontines were never forbidden in Germany. This is consistent with the above findings on U.S. tontines:[457] it was not so much the product itself which raised concerns but rather the marketing strategies and accounting practices that met criticism. In 1891, Prussia ordered the U.S. life insurance companies to meet special accounting standards for their tontine products. In 1894 the Equitable Life Assurance Society of New York pulled out of the Prussian market. The New York Life Insurance Company and the Mutual Life Insurance Company of New York lost their concessions in 1895 for non-compliance with the order. The New York Life Insurance Company was readmitted in Prussia in 1899, and it was allowed to sell its products even after the introduction of the VAG of 1901. It left the German market only in 1914, and as late as the 1930s there is case law concerning a tontine product of the New York Life Insurance Company which looks upon a tontine as a permissible transaction.[458] Tontines were never forbidden. They simply became unfashionable.

The fact that modern literature classifies tontines as a form of gambling or a manner of lottery and the fact that modern literature expresses moral reservations against tontines may be explainable simply on the basis that tontines often exhibited lottery elements, that the word tontine was often used very loosely to refer to annuity lotteries which did not adopt the hereditary principle, that today's literature often refers to those early examples of tontines which allowed the last annuitant to receive exorbitantly high annuities disproportionate to his or her initial investment, and finally that modern literature, as well as the literature of the late 19th century discussing U.S. tontine life insurance products, does not clearly distinguish between tontines as pension products on the one hand and tontine life insurance products as well as so-called *Sparkassen Tontinen* on the other hand – a distinction to which I will return in the conclusion of this volume.[459]

Nevertheless, to the modern eye it seems to raise special concerns that it was possible to speculate on other peoples' lives in cases where the payee and the nominee were not the same person, and it is said that it was this detail which tainted tontines.[460] However, the announcement for the life annuity lottery of

[457] See the text corresponding to n. 317–319, above.

[458] *Reichsgericht* (*Imperial Court*), (1930) 129 Entscheidungen des Reichsgerichts in Zivilsachen (RGZ) 134–143.

[459] See the text corresponding to n. 579, below.

[460] *Ogris*, Leibrentenvertrag, 132.

Murcia issued in 1775 explains why such a design made sense:[461] in order to collect the annuity one had to present a certificate that the nominee was still alive. The costs of generating such a certificate were high. The Spanish lottery made the following provision: the total amount of an annuity was fixed after the lottery. Only then did the contributor have to name the nominee. In order to avoid the costs of generating the aforementioned certificate each year, those who had a right to an annuity of only less than 100 livres could name only a king, a sovereign prince, or a prince of royal descent. With such a nominee a certificate was dispensable because it was generally known whether the person was still alive. Only where the annuity was above the sum of 100 livres was it open to the contributor to name himself or some other third party as nominee. Thus, the possibility to name a nominee other than the payee could make sense. I will at a later point return to the question of how the different tontine regulations reacted to the problem of the costs of a life certificate.[462] Nevertheless, the possibility to name a person other than the payee as nominee opened the door to speculation. Indeed, it apparently occurred that Swiss inhabitants invested in European tontines, named young Swiss children as nominees, had these children picked by medical doctors from families with high life expectancies, and had these children receive thereafter special attention by medical doctors to safeguard a long and healthy life.[463]

2. Financial soundness, solvency, securities, and transparency: the development of insurance supervision and insurance regulation

a) The first phase: self-contained tontines in the 17th and 18th centuries

In the 17th and 18th centuries tontines were primarily issued by the public hand to raise capital on a European financial market. Contributors had to make their investment when the tontine was issued. In return the payee received the right to annuities until the death of the nominee on which the payee's right was based. If the nominee was of a very young age when the tontine was issued, the tontine could easily run 90 years or more. It is obvious that a contributor was only inclined to invest in a tontine if he was convinced that the issuer was willing and financially able to pay the annuities until the death of the last surviving nominee. And the contributor wanted to be certain that the tontine would be run properly.

[461] (1776) Gnädigst privilegirtes Leipziger Intelligenz-Blatt 301. See also *Braun*, Geschichte, 67; *Du Pasquier*, (1910) 46 Zeitschrift für Schweizerische Statistik 489.

[462] See the text corresponding to and following n. 561, below.

[463] *Kürble*, (1990) 79 Zeitschrift für die gesamte Versicherungswissenschaft 594.

Such concerns were present given that the 17th and the 18th centuries experienced some spectacular speculative bubbles, such as the Dutch tulip mania in the 17th century, the English South Sea bubble in the 18th century, and the French Mississippi bubble of about the same time. Furthermore, the interest rates which were promised by issuers of tontines and other life annuity schemes were often so high that they caused legitimate worries about the soundness of the plan.[464] Finally, the 18th century experienced frauds on the sides of both privately run funeral funds and the investors in these funds.[465]

Consequently, the tontines of the 17th and the 18th centuries had to allay these concerns if they wanted to be successful and raise the projected capital. A modern lawyer will look upon these issues as problems of insurance regulation and insurance supervision:[466]

> Insurance regulation is the collection of all laws dealing with the regulation of insurance markets. First and foremost, it aims to protect the insured person (policyholder, other entitled person and injured party) from insolvency (corporate) of the insurance company. In addition, it also aims to provide protection from abusive business conduct by the insurers. Insurance regulation is part of the broader law regulating the financial market.

Modern research on the history of insurance regulation in Germany usually starts with the Prussian *Wiederholtes Verboth aller und jeder Collecten, wozu keine Königl. Approbation ertheilet ist* (Repeated Prohibition of all Collections without Royal Approval) of 1781[467] and analyses developments up to the *Versicherungsaufsichtsgesetz* (Insurance Regulation Act) of 1901.[468]

For a historical analysis of the development of insurance regulation and insurance supervision, 17th- and 18th-century tontines seem to be of no relevance in that they were issued by the public hand. Questions of regulation and supervision seem to arise only if tontines are operated by private entities.

Nevertheless, the tontine plan of the city of *Danzig* (Gdańsk) of 1657 clearly addressed the concerns of potential investors. Article 11 provided that the tontine had to provide each year an estimate of the annuities which were to be paid out the following year.[469] Article 12 aimed at transparency: each year the tontine had to publish a list of the names of all payees/nominees so that each member was in

---

[464] *Vogel* (1843), 121 f.; *Schöpfer*, 143.

[465] *Vogel* (1843), 113, refers to the case of the Bassumer Trauerpfennigs- und Sterbethaler-Gesellschaft in Bremen, which is said to have been prohibited by the city of Bremen in 1789.

[466] *Schnyder* and *Heierli*, 921.

[467] Novum Corpus Constitutionum Prussico-Brandenburgensium Praecipue Marchicarum, vol. 7 (1786), 181–186.

[468] See especially *Tigges*, passim; *Atzpodien*, passim; *Burger*, passim.

[469] The regulations are reproduced in: *Foltz* (1912), 459–461.

the position to understand the calculation of his or her annuity. Finally, Art. 14 stated that each payee was to receive an obligation/bond stamped with the official town seal so that every payee could be assured that he or she would receive the annuities each year until the nominee's death. The same provisions were adopted for the Gdańsk tontines of 1775 and 1792; however, with these tontines a secure fund was formed to guarantee the payments.[470]

With the exception of the Lübeck tontine plan of 1708,[471] security and transparency are the two components which continually reappear in the public tontine plans and regulations of the 17th and 18th centuries. Furthermore, elements of self-administration were incorporated in many of the tontine schemes. Such elements served to enhance trust in the administration of the tontine and fostered transparency.

According to the Bremen loan agreement of 1692, the city of Bremen pledged as security all assets of the city of Bremen ('Damit aber mehrberührter unser geliebter Syndicus und dessen Mitbeschriebene so wohl wegen Capitals als Zinse gnugsahm versichert seyn mögen / So verhypothesiren Wir Ihnen der besten Formb und Weise ... nicht allein alle unsere Stattgüther /gewisseste Renten und Einkommen / sondern assigniren Ihnen auch in specie unserer Statt Compter Güter und Wage und deren Intraden samt und sonders zu einem special Unterpfande ...').[472]

Article 8 of the Prussian tontine regulation of 1698 provided that a financial statement for the tontine had to be published each year in order to create clarity for the payees, and the issuer guaranteed the payment of the annuities in the preamble.[473] In addition, the income generated from the beer tax was pledged as security ('Bier-Gelde, welche dafür zur Sicherheit und Hypothec hafften').[474]

The Lübeck tontine plan of 1708 addressed only the question of self-administration. The plan seems to suggest that there was a clear divide in responsibilities: it was the city's obligation to pay the full interest rate of 300 talers per year until the death of the last nominee and it fell upon the members to distribute the annuity among themselves. For that reason the members had to elect a committee:[475]

470 See the plans as cited in n. 243.

471 Archiv der Hansestadt Lübeck, 3.4-2 Stadt-Cassa No. 483.

472 Staatsarchiv Bremen, No. 2-R.1.a.10.c.4.I.

473 Patent wegen der einzurichtenden Leib-Renten d.d. den 30. Decembr. 1698, (1736) 6/1 Corpus Constitutionum Marchicarum 654, 656.

474 On the beer tax in Prussia-Brandenburg see *Kriegk*, passim.

475 Archiv der Hansestadt Lübeck, 3.4-2 Stadt-Cassa No. 483.

Die Austheilung dieser Renten betreffend / müssen diese 100. Persohnen 4. oder 5. Persohnen unter sich wehlen / so die Renten von der Cassa abfordern / und die Distribution verrichten könten / auch unter sich die Rechnung wegen der etwa Abgehenden halten.

Concerning the distribution of the annuities / the 100 members have to elect 4 or 5 from among themselves / who have to claim the annuities from the town treasury / and who perform their distribution / also they have to calculate the annuities with respect to deceased members.

That explains why the tontine plan does not contain any provisions on transparency: the calculation of the annuities was not an obligation of the city of Lübeck as the issuer of the tontine but was rather a duty of the investors.

The regulations of the Bolzano tontine of 1737 were similarly clear in satisfying the two prerequisites for issuing a tontine and for making the tontine an attractive investment also for foreigners, namely that the funds have to be secure and the tontine has to be run by a trustworthy administration:[476]

Und wie Wir nun anbey … in die Erwegung gezogen/ daß zur Sicherheit einer solchneu-errichtenden Tontina, fürnehmlich zwey Stuck erforderlich: Als erstens / daß selbe mit einem sicheren Fundo versehen: Dann andertens / daß die Direction und Verwaltung derselben von einem solchen Corpore übernommen werden / welches dieses Werck nicht nur allein nützlich ein- und fortzuführen im Stande ist / sondern auch bey denen ausländischen Nationen in allgemeinem guten Credit stehet …

And we have taken ... into consideration / that to secure such a newly established tontine, foremost two things are necessary: As first / that it has to have a secure fund: then also / that the administration is taken over by a body / which is not only able to carry on the business / but which also stands in good credit with foreign nations ...

This was the reason why the *Mercantil-Magistrat* of the city of *Bozen* (Bolzano) was entrusted with the administration of the tontine. Furthermore, the income generated from the tax on salt from Hall in the Inn Valley in Tyrol ('Hall-Ynthalischen Salz Gefällen') was pledged as security.

Article 9 of the published plan of the Berlin tontine of 1747 set forth that a small number of investors had to be invited each year in December when the annuities were determined so that they were able to oversee the process of calculation.[477] Furthermore, the details of the calculation had to be sent to all investor each year in January. Finally, the governing board guaranteed the payment of the annuities and pledged as security all immovable and movable property of the church and all future income ('Gefälle').

According to Art. 24 of the regulations of the Wied tontine of 1749, the members of the scheme had a right to appoint one director to the commission whose

---

476 Nachtrag zu denen wöchentlich-kurzgefaßten Historischen Nachrichten der Neuern Europäischen Begebenheiten, 1stes Stück (Regensburg 1738), 17.

477 Brandenburgisches Landeshauptarchiv, No. 23A C.2720, fol. 79^{r}–80^{v}.

task was the administration of the tontine. The members' director had full rights in the commission, and he had the right to inform all members of all concerns. Furthermore, all members had a right to inspect the books and accounts of the tontine at any time. According to Art. 9 and Art. 47, the shire guaranteed the payment of the annuities, and it pledged the income generated from specifically enumerated farms, mills, and tenths as security. According to Art. 33 each payee was allowed to demand each year a list of all surviving members of that class and an exact calculation of the annuity. Furthermore, the plan addressed the question of the costs of administration: for each invested taler a non-recurring fee of 6 kreuzers was to be paid, and for each taler of received annuities a charge of 8 kreuzers had to be paid. The fact that the members had a right to appoint a director and had a right to inspect all books and accounts is surprising because the tontines issued by public bodies in the 17th and 18th centuries can hardly be characterized as mutual societies or as corporations: the public hand wanted to raise capital, the public hand was obliged to pay out the annuities, and the public hand gave security for its obligations. It was rather a multitude of bilateral agreements between the public hand on the one side and numerous investors on the other side.

According to Art. 19 of the regulations of the Gotha tontine of 1752, the state treasury guaranteed the payment of the annuities.[478] The East Frisian tontine plan of 1755 wanted to secure the payment of the annuities with the income flowing from the impoldered land.[479] The tontine plan for the Duchy of Cleves of 1763 provided that each year a list of the deceased members and a calculation of the annuities had to be published (Art. 9). And according to Art. 11, the annuities were paid out of a secured fund so that the annuities were treated preferentially over other debts of the Duchy. In the published plan for the 1767-tontine, the city of Bremen pledged the income generated from the tax on wine and spirits as security, and at the same time it promised to publish each year a list of all deceased nominees.[480]

The estates of Mecklenburg-Strelitz offered according to Art. 4 of the published 1776-tontine plan all their income generated in the Duchy as security.[481] According to Art. 17 the society had to publish a full list of all members and all nominees when the shares were issued and then annually a list of all deceased together with an exact calculation of the annuities.

---

478 The regulations are reproduced in: *Krünitz*, Encyclopädie LXXI (1796), 295–303.

479 *Wiarda* (1798), 379 f.

480 Niedersächsisches Landesarchiv (Osnabrück), Depositum 3 b IV No. 5759.

481 Landeshauptarchiv Schwerin, 3.1-1 (Mecklenburgische Landstände mit Engeren Ausschuß der Ritter- und Landschaft zu Rostock) No. 20 Anhang 29, fol. 691–705.

According to Art. 11 of the statutes of the 1777-tontine, the city of Stade pledged all its income as security ('Damit die Interessenten der jedesmaligen richtigen Einhaltung des Zahlungs-Termins destomehr versichert seyn können; so sollen alle gemeiner Stadt zustehenden Einkünfte hiemit dafür verpfändet seyn'). And according to Art. 12, the city had to publish each year at Easter a complete list of those nominees who had died in the past year.

The city of Nuremberg guaranteed the payments of the annuities in Art. 30 of the tontine regulations of 1777,[482] and a similar guaranty is found in the preamble of the tontine regulations of 1783.[483] The tontine regulations of 1783 also provided for transparency: under Art. 26 each member was to receive a list of all members of the same class, and under Art. 29 once a year the names of the surviving members and those of the deceased members were to be published alongside a calculation of the annuities.[484] In 1776, two plans for tontines were published in Hamburg. The second plan of October adopted the principle of self-administration:[485] each class had to elect an administrator who had to be a citizen of Hamburg (Art. 7). The Oldenburg ordinance of 1782 set forth that the funds of the different classes of the widow and orphan assurance had to be accounted for separately. And again, the payment of the annuities was guaranteed.[486] Article 21 of the regulations of the Prussian tontine of 1788 made the costs of administration transparent and the preamble stated that the Prussian state guaranteed the payment of the annuities:[487]

> Wir ertheilen allen und jeden die sich bey dieser Anstalt interessieren werden, für Uns und Unsere Nachfolger die bündigste und unwiderruflichste Versicherung, daß die ihnen einmal versicherte jährliche Renten bis an ihren Tod unverkürzt bezahlt werden sollen, auch die dazu alljährlich erforderliche Summe, für jetzt und für die Zukunft, bis zu dem Zeitpunkt wo alle Rentenierer abgestorben seyn werden, auf Unsre Fonds in der Haupt-Banque zu Berlin, ganz bestimmt und etatsmäßig angewiesen ist.

---

[482] Gründliche Nachricht von einer neuen sehr vorzüglichen und vortheilhaften Reichs-Stadt Nürnbergischen Leib-Renten Gesellschaft (Nürnberg 1777), 30.

[483] See also *Schöpfer*, 139.

[484] Gründliche Nachricht von einer neuen sehr vorzüglichen und vortheilhaften Reichs-Stadt Nürnbergischen Leib-Renten Gesellschaft (Nürnberg 1777), 36, 39.

[485] Sammlung Hamburgischer Verordnungen, vol. 1 (Hamburg 1783), 125–136. The plan is also reproduced in: *Krünitz*, Encyclopädie LXXI (1796), 312–319.

[486] Verordnung wegen Erweiterung der Wittwen- und Waisen Casse auf Leibrenten, (1782) 5/2 Schlözer's Stats-Anzeigen 38–43; Verordnung wegen einer errichteten Witwen- und Waysen-Casse für die Hochfürstl. Bischöfl. Lübekschen und Herzogl. Holstein-Oldenburgschen Lande (Eutin 1779); Niedersächsisches Landesarchiv (Oldenburg), Best. 222 No. 41.

[487] Patent wegen Errichtung einer wachsenden Leibrenten-Anstalt zum Betrieb des Chaussee-Baues im Magdeburgischen und Halberstädtschen, (1788) 8 Novum Corpus Constitutionum Prussico-Brandenburgensium Praecipue Marchicarum 2257–2258.

> We grant to everyone who is interested in the present institution the clearest and the most irrevocable assurance on our own behalf and on behalf of our successors that the promised annuity will be paid without any reductions until their death and that the sum which is required each year for that purpose, now and in the future until the death of the last nominee, will be assigned most certain and in accordance with our budget to our funds at the central bank at Berlin.

The Hamburg tontine plan of 1807 simply stated:[488]

> Für die Sicherheit der Zahlung der Renten dieser Tontine ist das Vermögen der ganzen Stadt verhaftet.

> As security for the payment of the annuities of this tontine all assets of the city are arrested.

In order to be able to pay the rents the city of Hamburg raised its tax on wine.[489] The tontine was administered by six directors, two of which were to be elected by its members. The costs of administration were carried by the city. And the plan also reflected the usual provisions on financial statements which had to be published together with the names of all surviving and deceased nominees.

The contemporary literature was in favour of these provisions. Bergius and von Justi argued that with life annuities and tontines it was of utmost importance that the public hand was creditworthy because people of only moderate wealth would use them, too, in order to provide for their own financial support or the financial security of their dependants.[490] Bergius furthermore stressed that the prospectus advertising the tontine had to be clear and transparent:[491]

> Man muß sich so gar hüten, dem Publico allzugekünstelte und versteckte Plane vorzulegen. So bald die Gründe, nach welchen die Einrichtung gemacht ist, schwer zu entdecken sind; so erwecket es bey dem Publico Verdacht, als wenn Betrug darunter verborgen liege, und man wird abgeschreckt, an dergleichen Leibrente oder Tontine Antheil zu nehmen. In dergleichen Dingen ist die Einfalt allezeit besser, und erweckt mehr Zutrauen.

> One has to beware of presenting to the interested public a plan which is far too stilted and cryptic. As soon as the plan underlying the institution is difficult to comprehend it will raise suspicions among the interested public, as if some fraud is hidden beneath the plan, and one will be deterred from participating in the life annuity or the tontine. In these matters plainness is always to be preferred and will create trust in the plan.

And finally, German authors of the 18th century were clear that a tontine should be run by the public hand for the very reason that the public hand was able to guaranty the payment of the annuities:[492]

---

488 (1807) 7/3 Sammlung Hamburgischer Verordnungen 157–164, 161.

489 (1807) 7/3 Sammlung Hamburgischer Verordnungen 165 f.

490 *Bergius* (1771), 150; *von Justi*, Finanzwesen (1766), 578.

491 *Bergius* (1771), 150 f.

492 *Michelsen* (1784), 180.

> Ob ein Jeder für sich das Recht habe, Rentengesellschaften jeder Art zu errichten, und sich zum Entrepreneur aufzuwerfen? scheint mehr zu verneinen als zu bejahen zu seyn. Denn wäre solches einem jeden erlaubt; so könnte sehr leicht dies Recht von manchem zum Schaden der Rentenirer gemißbraucht werden, oder wenigstens zum Schaden der Rentenirer ausschlagen, indem dieselben oft durch scheinende Sicherheit sich verleiten lassen könnten. Da der Entrepreneur aus mehr denn aus einem Grunde die größte Sicherheit zu geben im Stande seyn muß, so sind Rentenentreprisen … vorzüglich Sache des States oder des Landesherrn, der aber, weil manche Bürger dadurch zum müssigen Leben verleitet werden, oder ihre Erben dessen, was dieselben sonst zu hoffen hätte, berauben, dazu ebenfalls nicht anders, als wenn anderweitige wichtige Gründe es rathen … schreiten sollte.

> It seems that the question whether everybody should have the right to found an annuity society and to make himself an entrepreneur should be answered in the negative rather than the positive. For if everybody was allowed to do so this right could easily be abused to the disadvantage of the annuitants or the use of this right could at least cause damage to them as they could fall for a deal which only appears to be safe. As the entrepreneur has to offer for more than one reason the utmost security, annuity schemes should primarily be run by the state or the ruler of the state; and as some annuitants will be misled to lead a too leisured life or as some will deprive their heirs of what they had hoped to receive, the state and the ruler of the state should issue annuity schemes only when important reasons demand to do so.

Another reason why private entities were not allowed to issue tontines may have been that the public hand used them as a means to raise capital: tontines were akin to state bonds. It is likely that the public hand wanted to have exclusive use of this transaction.

The printed financial statements for the years between 1780 and 1806 for the tontine of the city of *Nürnberg* (Nuremberg) of 1777 have survived in the *Stadtarchiv Nürnberg* (Archive of the city of Nuremberg),[493] and they thus exemplify the practice of such statements. The shares in the tontine were numbered. The annual financial statement contained for each class a list of the numbers of those shares of which the nominees had died in the preceding year. At the same time the total number of surviving shares per class was listed, and on the basis of these figures the annuities were calculated for each class. Thus, the names of the deceased were not published in the annual financial statements. However, the financial statement for the year 1806 also contains a number of corrections of printing errors in the members' list. It seems that each member of the tontine had received a list of members indicating also the share number. Thus, each member was able to identify which member had died in the preceding year.

A similar practice was followed in Bremen. The financial statement for the year 1799, for example, expressly named the nominees that had died in the past year together with the respective share number. Furthermore, it specifically pointed out the number of surviving shares and calculated the annuity per

[493] Stadtarchiv Nürnberg, E 6/125 No. 1.

share.[494] However, apparently there were two different sets of statements published: a second set of publications simply named the names of the deceased nominees together with the respective share number without indicating the number of surviving shares and without calculating the annuity per share.[495] For the 1767-tontine the *Staatsarchiv Bremen* holds these publication until the year 1842, when the first three classes of the tontine were still in operation; for the 1772-tontine there are archived materials up until the year 1843, when the first two classes were still in operation.

b) The second phase: tontines issued by pension funds in the 19th century

In the late 18th and early 19th centuries, we then observe a shift in the discussions: life annuity schemes should primarily be run by the state and only exceptionally may a private entity be granted the permission to do so, and here only if the payment of the annuities is secured. Kritter wrote in 1786:[496]

> Ob auch wohl eine Gesellschaft reicher Privatpersonen Entrepreneur einer Tontine seyn könne, kommt auf die Erlaubniß der Landesregierungen an. Insgemein aber eignen sich diese allein dieses Recht zu, und machen Gebrauch davon, wenn dringend Bedürfnisse des Staats sogleich grosse Geldsummen erfordern. Es verstehet sich aber von selbst, daß in allen Fällen genugsame Sicherheit wegen richtiger Bezahlung der Renten gemacht werden müsse.

> Even though an association of rich persons can issue a tontine, too, a concession by the state is necessary. However, usually it is only the public hand which will issue tontines if it is in need of a great amount of capital. Of course, *in all cases* the obligation to pay the annuities has to be secured.

In the 18th century, widow and orphan assurances were often run or at least initiated by the public hand. In the late 18th and early 19th centuries private pension funds were founded. With a public pension fund there was the risk of an intervention by the sovereign prince of the state. To have private pension funds under the supervision and regulation of the authorities guaranteed more stability and trust in these funds.[497]

In the modern historiography, the aforementioned Prussian Act of 1781 – introducing allegedly for the first time the requirement of a concession or state permission for the initiation of certain funds – is presented as a very modest starting point in the development of insurance regulation and insurance supervision.

---

494 Staatsarchiv Bremen, No. 2-R.1.a.10.c.4.I.

495 Staatsarchiv Bremen, No. 2-R.1.A.10.c.4.II.b.1.d and No. 2-R.1.A.10.c.4.II.c.1.b.

496 *Kritter*, (1786) Leipziger Magazin für reine und angewandte Mathematik 501 f. (emphasis added). See also *Oeltermann* (1805), 8 f.

497 *Ventzke*, 356.

However, if we put this act into the context of the discussions surrounding tontines, it seems clear that the public hand had developed very precise ideas on how to run tontines, that it had prohibited tontines from being initiated by private entities in order to see these ideas being implemented, and that it, as seems likely, permitted private entities to run tontines only if they also implemented these ideas. But how effective was the state supervision? The Prussian lawyer C.F. Koch claimed in 1859 that the call for effective state supervision of tontines was not implemented.[498] By contrast, the influential Hamburg commercial lawyer Meno Pöhls (1798–1849) made clear that the regulatory authorities had to screen a projected tontine more thoroughly than any other corporation before granting a concession:[499]

> Die Autorisation … ist hier aber noch durch ein Erforderniß bedingt, welches gewöhnliche Gesellschaften nicht kennen. Die Basis der Gesellschaft muß eine richtige seyn. Da alles auf einer Berechnung der Wahrscheinlichkeit beruht, so muß die Grundlage dieser Berechnung untersucht und eine Gesellschaft nur dann autorisiert werden, wenn jene Grundlage sich als richtig ausweiset …

> Granting a concession ... is dependent on a further requirement which is unknown to other corporations. The [financial] foundation of the company needs to be sound. As all is based on calculating probabilities, the very basis of this calculation has to be screened and a company may only receive a concession if everything turns out to be correct ...

Furthermore, the plans and statutes of tontines of the late 18th and early 19th centuries indicate that the state supervision of tontines was taken seriously and that the private pension funds and savings banks who issued tontines had to meet standards of financial soundness, solvency, and transparency.[500]

§ 9 of the terms of the Lübeck tontine of 1809 makes clear that the *St. Annen Armenhaus* which benefited from the raised capital of that tontine had to pledge parts of its real estate as security.[501] The tontine had six directors; two were appointed by the *St. Annen Armenhaus*, and the others were elected by the shareholders (§ 10). According to § 17, the tontine had to submit an annual financial statement to a commission which was to be appointed by the city of Lübeck, and the financial statement had to be published annually. These financial statements continued to follow earlier examples: the numbers of those shares to which the nominees had died were included; the numbers of surviving shares were spelled

498 *C.F. Koch*, Recht der Forderungen (1859), 856.

499 *Pöhls* (1842), 70.

500 See also the discussion by *von Littrow* (1832), 22.

501 Archiv der Hansestadt Lübeck, 05.4-4 Tontine-078 No. 01.

out; and the annuity was calculated.[502] Furthermore, a full list of all members, together with their share numbers, was published.[503]

Under § 4 of the original articles of the *Hamburgische Allgemeine Versorgungs-Tontine* (Hamburg General Pension Tontine) of 1822, the general assembly of the members of each class had the right to elect two auditors who would have the responsibility of checking the accounts annually.[504] According to § 5, the financial statements had to be submitted to the general assembly of the tontine, which had to be held in the beginning of each year. In addition, the financial statements together with a list of all deceased members had to be sent to all members. In 1832 the articles were amended: according to the revised § 29 the capital had to be invested in real property, except for 100,000 marks that had to be invested in bonds. The decision as to what kind of bonds the tontine was allowed to invest in had to be made by unanimous vote of the board of directors.[505]

The concession for the *Würtembergische Leibrenten-Bank* (Württemberg Life Annuity Bank) of 1822 made explicit that the bank was subject to continuous state supervision and that a special commission under the secretary of the interior was to be established for that purpose; the articles of the bank provided that the bank had to publish each year an exact calculation of the annuities for each class and for each division and that the terminate shares – i.e. the names of the deceased – had to be published as well.[506] The terms of the Austrian *Allgemeine Versorgungsanstalt* (General Pension Fund) of 1823 provided that the fund had to publish annually its accounts, the amount of annuities per class, and the names of all deceased members; it also contained rules on the costs of administration and on how to invest the capital. The terms of the Hamburg *Allgemeine Versorgungs-Anstalt* (General Pension Fund) of 1778 clearly followed the principles of self-administration.[507] The tontine had five directors, who had to be members of the tontine and who were elected by all its members. The costs of administration were covered by a fund into which each member had to pay a predefined sum when joining the fund. The Senate of the city of Hamburg supervised the administration of the fund and had to approve all changes to the terms. A planned tontine to be issued by the Leipzig *Assekuranzgesellschaft auf das Leben* (Life Insurance Society) in 1791 was secured by 'Capitale und beträchtliche Grundstücke' ('capital and a considerable amount of real estate'), and the society invited members of the public who were interested in the tontine to examine these

502 Archiv der Hansestadt Lübeck, 05.4-4 Tontine-078 No. 01.

503 Archiv der Hansestadt Lübeck, 05.4-4 Tontine-078 No. 01.

504 The plan can be found in: Staatsarchiv Hamburg, No. 613-3/91_I A 3.

505 The plan can be found in: Staatsarchiv Hamburg, No. 613-3/91_I A 3.

506 Landesarchiv Baden-Württemberg (Hauptstaatsarchiv Stuttgart), E 146 No. 8972.

507 See the discussion by *Krünitz*, Encyclopädie LXXI (1796), 192.

securities.[508] The articles of the *Preußische Renten-Versicherungs-Anstalt* (Prussian Pension Insurance Fund) of 1838 made clear in its preamble that the fund was subject to state supervision.[509] The articles provided for clarity as to how the administration costs of the tontine were paid for: each member had to pay 15 silver pennies as admission fee; furthermore, a reserve fund was applied to cover the costs of administration. The annual financial statement had to be published in the official governmental journals. The governmental department which was in charge of supervision had to name a commissioner who had the right to attend all meetings of the fund and who had the right to order the board of trustees to examine all accounts. The president and the vice-president of the board of trustees which supervised the administration of the fund were appointed by the Prussian King on recommendation of the governmental department. The other six members of the board were elected by a general assembly of all members of the fund. The general assembly met once a year, and the invitation had to be published in Berlin newspapers and in the official governmental journals. Furthermore, the statute had detailed provisions on how to invest the assets. Finally, there were detailed provisions for the eventuality that the fund wanted to change the amount of annuities which it paid out. It could only implement such a change for new members of the tontine, and it could only do so if there was a material change in the market interest rate. The change had to be approved of by the responsible governmental department. Further, the change had to be published in Berlin newspapers and official governmental journals so that the general public would be informed about this change before joining the tontine.

c) The third phase: tontine life insurance products in the late 19th century

The tontine business of the U.S. life insurance companies in the late 19th century was subjected to harsh criticism. It was argued that the tontines were financially unsound in the sense that they had promised a much higher dividend than could realistically be paid out. It was alleged that they did not provide the appropriate transparency and did not open their books to the tontine members. Indeed, under U.S. law, individuals insured under tontine life insurance did not have a right to examine the books.[510] Furthermore, it was assumed that the U.S. life insurance companies in Germany did not maintain separate accounts for either their tontines or for the different tontine classes. It was criticized that, in comparison to German tontines and life insurance companies, they invested their capital in less secure investments with the hope of realizing higher dividends – and with a

---

[508] (1792) Münchener Intelligenzblatt 34.

[509] Statuten der Preußischen Renten-Versicherungs-Anstalt zu Berlin (1838).

[510] *McKeever*, Evolution of the Tontine in North America, 248 f., citing *Uhlman* v. *New York Life Insurance Co.*, 109 N.Y. 421 (N.Y. 1888), 428 f.

corresponding risk of loss. And it was argued that they paid overly high commissions to their agents, thus increasing the (non-transparent) costs of administration.[511] The discussions in contemporary publications were heated, and it was again forcefully argued that tontines were nothing but gambling.[512] The U.S. life insurance companies countered that the criticism was unfounded and discriminatory. However, if one considers the German discourse spanning over 200 years on how to run a tontine soundly, it seems that the criticism was well justified.

In reaction, Prussia ordered these companies to meet specific accounting standards for their tontine products and to raise their deposits with the Prussian state. Tontines were not, however, forbidden. It was simply ensured that those standards to which the German market was accustomed were also observed by foreign insurers. The same is true for Austria, as § 19 of the *Verordnung betreffend die Errichtung, die Einrichtung und die Geschäftsgebarung von Versicherungsanstalten* (Ministerial Order concerning the Incorporation, Organization, and Operation of Insurance Institutions) of 1896 proves:[513]

> Lebensversicherungsanstalten können berechtigt werden, Erbgesellschaften (Überlebensassociationen, Tontinen) unter ihrer Leitung zu bilden, bei welchen die Anstalt nicht selbst als Versicherer erscheint, sondern nur deren Geschäftsführung und Vermögensverwaltung unter Controle der versicherten Mitglieder übernimmt. Das Vermögen solcher Associationen ist als ein der Anstalt anvertrautes Gut zu behandeln und unter Angabe der das Eigenthum der Associationen nachweisenden Daten getrennt zu verwalten.

> Life insurance companies may receive the permission to form and to administer hereditary societies (survivorship societies, tontines). With such societies the company does not act as the insurer, instead only undertaking the societies' administration and asset management. The company is supervised by the members of that society. The society's assets are to be treated as entrusted assets which have to be administered separately acknowledging the society's proprietary rights.

This text also raises another question: who is owner of the invested capital? For the 17th and 18th centuries, the answer seems to be straightforward: the issuer. The public hand issued tontines in order to raise capital, and in return it was obliged to pay out annuities. However, all along it was accepted that the investors had a strong interest in how the tontine is run. Thus, they were allowed to name co-directors, they had the right to inspect the accounts etc. By the end of the 19th century, Austria had settled on the solution that the invested capital was that of the members of the tontine.

---

[511] *Kürble*, (1990) 79 Zeitschrift für die gesamte Versicherungswissenschaft 605, 609–611; *Taussig* (1885), 3–26; *Wiese*, Treu und Glauben (1892), 3–32; *idem*, Tontinen-Versicherung (1892), 1–40 (the author was a former employee of Equitable); *Mancke* (undated), 5–26.

[512] *Wiese*, Tontinen-Versicherung (1892), 1.

[513] (1896) Reichsgesetzblatt 63–92, 67.

d) Conclusion and comparative observations

These findings make it necessary to reassess the history of insurance regulation and insurance supervision. Modern research suggests that the history of insurance regulation and insurance supervision in Germany starts with the Prussian *Wiederholtes Verboth aller und jeder Collecten, wozu keine Königl. Approbation ertheilet ist* (Repeated Prohibition of all Collections without Royal Approval) of 1781.[514] This act introduced the requirement of a concession for establishing certain funds. However, what we see is that the ideas on how to guaranty financial soundness, solvency, proper administration and transparency for investors had already been developed in the context of tontines in the middle of the 17th century. These ideas were developed in the context of state finances which saw the use of an early form of a state bond. They were not rules on regulating and supervising private entities running an investment or insurance business; rather, they were rules which the states themselves adhered to in order to attract capital from private investors.

The origins of these rules deserve further research. It could perhaps be feasible to understand the provisions on self-administration, the need to send out annual financial statements and the members' rights to examine the books as an application of the rules on *societas*,[515] but it is unclear whether it is possible to characterize all tontines as a *societas*.[516] Two points are, however, clear. First, the issuers of simple life annuity contracts had in practice offered some kind of security since the Middle Ages, and Ogris discusses the different kinds of securities given in the context of life annuities.[517] They very much resemble the different forms of securities in the context of tontines. Secondly, the ideas on how to guaranty financial soundness, solvency, proper administration, and transparency for investors were not restricted to Germany. During the 18th century, foreign tontines published financial statements in German newspapers and magazines.[518] Krünitz gave a detailed overview of how the Hague tontine of 1771 was run,[519] and the details of his overview resemble the rules applied in Germany. The proposition that these ideas were not restricted to Germany is further supported by the research undertaken by Gallais-Hamonno and Rietsch, Sirks, and

---

514 Novum Corpus Constitutionum Prussico-Brandenburgensium Praecipue Marchicarum, vol. 7 (1786), 181–186.

515 Compare *Coing*, vol. 1, 466 f.; *Lepsius*, in: Historisch-kritischer Kommentar, vol. 3/2, §§ 705–740 para. 113 f., 119–122.

516 See the text corresponding to and following n. 529, below.

517 *Ogris*, Leibrentenvertrag, 251–262.

518 See the reference in n. 91, above.

519 *Krünitz*, Encyclopädie LXXI (1796), 136–142.

Sunnqvist.[520] And according to the act establishing the English tontine of 1692, the Office of the Clerk of the Pells had to keep books with the names of all contributors and of all nominees, to 'which … it shall be lawfull for the respective Contributors their Executors Administrators and Assignes from time to time att all seasonable times to have resort and to inspect the same without fee or reward'; furthermore, the act made clear that the costs of administration were not charged to the fund.[521]

However, according to the present state of research it seems that it was only in Germany that these means had a lasting impact on the further development of insurance regulation and insurance supervision: when in the second phase of their development tontines were issued as pension insurance products by private pension funds, the state ensured that the rules which it had imposed upon itself for running a tontine were also observed by these private pension funds. Against this background it is clear why the U.S. life insurance companies ran into problems when offering tontine life insurance products in Germany.

The reflections on the development of the ideas on the financial soundness, the solvency, the proper administration, and the transparency of tontines suggest one final point. The discourse on tontines in the late 19th century was 'overshooting'. The tontine life insurance products of the U.S. life insurance companies raised very specific regulatory problems. It was not that the tontine raised these problems as an investment product. Only the specific U.S. tontine life insurance products raised these problems. And these problems had been solved by the regulatory bodies. However, as a consequence the tontine as such was discredited. And this is why the discourse was 'overshooting': it was claimed that tontines were nothing but a form of gambling even though the designs of tontines had been refined to turn them into a pension insurance product: lottery elements had disappeared (with the exceptions of the *Hamburgische Allgemeine Versorgungs-Tontine* (Hamburg General Pension Tontine) of 1822 and the *Rostocker Versorgungs-Tontine* (Rostock Pension Tontine) of 1831); the Nuremberg tontine of 1777 had introduced a system according to which all investors (or their heirs) received back at least their initial investment; and the increase in the annuities was either capped or was predetermined. This 'overshooting' discourse understandably had the consequence that tontines went out of fashion. However, the 'overshooting' discourse also resulted in claims that tontines as such should be banned altogether, and it resulted in the misperception that tontines in fact were banned. A possible distinction is and was not made by modern literature – that

---

520 *Gallais-Hamonno* and *Rietsch*, Financial Engineering, 61 ff., 71 f.; *Sirks*, 130 f.; *Sunnqvist*, 160 f.

521 An Act for granting to Their Majesties certain Rates and Duties … and Advantages in the said Act mencoed to such Persons as shall voluntarily advance the Sūme of Ten hundred thousand Pounds towards carrying on the War against France, 4 Will. & Mar. c. 3.

between, on the one hand, tontine pension products which should have not raised any concerns and, on the other hand, tontine life insurance products as well as *Sparkassen Tontinen* which may be looked upon as problematic. I will return to this possible distinction in the conclusion of this volume.[522]

3. Alteri stipulari nemo potest?

Today, contracts in favour of third parties are permissible under German law, and they are of great importance. Moreover, a prime example of their importance is the life insurance contract.[523] Under Roman law, however, the rule *alteri stipulari nemo potest* applied.[524] Still, even in Roman times, exceptions to this rule had been acknowledged and one of these exceptions concerned, arguably, the case of funeral funds.[525] These exceptions had been expanded since the Middle Ages, but only since the 17th century had the rule been overcome so that contracts in favour of third parties generally became permissible.[526] It seems clear that in the context of life annuity contracts and tontines the rule was not applied.[527] Article 2 of the Gdańsk tontine regulations of 1657 allowed investors to name themselves, their wives, or their children as payee. But it was only the literature of the 19th century which clearly saw that tontines, widow assurances, and pension funds were examples of contracts in favour of third parties in cases where the investor and the payee were not the same persons.[528]

4. Explaining the hereditary principle

Is a tontine enterprise nothing but a multitude of bilateral contracts between an issuer, on the one hand, and a number of investors on the other hand? Or is a tontine some kind of (mutual) society, a *societas*? These questions have never received an explicit answer. In the 17th and 18th centuries, self-contained tontines

---

[522] See the text corresponding to n. 579, below.

[523] See e.g., *Vogenauer*, 386.

[524] *Kaser*, vol. 1, 491, vol. 2, 339 f.

[525] On the details and the problems concerning the interpretation of that case as an exception to the rule see *Wesenberg*, 63–65.

[526] See on this development *R. Zimmermann*, Law of Obligations, 34–45, *Vogenauer*, in: Historisch-kritischer Kommentar, vol. 2/2, §§ 328–335 paras. 5–45; *Coing*, vol. 1, 423–430, vol. 2, 452–455; *Müller*, 98–151; *Scheuermann*, 103–110.

[527] *Ogris*, Leibrentenvertrag, 158 f.

[528] *Gareis* (1873), 275 f.; *von Kübel*, 1188; *von Buchka* (1852), 187; *Hellwig* (1899), 157 (referring only to life annuity contracts); *Dernburg*, Obligationenrecht (1882), 47 (with reference to life annuity products offered by life insurance companies). See also the discussion of *von Wächter* (1881), 390. See also with reference to widow and orphan assurances *Vogenauer*, in: Historisch-kritischer Kommentar, vol. 2/2, §§ 328–335 para. 49.

were issued to raise capital. They were used as an early form of a state bond. It was generally accepted that the issuer and the investor concluded a contract,[529] and it seems that a tontine scheme was nothing but a multitude of bilateral contracts between an issuer on the one hand and a large number of investors on the other hand. But how then was the hereditary principle explained doctrinally? A number of different explanations would have been possible. The problem with a historical analysis of the question is that while each explanation finds some support in the historical materials, no explanation is able to fully explain the hereditary principle.

(1) One could have explained the hereditary principle as some kind of singular succession.[530] Each investor appointed all other surviving members of the tontine as successor to his rights in the tontine. Indeed, the word 'hereditary principle' suggests explaining it in terms of the law of succession. Furthermore, tontines were also called *Erbklassenrenten* (hereditary class annuities).[531] Sirks points out that Dutch investors in tontines feared an explanation in terms of the law of succession. They were afraid that the inheritance tax would be imposed on the increase in the annuities.[532] Furthermore, explaining the hereditary principle as a form of singular succession should have led to discussions whether the act of subscribing to a tontine met the formal requirements of the law of succession. A tontine could, for example, have been looked upon as a contract as to succession: an inheritance contract.[533] However, such an analysis would have faced two problems. First, Part I, Title 12, § 617 of the *Allgemeines Landrecht für die Preußischen Staaten* (General Prussian Territorial Law – ALR) of 1794, for example, suggests that the contract had to be concluded between the parties making dispositions in each other's favour. Yet in the case of tontines the contract was concluded between the issuer and the different investors. Secondly, the formal requirements of § 621 would not have been met in the case of tontines. Furthermore, if the investor invested all his assets into a tontine and if the other members of the tontine profited from the annuity of the deceased member via the law of succession, then it should have been discussed whether the heirs who were left with nothing had some rights, too, via the rules on forced heirship or compulsory portion.[534] However, there are no signs of such discussions. Finally, an explanation in terms of the law of succession was simply impossible if a third party was named as nominee who was not identical with the investor or payee.

---

[529] See the text corresponding to n. 442, above.

[530] Compare *Coing*, vol. 1, 562 f.

[531] See the text corresponding to n. 117, above.

[532] *Sirks*, 128, 131.

[533] Compare *Coing*, vol. 1, 587–593.

[534] Compare *Coing*, vol. 1, 576, 610–618. See also the text corresponding to n. 553, below.

(2) It would have been possible to explain the hereditary principle on the basis of a stipulation in favour of third parties: the issuer promised to each investor that, in the case of the nominee's death, the respective annuity would not, as is the case with a standard life annuity, terminate, but that it would benefit the other surviving investors. However, here again the contemporary literature does not adopt this explanation.

(3) Many tontines were called a society. The Schweinfurt tontine of 1735, for example, was titled a *Leib-Renthen-Societät* (Life Annuity Society).[535] Thus, could one apply the rules on the *societas* to tontines, and is it thus possible to explain the hereditary principle on the basis of these legal rules?

Some tontines had general assemblies of all investors. And there were elements of self-administration. Thus, one could indeed argue that all investors formed a *societas*. And some of the above mentioned schemes could be explained on these grounds. The Bremen loan of 1692 consisted of two contracts: one contract concerned the terms of the loan with the city of Bremen; the other contract was made between the ten investors, and it concerned the question of how to apportion the interest and the capital.[536] Thus, it seems that a *societas* was formed between the ten investors. The Lübeck tontine plan of 1708 adopted a similar approach:[537]

> Es würde 100. Portiones auff junge Leute / jede auff 100. Rthlr. gesetzet / so ein Capital von 10000. Rthlr. ausmachen / wovon die Cassa jährlich 3. pro Centum zahle / insgesammt 300. Rthlr. und müsten diese Persohnen / so solche Portiones nehmen / den Vortheil unter sich selbst suchen ...
>
> There are 100 shares on young people / each at a cost of 100 talers / so that there is a capital of 10,000 talers / on which the treasury pays annually 3% / in total 300 talers and the persons / who buy the said shares / have to look for their advantage among themselves ...

The city's only obligation was to pay the full interest rate of 300 talers per year to the entirety of the tontine members until the death of the last nominee. The distribution of the annuities was exclusively in the hands of the tontine members. For this purpose they had to elect a committee:

> Die Austheilung dieser Renten betreffend / müssen diese 100. Persohnen 4. oder 5. Persohnen unter sich wehlen / so die Renten von der Cassa abfordern / und die Distribution verrichten könten / auch unter sich die Rechnung wegen der etwa Abgehenden halten.
>
> Concerning the distribution of the annuities / the 100 members have to elect 4 or 5 from among themselves / who have to claim the annuities from the town treasury / and

---

[535] See the text corresponding to n. 166, above.

[536] See the text corresponding to n. 135, above.

[537] Archiv der Hansestadt Lübeck, 3.4-2 Stadt-Cassa No. 483.

who perform their distribution / also they have to calculate the annuities with respect to deceased members.

One could thus argue that the investors in the Lübeck tontine formed a *societas*. However, with many tontines it did not fall on the investors to administer the tontine and to distribute the annuities, but on the issuer. Nevertheless, with many tontines its members were allowed to appoint a specified number of members to the board running the tontine. Was the issuer then simply managing the *societas* of the investors? Or was the *societas* formed not only between the investors but also between the issuer and the investors? And did the legal analysis depend on the specific tontine design? The tontines outside Germany leave similar room for interpretation.[538]

The immediate problem with the second explanation is, however, that the issuer on the one hand and the investors on the other hand were not pursuing a common purpose, having instead entered into a pooled life annuity contract. With a compound tontine the picture was slightly differently: it was not only the surviving members who profited from the annuities of a deceased member; a portion of the annuities of the deceased member was lost to the issuer. Yet, is the fact that the issuer also profited from the annuities of a deceased member enough to speak of a common purpose? I do have doubts: the term 'compound tontine' rather refers to a combination of a simple life annuity contract with a pooled life annuity contract.[539]

Furthermore, Sirks reminds us of the problems associated with explaining a tontine as a form of a *societas*: normally 'a partnership would dissolve at the death of a partner, but, as Voet says, one could agree that it would continue with the remaining partners.[540] But this is never stated in the advertisements and brochures for tontines.'[541] Thus, the hereditary principle would not have been explainable by reference to the legal rules on *societas*. The hereditary principle would have been an exception to the rule that a *societas* dissolved at the death of one of the parties. Furthermore, with many tontines the shares were freely negotiable, again a detail which is hardly in line with the rules on *societas*. And the way the contract was concluded – or the way the contracts were concluded – does not suggest that any form of a *societas* was formed: each investor subscribed to a pooled life annuity contract with the investor. An additional problem in analysing the hereditary principle in terms of the rules on *societas* would have arisen where the investor, the payee, and the nominee were different persons. Finally,

---

538 *Sirks*, 134 ff.; *Gallais-Hamonno* and *Rietsch*, Financial Engineering, 72 f.

539 See the text corresponding to n. 126, above.

540 *Voet* (1698), 1704, ad D. 17,2 n. 23.

541 *Sirks*, 134 f. So also *R. Zimmermann*, Law of Obligations, 455 f.; *Coing*, vol. 1, 469; *Lepsius*, in: Historisch-kritischer Kommentar, vol. 3/2, §§ 705–740 para. 195–204.

it seems odd to define the hope for the early death of the other partners as a common purpose of a *societas*.

Most probably, the question of how to explain the hereditary principle would have confused contemporary lawyers. Claproth made clear why the legal discussion on tontines, as well as on life annuity societies and widow assurances, could be so brief in treatises: the rules governing tontines were fully contained in the plans, statutes, or regulations of the different tontines.[542] Put differently: it was a matter left to the freedom of contract of the parties engaging in a tontine transaction,[543] and thus there was no need to develop a doctrinal explanation of the hereditary principle. And even if contemporary lawyers had developed such an explanation, everything would have depended on the exact design of the tontine as there was, most probably, more than one possible explanation of the hereditary principle.

5. Preventing fraud on the side of the investor

According to modern life insurance law the insured has to disclose his or her true age before the contract is formed. In a different contribution I have analysed the development of the duty of disclosure in the terms and regulations of German widow and orphan assurances, death funds, and life insurance companies in the 18th and early 19th centuries.[544] In that contribution it became obvious that the insured was early on burdened with a duty of disclosure. Article 1 of the regulations of the Berlin *Sterbe-Kasse* (Death Fund) of 1710 required the insured to be of a certain age in order to be admitted to the fund.[545] Article 5 provided for a relatively mild legal consequence if it later turned out that the insured was older: the insured was burdened with a penalty of 10 talers but did not lose coverage under the insurance. By the middle of the 18th century a different legal consequence had developed, as becomes obvious from the regulations of the Württemberg *Allgemeine Freywillige Wittwen- und Waysen-Cassa* (General Voluntary Widow and Orphan Assurance) of 1756.[546] Under Art. 10 of its regulations the insured had to prove his or her age by presenting his or her certificate of baptism; if it later turned out that the certificate was incorrect, the insured forfeited insurance coverage and all paid premiums. These consequences – loss of coverage

---

[542] *Claproth* (1798), 1084.

[543] Compare *Coing*, vol. 1, 465.

[544] *Hellwege*, (2014) 131 Zeitschrift der Savigny-Stiftung für Rechtsgeschichte (Germanistische Abteilung) 247–250.

[545] The regulations are reproduced in: *Schöpfer*, 214.

[546] Herzoglich-Würtembergische Ordnung für die allgemeine freywillige Wittwen- und Waysen-Cassa von 1756 (Stuttgart 1756).

and loss of all paid premiums – appeared in most widow and orphan assurances regulations since the middle of the 18th century.

In tontines, too, it was material for the issuer to know the age of the nominee. However, whereas in the case of life insurance and widow and orphan assurance the insured had the incentive to feign a younger age, in tontines the contributor would have the incentive to pretend that the nominee was older than his or her actual age. The nominee would then be assigned to a class of older nominees, and consequently the payee would receive a higher interest rate to start with and the chances would be higher that the nominee would be the last survivor of his or her class.[547] Furthermore, an issuer who utilized a tontine in order to raise capital would not be able to close the class of that age group until later than anticipated. The problem did, however, not arise with all tontines: the classes of the Gotha tontine of 1752 were, for example, not divided according to the nominee's age.[548]

The problem is only rarely discussed in the literature.[549] The reason for this silence has already been pointed out above: Claproth clarified that academic discussions on the legal regime concerning tontines, as well as life annuity societies and widow assurances, could be brief because these regimes were fully specified in the terms, regulations, and statutes of the different tontine ventures.[550] Nevertheless, Claproth is one of few authors who discussed the problem:[551]

> Wäre nun in der Angabe der Jahre ein Betrug oder ein beträchtlicher Irrthum vorgegangen, so kann es bey dem Contract nicht bleiben, woferne nicht dieser Unterschied auf andere Weise wieder gut gemacht wird. Bey Wittwencassen und Tontinen müssen die Vorschriften, welche die Aufnahme der Candidaten betreffen, auf das pünctlichste beobachtet werden.
>
> If in the declaration of age there is any fraud or any substantive error, then the contract cannot stand if the difference cannot be made up in any other way. With widow assurances and tontines, the regulations which concern the admission of members have to be observed in the most accurate way.

Thus, it does not come as a surprise that the tontine regulations of the 17th, 18th and 19th centuries required contributors to disclose the nominees' true age. Article 3 of the regulations of the Gdańsk tontine of 1657 stated, for example, that all investors had to disclose the nominees' ages faithfully ('Bei der Einteilung der Personen wird man das Alter, welches ein jedweder treulich kund zu tun

547 *Krünitz*, Encyclopädie LXXI (1796), 10.

548 See the text corresponding to and following n. 190, above.

549 It is, for example, discussed by *Ayrer* (1750), 36–39, with reference to Art. 32 of the regulations of the tontine of the shire of Wied. It is also discussed from a more pragmatic point of view by *Marperger* (1715), 282.

550 See the text corresponding to and the reference in n. 390, above.

551 *Claproth* (1798), 1085.

… verbunden sein wird').[552] The article further specified the legal consequences if someone was in breach of this obligation: the money was lost ('bei Verlust seines gelegten Geldes, dafern ein anders an den Tag käme'). Finally, Art. 3 explained the rationale behind this rule: only nominees of a similar age should be grouped together in the same class. It is, however, surprising that the harsh legal consequences – loss of the investment and loss of the right to all annuities – had been made explicit in the context of tontines already in the middle of the 17th century, whereas in the context of widow and orphan assurances the equivalent legal consequences appeared only 100 years later.

6. Protecting the investor's heirs and creditors

A problem which was regularly discussed in the context of life annuity contracts was that of how to protect the buyer's heirs and creditors. If the buyer of a life annuity paid out the entirety of his or her assets in return for the right to the annuities, the interests of his or her creditors and potential heirs may have been affected. Nevertheless, in the context of life annuity contracts the general position was clear:[553] neither creditors nor potential heirs had any special right to rescind a life annuity contract. In favour of creditors, the general *actio Pauliana*, of course, applied. This position was also reflected in § 1286 of the Austrian *Allgemeines Bürgerliches Gesetzbuch* (General Civil Code – ABGB) of 1811. The Prussian position was different. According to Part I, Title 11, §§ 637–641 of the *Allgemeines Landrecht für die Preußischen Staaten* (General Prussian Territorial Law – ALR) of 1794, creditors had a special right to rescind a life annuity contract, and the heirs were protected, too. These provisions raised complex problems, e.g., on how to unwind the rescinded contract.[554] With tontines, too, the interests of creditors and heirs may have been affected if the contributor invested a large portion of his or her assets in a tontine. And the rights of potential heirs were one of the main concerns raised by the *Kameralisten* against tontines.[555] Were the special provisions of the Prussian ALR introduced in reaction to these concerns? I was not able to find an answer to this question.

[552] The regulations are reproduced in: *Foltz* (1912), 459–461.

[553] *Mittermaier* (1843), 81 f.; *Bluntschli* (1854), 81; *Winiwarter* (1844), 539. See also the discussion of a rather special case by *Claproth* (1798), 1085.

[554] *Hiersemenzel* (1855), 356 f.

[555] See the text following n. 417, above.

7. Usury and laesio enormis

The issuer of a tontine paid interest on the invested capital to the contributor. This raises the immediate question of whether the rules against usury applied to tontines. Dietrich Gotthard Eckard (1696–1760) observed that this question regularly worried parties to a life annuity contract.[556] The question received a clear answer in the context of life annuity contracts, and one may assume that this answer equally applied to tontines: the rules against usury were not applicable because the capital remained with the issuer.[557] The classification of non-gratuitous life annuity contracts as contracts for the sale of rights to the annuities, and not as a credit agreement, was thus of importance.[558]

Furthermore, it was generally accepted that the principle of *laesio enormis* was not applicable to life annuity contracts and tontines, but this position was not uncontested.[559] It was generally thought that the principle is of no relevance to aleatory contracts. Furthermore, the principle of *laesio enormis* was only applicable if the values of both performances were quantifiable when the contract was concluded. With life annuity contracts it was impossible to quantify the performance of the seller as it was unclear how long he had to pay the annuities to the buyer. Nevertheless, it was accepted that the principle of *laesio enormis* could apply under exceptional circumstances, e.g. if the total amount of the promised annuities based on the highest possible age was still less than half of the purchase price.[560]

8. Preventing fraud on the side of the payees

In a tontine, the payee's right to the annuity was dependent on the nominee's life. Consequently, the payee had the incentive to pretend that a deceased nominee was still alive. Such a fraud was not at the expense of the issuer of the tontine

---

556 *Eckard* (1733), 902.

557 *Eckard* (1733), 902; *Gengler* (1892), 439 f. *Mittermaier* (1843), 80 f.; *C.F. Koch*, Recht der Forderungen (1859), 842; *Winiwarter* (1844), 536. See also *Ziegler* (1708), Th. XIX; *Seyberth* (1768), 12–14. In detail on the discussions and problems with respect to life annuity contracts see *Ogris*, Leibrentenvertrag, 104–108.

558 On the classificatory problems see the text following n. 423, above.

559 *Linck* (1682), 65 f.; *Eckard* (1733), 900; *Gengler* (1892), 439 f.; *C.F. Koch*, Recht der Forderungen (1859), 842; *Mittermaier* (1843), 72, 81 *Förster* (1873), 131; *Winiwarter* (1844), 536; *Runde* (1791), 140 f.; *Danz* (1797), 305; *Claproth* (1798), 1091; *von Holzschuher* (1864), 760; *Hillebrand* (1864), 400. See also the discussion of *Ayrer* (1750), 51–54; *Struben* (1772), 332–324; *Schneidt* (1789), 3201 f.; *Glück* (1815), 85 f.; *Rückert* (1857), 20 f.; *Gründler* (1833), 168 f.

560 *C.F. Koch*, Recht der Forderungen (1859), 842; *Waldeck* (1827), 268–278; *Hillebrand* (1864), 400.

unless it related to the last surviving nominee or unless it was a compound tontine. Rather, in most cases the fraud would be at the expense of other payees as it would interfere with the hereditary principle.

Early on, the tontine regulations addressed this problem. Article 10 of the regulations of the Gdańsk tontine of 1657, for example, provided that each payee was obliged, when collecting the annuity, to present an *attestatum vitae* – a certificate that the nominee was still alive – if the nominee was a foreigner or for any other reason unknown to the issuer ('Damit man auch Gewißheit habe, wer von den Interessenten annoch lebet oder Todes verfahren ist, so soll ein jedweder Frembder oder sonsten Unbekannter eine Attestation seines Lebens von seinem Magistrat bei Hebung der Zinser beizubringen gehalten sein').[561] If the payee did not present such a certificate, he was barred from collecting the annuity in that year.

Such a provision was widespread in the tontine regulations of the 17th to the 19th centuries, and legal commentators were in agreement with them.[562] Again, the provision had been known since the Middle Ages in life annuity transactions.[563] In those situations any fraud was at the expense of the issuer and not, as with tontines, at the expense of the other payees.

It was clear that anyone who collected annuities fraudulently was liable in damages, as the regulations of the Hamburg tontine of 1776 made explicit.[564] Article 10 of the Stade tontine of 1777 introduced a penalty: if a payee had collected the annuities on the basis of a false certificate despite the nominee having already passed away, the payee was liable to repay twice the amount of the collected annuities.[565]

An *attestatum vitae* was usually costly. The plan of the Cleves tontine of 1763 stated in Art. 8 that all civil servants, judges, and magistrates of the Duchy had to issue an attestation free of charge.[566] The plan for the Wied tontine of 1749 and the life annuity lottery of Murcia of 1775 had introduced different solutions to the problem of costs:[567] according to the Wied tontine plan the payment of small annuities was postponed; according to the Spanish lottery, the payees of

---

[561] The regulations are reproduced in: *Foltz* (1912), 459–461.

[562] See e.g., *Marperger* (1715), 283; *C.F. Koch*, Recht der Forderungen (1859), 850.

[563] *Ogris*, Leibrentenvertrag, 170–172.

[564] The plan is reproduced in: *Krünitz*, Encyclopädie LXXI (1796), 308–312.

[565] Stadtarchiv Stade, St.H. 51–52 No. 18.

[566] Plan zu einer Geld-Negotiation, in Form einer Tontine, zum Besten des Herzogthums Cleve und der Graffschaft Marck; vertheilet in vier Classen, ausmachen eine Summe von 300,000 Reichsthalern (Cleve 1763).

[567] See the text corresponding to n. 185 and following n. 461, above.

small annuities had to name a public person as nominee; it was generally accepted that an *attestatum vitae* was dispensable if the nominee was known to the issuer, as was the case with public persons. The report on the planned Augsburg tontine of 1753/55 explains:[568]

> Es ist auch noch ein allgemeiner Nutzen dabey zu finden, wann die Tontinenzettel nach hohen Standespersonen benennet werden. Mit diesen kann der wenigste Betrug gespielet werden. Jedermann kennet solche Personen, und ihr Tod wird, so zu reden, in einem Augenblicke durch ein ganzes Land bekant und ruchbar: da hingegen manche Privatperson lange gestorben seyn kann, ehe es alle Einwohner eines Ortes erfahren werden.
>
> There is a general advantage if the nominee in a tontine is a public person. No fraud can appear. Everybody knows such a person. When they die, this will be generally known. By contrast a private person can long be dead before even the inhabitants of a community will know about it.

The Nuremberg tontine of 1777 wanted to be more attractive to investors and, therefore, tried to introduce procedures which were easy to comply with. According to Art. 28 of its regulation, it was sufficient if the nominee him- or herself signed a certificate that he or she was still alive. However, the regulations made clear the consequences of fraud: the payee lost all rights in the tontine, was liable to repay any annuities which were collected wrongfully, and was exposed to criminal proceedings.[569] Finally, according to Art. 10 of the published plan of the Bremen tontine of 1767 and according to Art. 8 of the tontine plan of the Bremen tontine of 1805, a certificate was necessary only if the nominee was not living in the city of Bremen.[570] A similar provision can be found in Art. 6 of the Stade tontine regulations of 1777, according to which a certificate was required only for unknown nominees and those nominees who lived in 'fremde Gebiete' ('foreign territories').[571] The statutes of the *Würtembergische Leibrenten-Bank* (Württemberg Life Annuity Bank) of 1822 addressed the problem as well:[572] in principle a certificate issued by the local authority had to be presented. If the annuity was below 100 gulden then it was possible to present a certificate of a simple witness for three consecutive years. The witness had to be respectable and had to be known to the bank. Furthermore, the witness had to guarantee the correctness of the certificate in the sense that he or she promised to repay any annuity wrongly claimed on the basis of an incorrect certificate. Every fourth year, however, a certificate issued by the local authority was indispensable.

---

568 (1757) Das Neueste aus der anmuthigen Gelehrsamkeit 754.

569 Gründliche Nachricht von einer neuen sehr vorzüglichen und vortheilhaften Reichs-Stadt Nürnbergischen Leib-Renten Gesellschaft (Nürnberg 1777), 28 f.

570 Staatsarchiv Bremen, No. 2-R.1.A.10.c.4.II.d.2 vol. 1; Niedersächsisches Landesarchiv (Osnabrück), Depositum 3 b IV No. 5759.

571 Stadtarchiv Stade, St.H. 51–52 No. 18.

572 Landesarchiv Baden-Württemberg (Hauptstaatsarchiv Stuttgart), E 146 No. 8972.

9. The nominee's death

Usually, the nominee on whose life the contract was based was the payee or a third person. However, it was generally accepted that the parties to a life annuity contract could also agree to base the contract on the life of the payor or to agree on other resolutive conditions, such as the remarriage of the payee.[573] In the context of life annuity contracts, basing the right to the annuities on the life of the payee, a third person, or the payor raised a number of problems. What happened if the payor killed the payee nominee or a third party nominee? And what happened if the payor nominee committed suicide or was subject to a death penalty? These questions received extensive discussion. Most authors distinguished between the different situations, and some territorial laws provided for special solutions.[574] Some authors argued and some laws held that the contract did, nevertheless, come to an end and that the payee's heirs had a delictual claim for damages; yet, this solution raised numerous problems as to how to quantify the damages. Others argued that the contract did not come to an end as the condition had been fulfilled by an act of the party to whose advantage the fulfilment of the condition operated. Again others were of the opinion that the payee's heirs had a right to the capital, and it was this latter position that was followed by the *Allgemeines Landrecht für die Preußischen Staaten* (General Prussian Territorial Law) of 1794. The problem that the issuer killed the nominees in order to escape his or her obligation to pay annuities did not arise in the context of tontines, as they were issued by the public hand, pension funds, and life insurance companies. In a tontine it could, however, have happened that one payee killed other nominees in order to receive an increase in his or her annuities. However, this was probably a rather theoretical scenario: tontines had a very large number of nominees, and they were marketed internationally. Most probably this explains why the problem did not receive any discussion in the literature in the context of tontines.

---

[573] *Hillebrand* (1864), 399; *O. von Gierke* (1917), 798; *Oertmann* (1899), § 759 para. 1; *Dernburg*, Schuldverhältnisse (1915), 142; *C.F. Koch*, Recht der Forderungen (1859), 841; *Mittermaier* (1843), 81.

[574] *Winiwarter* (1844), 538; *Dernburg*, Schuldverhältnisse (1915), 144; *Hiersemenzel* (1855), 356–357; *Haberstich* (1885), 330; *Crome* (1902), 608; *Förster* (1873), 130; *C.F. Koch*, Recht der Forderungen (1859), 848; *Oertmann* (1899), § 759 para. 1; *Sepp*, Leibrente (1903), 48–55; *Eccius*, (1901) 45 Beiträge zur Erläuterung des deutschen Rechts 11–28, 23; Part I, Title 11, §§ 626–630 Allgemeines Landrecht für die Preußischen Staaten (General Prussian Territorial Law – ALR).

10. The payor's default and insolvency

If the payor was in default, it was generally thought in the context of life annuity contracts that the annuitant could only claim the outstanding annuities.[575] However, some authors argued that the annuitant should have a right to rescind the contract if the payor had failed to make annuity payments for three consecutive years and this position resulted in restitutionary difficulties as rescission would have been followed by unwinding the entire contract. The latter position was also adopted by Part I, Title 11, §§ 647 f. *Allgemeines Landrecht für die Preußischen Staaten* (General Prussian Territorial Law) of 1794. If the payor was insolvent, the annuitant's rights were capitalized and he did not receive any preferential treatment.[576]

IV. Conclusion and comparative observations

With respect to the development of tontines in England and Scotland, MacLeod observes, that '[p]erhaps the most striking thing about tontines is how little material there is on them in the legal sources'.[577] A similar observation can be made with respect to many other European legal systems. Above, I have asserted that the German-language literature of the 17th, 18th, and 19th centuries rarely thoroughly discussed tontines. Nevertheless, the German legal literature at least widely took notice of tontines. First, there is the question of whether tontines were a variance of life annuity schemes or lotteries, or whether they count as insurance. From the 17th century up to today, tontines have been and are qualified as a variance of life annuity contracts. In the 19th century, when tontines had been turned into pension products, they were additionally looked upon as an insurance product. And it was accepted that tontines are – just like lottery contracts, life annuity contracts, and insurance contracts – aleatory contracts. It was only at the end of the 19th century, and in the context of the U.S. tontine life insurance products, that tontines were heavily criticized as being nothing but lotteries on lives. In Germany, it is in the context of insurance supervision and insurance regulation where tontines had a lasting impact. In the 17th and 18th centuries tontines were issued by the public hand as a means to raise capital. The public hand developed

---

575 See on the following positions: *Hillebrand* (1864), 400; *Hiersemenzel* (1855), 356 f; *Förster* (1873), 131; *von Holzschuher* (1864), 762; *Fischer* (1887), 411; *Mittermaier* (1843), 81 f.; *C.F. Koch*, Recht der Forderungen (1859), 852; *Sepp*, Leibrente (1903), 46–48. The predominant view is reflected in Art. 1978 of the French Code civil.

576 See the discussions of *Bluntschli* (1854), 82; *von Holzschuher* (1864), 763 f.; *Haberstich* (1885), 329; *Gengler* (1892), 440; *O. von Gierke* (1917), 803; *Förster* (1873), 132; *Mittermaier* (1843), 83; *Weishaar* (1833), 181 f.; *Sepp*, Leibrente (1903), 22–34; *Schneidt* (1789), 3213. See also *Harpprecht* (1754).

577 *MacLeod*, 144.

specific practices in order to offer trustworthy products to the general public: the public hand pledged securities; it introduced measures to guarantee transparency (e.g. financial reports had to be published and sent to members); members had the right to examine the books; and measures of self-administration were introduced. Although these means were not restricted to Germany, it seems that it was primarily in Germany that they were, in the late 18th century and then throughout the 19th century, imposed on those private pension funds which offered tontine products. Thus, the rules which the public hand had placed upon itself when offering tontines in the context of public lending were transformed into rules on the supervision and regulation of pension funds. These findings make it necessary to reassess the German history of insurance regulation and insurance supervision. In France, the rules on tontine supervision and regulation began to be developed in the early 19th century, and these rules, of course, influenced the development in the Netherlands, too. However, it is unclear whether there are in France, as well, any lines of continuity with earlier developments. And in other countries the regulatory discussions started only in the second half of the 19th century.

F. Conclusion

With respect to (i) the practical importance and occurrence of tontines in German-speaking territories, (ii) their designs, and (iii) the purposes which they served, it is possible to distinguish three phases of development.

The first phase of development stretches from the middle of the 17th century to the early 19th century. I was able to identify a larger number of tontines and tontine plans than are mentioned in modern literature. Nevertheless, I am not able to claim that I have identified all tontines that existed or were planned during the first phase of their development. There is simply the problem of finding the relevant archival materials on those tontines which are not mentioned in modern or contemporary literature. Furthermore, it became apparent that tontines were marketed on a European scale. Germans invested in foreign tontines, and many German tontines were marketed internationally. In conclusion, in the first phase of their development tontines played a much more important role in Germany as an investment product than is generally acknowledged.

In the first phase of their development, tontines were predominantly issued by the public hand as self-contained investment schemes. Their designs differed greatly. Today, we define tontines as pooled life annuity schemes: the characteristic feature is that the annuities of deceased members accrue to surviving members, so that the annuities increase over time; this is generally called the hereditary principle. However, in the 17th and 18th century the term 'tontine' was used more loosely. Foremost, many lotteries were called tontines. A number of these lotteries paid out tontine-based annuities. Others were life annuity lotteries which did not apply the hereditary principle. Again others were simple lotteries. And there were loan agreements which included a lottery element and which were also referred to as tontines.

In the first phase of their development, tontines were a multi-purpose investment product: the public hand issued them for the purpose of raising capital, foremost to cover the costs of wars. For investors, tontines functioned primarily as a means to generate a pension either for themselves or for dependants. In addition, investors could invest in a tontine simply for the purpose of speculation. Specifically, they could hope to sell the right in the tontine for a profit. Finally, those tontines involving a lottery element also served the purpose of gambling.

The assertion that the number of tontines was in decline in the 19th century due to the emergence of modern life insurance schemes seems to be wrong. Throughout the 19th century, pension funds and savings banks offered tontines.

This is the second phase in the development of tontines. In the second phase of their development, tontines were turned into single-purpose financial products: they were only a means to generate a pension or they were utilized as a savings plan. Thus, Germany had two single-purpose financial products with two distinct purposes.

In the third phase of their development, occurring in the late 19th and early 20th centuries, U.S. life insurance companies offered tontine life insurance products throughout Europe (including in Germany). Tontines were reduced to being an add-on to a standard life policy for the purpose of marketing. The tontine mechanism was not used, as it was in the second phase, to generate a pension. It was a means to distribute the dividends to surviving insured.

With respect to the importance of tontines for the development of life insurance, it is generally claimed that tontines were of utmost importance in the further development of mortality tables and actuarial science. However, the German-language 18th-century literature discussed mortality tables and actuarial problems not only in connection with tontines but also in connection with other life annuity schemes as well as with widow and orphan assurances and funeral funds. Tontines were one out of many relevant products.

Furthermore, it is alleged that tontines 'helped spread the idea of insurance and made wider circles receptive for the idea of life insurance'.[578] If it all, this assertion is valid only for the tontines of the first phase and the tontine based pension products of the second phase. Yet here again, there are other institutions which could have had the same effect, e.g. widow and orphan assurances. Thus, in order to prove the special importance of tontines, further research is needed. One would need to undertake statistical research on the number of people participating in tontines as compared to widow and orphan assurances. Furthermore, it would be of interest to know which social classes participated in the different schemes and how these numbers and the social composition developed in the course of the 18th century.

Finally, modern literature claims that tontines were of importance for the development of life insurance law, but a detailed analysis of their impact on the history of insurance law is still missing. It has, however, become clear that tontines were of utmost importance for the development of the rules on insurance supervision and insurance regulation. In the first phase of the development of tontines, the public hand developed specific practices on how to run a tontine: the rights of the members had to be secured; the tontine plans needed to be transparent; the administration and the costs of administration needed to be transparent; issuers needed to send financial statements to members annually; members

---

[578] See the references in n. 14, above.

had a right to examine the accounts of the tontine; and members were often involved in the administration of tontines. Some of these practices have a longstanding history. Since the Middle Ages, for example, it was common in the context of life annuity transactions that the issuer pledged some kind of security. When in the second phase of their development tontines were issued by pension funds, the public hand made sure that these funds implemented the same practices which had been observed by the public hand in the first phase of development. This explains why the tontine life insurance products of the U.S. life insurance companies in the third phase of the development of tontines met with so much opposition. Foremost, the administration of these tontine life insurance products was not transparent.

Pursuant to modern life insurance law the insured has to disclose his or her true age before the contract is formed. This duty of disclosure is found early on also in the context of widow and orphan assurances. However, it seems that the harsh legal consequence whereby the insured lost his coverage and forfeited all paid premiums was introduced in the context of widow and orphan assurances only in the middle of the 18th century. Tontine regulations of the 17th, 18th and 19th centuries similarly required contributors to disclose the nominees' true age. But, the harsh legal consequences – loss of both the investment and the right to all annuities – were made explicit in the context of tontines already in the middle of the 17th century.

Tontines raise a number of further legal questions. How is the hereditary principle explained? Is a tontine enterprise nothing but a multitude of bilateral contracts between an issuer on the one hand and a number of investors on the other hand? Is it in turn possible to explain the hereditary principle on the basis of a stipulation in favour of third parties? Or is a tontine some kind of *societas*? Classifying a tontine as some kind of *societas* would have the advantages that the member's rights to examine the accounts of the tontine, that their involvement in its administration, and that their right to receive financial statements would be doctrinally explainable. Nevertheless, the classification as some kind of *societas* would raise a number of other problems. The German-language legal literature of the 17th, 18th, and 19th centuries rarely thoroughly discussed tontines, and it does not address these questions. For that reason I was not able to develop a final answer to them.

It became clear, however, that the legal literature classified tontines of the first phase and the tontine base pension products of the second phase as life annuity transactions. As life annuity transactions, tontines were legally permissible. And contrary to what modern literature claims tontines were never banned in Germany. They simply went out of fashion.

Finally, the assertion that tontines are a manner of gambling is outdated – at least, this assertion needs to be qualified. In the 17th and 18th centuries tontines often involved a lottery element; the last surviving annuitant frequently received exorbitant annuities which were out of proportion to his or her investment; and it was possible to name third parties as nominees. Modern literature often refers to these features of early tontines when arguing that tontines were a manner of gambling. However at the time, naming a third party as nominee made sense to prevent fraud and to avoid the costs of a certificate of life. Furthermore, the 17th and 18th centuries saw a number of improvements and novelties in tontine designs. Three improvements seem to have been of importance for the further development of tontines. (1) Foremost, the Nuremberg tontine of 1777 introduced a scheme under which the invested capital was not lost: if the annuities which the payee received did not amount to the invested capital before the nominee died, the heirs were reimbursed the balance. (2) The Prussian tontine of 1788 applied the hereditary principle in a typified way: the increase in the annuities was predetermined and the increase was capped. (3) Finally, the possibility to pay the investment in instalments opened tontines to poorer populations of inhabitants. On the basis of these innovations, tontines were turned into true pension insurance products. The risk against which the investor seeks coverage is that his or her assets will not be sufficient to support him- or herself upon reaching a high age. Thus, there are no arguments against re-introducing tontines as pension products in the future. If at all the argument that tontines are a form of gambling could be raised against so called *Sparkassen Tontinen* as well as tontine life insurance products of the late 19th century. I am now returning to the distinction between tontine pension products on the one hand and *Sparkassen Tontinen* as well as tontine life insurance products on the other hand.[579] The former is a form of insurance, the latter two arguably are not. The latter two are savings products imitating the mechanism of much older dowry insurance products. The invested capital or, in the case of tontine life insurance products, the accumulated dividends were paid out to the surviving investors or insured after a fixed period of time – usually between 5 and 20 years. There is no risk involved with these products. In the case of tontine life insurance products the insured risk does not concern the tontine scheme which is simply added to a life insurance policy. These products may be looked upon as a means of gambling or as a means of speculating on other peoples' lives. The fact that in the case of the U.S. tontine life insurance products the tontine element was added to a life insurance policy does not change this qualification. In conclusion, there may be valid arguments against re-introducing tontines as savings products and against re-introducing tontine life insurance products. There are, however, no arguments against re-introducing tontines as pension insurance products.

---

[579] See the text corresponding to n. 291, 320, 459, and 522, above.

Archival Sources

Archiv der Hansestadt Lübeck

- 05.4-4 Tontine-078, No. 01, 1809–1896.
- 05.4-4 Tontine-078, No. 04, 1896.
- 3.4-2 Stadt-Cassa, No. 482: Projekte zu Tontinen und Leibrenten, o.D.–1715.
- 3.4-2 Stadt-Cassa, No. 483: Plan einer Tontine, 1708.
- 5.1-1/04 Bergenfahrerkompanie, No. 2896: Errichtung einer Tontine, 1790–1809.
- 5.1-1/08 Krämerkompanie, No. 1552: Verhandlung über Zulage und Tontine, 1712, 1714.

Augsburger Stadtarchiv

- 00059 Kaiserliche Franciscische Akademie der freien Künste, No. 1.

Brandenburgisches Landeshauptarchiv

- No. 23A C.2720: Forderung Kurfürst Friedrichs III. zur Aufbringung von 200 000 Reichstalern als eine sogenannte Tontine oder Leibrente und Genehmigung zur Errichtung einer Tontine von 30 000 Talern Kapital zum Wiederaufbau der Schloß-, Oberpfarr- und Domkirche, 1698–1747.
- No. 23B 1295: Plan zur Beschaffung von Geld in Form einer Tontine (Leibrente, hier ist die Lotterie gemeint) für das Herzogtum Cleve und die Grafschaft Mark.

Hessisches Staatsarchiv (Marburg)

- 17 II No. 383: Projekt einer zu errichtenden Tontine.
- 340 von Dörnberg No. 4311.
- 40 Rubr. 24 No. 462: Projekt einer Tontine oder Leibrentenkasse für das Hofhospital St. Elisabeth zu Kassel.
- 7 a No. 1/232/48: Unter dem Namen Tontine bestandene Gesellschaft der Marställer des ehemaligen Westfälischen Hofes.
- 80 No. 6345: Verbot zur Einzahlung in die Tontine (Leibrentengesellschaft) der Fürsten zu Wied.

Landesarchiv Baden-Württemberg (Hauptstaatsarchiv Stuttgart)

- E 146 No. 8972: Errichtung einer Leibrentenbank (Tontinenanstalt), 1817–1827.
- E 146 No. 8974: Kommissionsakten zur Errichtung einer Leibrentenbank (Tontinenanstalt), 1821–1824.

Landesarchiv Mecklenburg-Vorpommern (Greifswald)

- No. 2145: Errichtung einer Fayance Tontine (Lotterie) auf den Landesjahrmärkten.

Landesarchiv Nordrhein-Westfalen, Abt. Ostwestfalen Lippe (Detmold)

– L 77 A No. 5744.

– L 92 A No. 5002: Anlegung einer Tontine auf 50 Jahre zur Finnazierung der Irrenanstalt zu Brake.

Landesarchiv Sachsen-Anhalt (Wernigerode)

– A 30aII, II No. 474: Stift-Merseburg Steuer-Cassen-Extrakt zum Landes-Bedürfnis, zur Tontine und künftigen Fonds d'Amortissement vom Jahr 1750 bis 1755.

Landeshauptarchiv Schwerin

– 3.1-1 (Mecklenburgische Landstände mit Engeren Ausschuß der Ritter- und Landschaft zu Rostock), No. 20 Anhang 27: Von dem Herrn Hofmeister von Vieregge in Vorschlag gebrachte Tontine oder Leibrenten-Sozietät, 1758.

– 3.1-1 (Mecklenburgische Landstände mit Engeren Ausschuß der Ritter- und Landschaft zu Rostock), No. 20 Anhang 29: Errichtung einer Tontine oder Leibrenten-Sozietät, 1763.

– 3.1-1 (Mecklenburgische Landstände mit Engeren Ausschuß der Ritter- und Landschaft zu Rostock), No. 20 Anhang 30: Errichtung einer Tontine oder Leibrenten-Sozietät, 1785.

Niedersächsisches Landesarchiv (Aurich)

– Dep. I, No. 3071: Die Ausschreibung einer Tontine zum Verkauf des künftig zu besiedelnden Neuen Bunder Polders (Landschaftspolders).

Niedersächsisches Landesarchiv (Oldenburg)

– Best. 222, No. 41: Verordnung wegen einer errichteten Witwen- und Waysen-Casse für die Hochfürstl. Bischöfl. Lübekschen und Herzogl. Holstein-Oldenburgschen Lande (Eutin 1779).

Niedersächsisches Landesarchiv (Osnabrück)

– Depositum 3 b IV No. 5759: Acten die Constituirung einer Tontine betreffend.

Niedersächsisches Landesarchiv (Wolfenbüttel)

– 4 Alt 1, No. 2668: Errichtung einer Tontine.

Österreichisches Staatsarchiv

– AT-OeStA/FHKA SUS Patente 70.5: Errichtung einer Tontine in Bozen.

– AT-OeStA/HHStA AKA 3-69: Auszug aus den Betrachtungen, Anmerkungen und dem Pro memoria über den Vorschlag einer Tontine (Rentenversicherung); mit kurzen Gegenanmerkungen, s.d.

– AT-OeStA/HHStA AKA 8-48: Vortrag Ludwig Graf von Zinzendorf betreffend den Vorschlag einer Tontine (Rentenversicherung). Weiterer Vortrag über dasselbe Thema, circa 1761.

Sächsisches Staatsarchiv (Hauptstaatsarchiv Dresden)

– 10015 Landtag No. 328 (H 108): Registraturen, Edikte und Beilagen, die Tontine, die 1747 errichtet worden, betreffend.

- 10025 Geheimes Konsilium Loc. 5350/08: Die zum Nutzen hiesiger Lande in Vorschlag gebrachte Anlegung [von] Lotterien und Tontinen.
- 10026 Geheimes Kabinett No. 530/02: Die Einrichtung der von Mackfail de Bischopfield [Mackphaile de Bishopfield] im Jahr 1747 in Vorschlag gebrachten Tontine.
- 10036 Finanzarchiv Loc. 41493 Rep. 59 Lit. D No. 1282: Lotterie oder Tontine zur Erweiterung des Steuerhauses in Dresden; Erweiterung des Steuerhauses in Dresden sowie die Lotterie bzw. Tontine.

Sächsisches Staatsarchiv (Staatsfilialarchiv Bautzen)

- 50001 Landstände der sächsischen Oberlausitz, No. 1166: Landeslotterie. Enthält u. a.: Lotterievorschläge, 1724, 1725; Errichtung einer oberlausitzischen Landeslotterie zur Tilgung der Landesschulden, 1765–1771; Avertissement über die Genehmigung der Lotterie, 1770 (Druck); Vorschlag einer Tontinen-Lotterie (Lotterie auf Renten) zur Tilgung der Landesschulden, 1766; Lotterielisten, 1771 (Druck), 1724–1774.
- 50009 Oberamt des Markgraftums Oberlausitz, No. 109: Errichtung eines Fonds d‘ amortissement (Abschreibungsfonds, Tilgungsfonds) für eine Tontine (Leibrente) durch die Oberlausitzer Landstände, 1777.

Staatsarchiv Bremen

- No. 2-R.1.a.10.c.4.I: Tontinen und Leibrenten im allgemeinen, 1692–1810.
- No. 2-R.1.A.10.c.4.II.b.1.a: Untersuchungen über die Zweckmäßigkeit einer Tontine (1728), 1757–1763.
- No. 2-R.1.A.10.c.4.II.b.1.b: Errichtung der ersten Tontine, 1767.
- No. 2-R.1.A.10.c.4.II.b.1.d: Verzeichnis der an der Tontine von 1767 beteiligten Personen und der unter ihnen eingetretenen Todesfälle, 1767–1842.
- No. 2-R.1.A.10.c.4.II.c.1.b: Verzeichnis der an der Tontine von 1772 beteiligten Personen und der unter ihnen eingetretenen Todesfälle, 1772–1843.
- No. 2-R.1.A.10.c.4.II.d.2, vol. 1–3: Verzeichnis der an der Tontine von 1805 beteiligten Personen.
- No. 2-R.1.B.4.e: Anleihe zum Neubau der Großen Weserbrücke und dem dabei erforderlichen Ankauf der Wassermühlen, 1838–1841.

Staatsarchiv Hamburg

- No. 613-3/91_I A 3: Pläne der Tontine, ab 1817.
- No. 613-3/91_I A 5: Literatur zur Tontine.
- No. 613-3/91_I E 1: Interessenten der Tontine.
- No. 613-3/91_I F 1: Liquidation der Tontine.

Staatsarchiv Nürnberg

- Reichsstadt Nürnberg D No. 4814.
- Reichsstadt Nürnberg D No. 4815.
- Reichsstadt Nürnberg D No. 4816.
- Reichsstadt Nürnberg Druckschriften No. 713.

- Reichsstadt Nürnberg Rentkammer No. 1950.

Stadtarchiv Nürnberg

- A 6 No. 2538.
- A 6 No. 2611.
- E 6/125 No. 1: Nürnberger Leibrenten-Gesellschaft.

Stadtarchiv Stade

- St.H. 51–52 No. 18: Acta die Anleihe eines Kapitals von 10,000 Reichstalern und Errichtung einer Leibrenten-Societät (Tontine) betreffend, 1775–1851.

Südtiroler Landesarchiv (Bozen)

- No. 3.23.1: Merkantilmagistrat Bozen. Akten und Verordnung über Tontinen, 1737–1740.
- No. 3.23.2: Merkantilmagistrat Bozen. Akten und Verordnung über Tontinen, 1737–1740.

Other Sources

An Act for granting to Their Majesties certain Rates and Duties … and Advantages in the said Act mencoed to such Persons as shall voluntarily advance the Sūme of Ten hundred thousand Pounds towards carrying on the War against France, 4 Will. & Mar. c. 3.

Anschreiben Von Errichtung einer Tontine oder Classen-Leib-Renten-Cassa (Neuwied am Rhein 1749).

Die schon längst von vielen eifrigst verlangte Nachricht von der Beschaffenheit, Einrichtung und Vorhaben der Kaiserl. privilegirten Gesellschaft der freien Künste und Wissenschaft (Augsburg 1753).

Edit de sa Majesté le Roi de Pologne, Electeur de Saxe concernant la negociation de rentes viageres et de famille ouverte a Leipsig au mois de Janvier 1748 (Dresde 1748).

Grundgesetzlicher neuer Erb-Vertrag der Durchlauchtigsten regierenden Herzogs und Herrn, Herrn Friederich Franz, Herzogs zu Mecklenburg … mit Ihro Erbunterthänigen Stadt Rostock, vollzogen zu Rostock, den 13ten May, 1788 (1788).

Gründliche Nachricht und Statuten von der sehr vorzüglichen und gemeinnützlichen Reichs-Stadt Nürnbergischen zweiten Leibrenten-Gesellschaft (Nürnberg 1783).

Gründliche Nachricht von einer neuen sehr vorzüglichen und vortheilhaften Reichs-Stadt Nürnbergischen Leib-Renten Gesellschaft (Nürnberg 1777).

Herzoglich-Würtembergische Ordnung für die allgemeine freywillige Wittwen- und Waysen-Cassa von 1756 (Stuttgart 1756).

Ihrer Königl. Majestät in Pohlen und Churfürstl. Durchl. zu Sachsen Edict wegen der im Monath Januario 1748 zu Leipzig eröffneten Leib- auch Familien-Renten-Negotiation (Dresden 1748).

Notification Von Der zu Dantzig Revidirten Leib-Rente im Monat Aprilis 1657 (Dantzig 1657).

Patent wegen der einzurichtenden Leib-Renten d.d. den 30. Decembr. 1698, (1736) 6/1 Corpus Constitutionum Marchicarum 653–658.

Patent wegen Errichtung einer wachsenden Leibrenten-Anstalt zum Betrieb des Chaussee-Baues im Magdeburgischen und Halberstädtschen, (1788) 8 Novum Corpus Constitutionum Prussico-Brandenburgensium Praecipue Marchicarum 2257–2268.

Plan d'une Tontine à etablir ou d'un fond à negocier sur rentes viagères sous la garantie des Ordres de la ville. Publié à Danzig le 13. du Mois de Mars 1775 (Danzig 1775)

Plan einer aus Schluß sämmtl. Löbl. OOgen dieser Stadt dem Publico zum Besten zu errichtende Tontine oder Negocirung auf Leibrenten, publicirt in Danzig den 27. Jan. 1792 (Danzig 1792).

Plan einer unter Assecuration der Landschafft des Fürstenthums Gotha zu entrichtenden Leib-Renten-Negotiation oder Tontine (Gotha 1752).

Plan von Ihro Churfürstl. Durchleucht genädigst-privilegierten und zum Nutzen des Publici errichteten Renntengesellschaft (München 1776).

Plan zu einer Geld-Negotiation, in Form einer Tontine, zum Besten des Herzogthums Cleve und der Graffschaft Marck; vertheilet in vier Classen, ausmachen eine Summe von 300,000 Reichsthalern (Cleve 1763).

Reglementäre Grundbestimmungen der bayerischen Hypotheken- und Wechselbank für die Renten-Anstalt (1839).

Statuten der Preußischen Renten-Versicherungs-Anstalt zu Berlin (1838).

Verzeichnuß Des halben Theils der, Von der Augspurgischen Gliederschaft Der Kayerlich Franzischen Academie freyer Künsten errichteten Tontine Oder Leib-Renten (Augsburg 1757).

Zweiter Rechenschafts-Bericht der Renten-Anstalt der bayerischen Hypotheken- und Wechselbank für das Jahr 1841 (1842).

Bibliography

Anonymous: Der redliche und aufrichtige Wirthschafter welcher weiset wie Regenten mächtig und Privat-Personen reich werden können (Jena 1745).

– Die Berliner Börsen-Zeitung und die Amerikanischen Lebens-Versicherungs-Gesellschaften (1888).

– Kritik und Erläuterung des Plans von 1859 der Hamburger Versorgungs-Tontine (1871).

– Ueber die Hamburgische Versorgungs-Tontine von 1817, (1817) 2/23 Lesefrüchte vom Felde der neuesten Literatur 353–362.

Asch, Ronald G.: Osnabrück zwischen Westfälischem Frieden und Siebenjährigem Krieg 1648 bis 1763, in: Gerd Steinwascher (ed.), Geschichte der Stadt Osnabrück (2006), 229–266.

Atzpodien, Hans Christoph: Die Entwicklung der preußischen Staatsaufsicht über das private Versicherungswesen im 19. Jahrhundert (1982).

Averdieck, G. F.: Beleuchtung des Berichts der Direktion der Hamburgischen allgemeinen Versorgungs-Tontine (1837).

Ayrer, Georg Heinrich: Dissertatio iuridica inauguralis de rescission contractus vitalitii (Göttingen 1750).

Bätge, Heinz: Leibrente, in: Franz Schlegelberger (ed.), Rechtsvergleichendes Handwörterbuch, vol. 5 (1936), 276–281.

Baumann: Kurze und faßliche Darstellung der Verträge über das menschliche Leben nach den Rechtsgerundsätzen. Zur Belehrung für Theilnehmer an Leibrenten-, Tontinen-, Lebensversicherungs- und Wittwenverpflegungs-Anstalten (1828).

Baumann, Horst et al. (eds.): Bruck/Möller. Versicherungsvertragsgesetz, vol. 8/1 (9th edn., 2013).

Baumstark, Edward: Staatswissenschaftliche Versuche über Staatskredit, Staatsschulden und Staatspapiere (1833).

Beckmann, Johann: Beyträge zur Geschichte der Erfindungen, vol. 5/3 (1804).

Beger, Carl Ludwig: Ueber die Allgemeine Versorgungsanstalt im Großherzogthum Baden (1835).

Bender, Wolfgang: "… aber die Anstalt wird darum nicht minder Statt haben". Fürstin Pauline und die Gründung der "Irrenanstalt" zu Brake, in: Jutta Prieur (ed.), Frauenzimmer – Regentin – Reformerin. Fürstin Pauline zu Lippe 1802–1820 (2002), 102–111.

Benecke, Wilhelm: Der jetzige Zustand der Hamburgischen Versorgungs-Tontine und die echten Grundsätze einer künftigen Verwaltung derselben (1832).

Berch, Andreas: Einleitung zur allgemeinen Haushaltung (Halle 1763).

Bergius, Johann Heinrich Ludwig: Policey- und Cameral-Magazin, vol. 6 (Frankfurt am Main 1771).

Bertheau, Heinrich August: Deutliche Darstellung der Hamburgischen Versorgungs-Tontine von 1817 (1817).

Beseler, Georg: System des gemeinen deutschen Privatrechts, vol. 1 (4th edn., 1885).

Bielfeld, Jakob Friedrich von: Lehrbegriff der Staatskunst, vol. 22 (Breslau 1761).

Bierer, Hermann: Handbuch des gesammten, in Württemberg geltenden Privatrechts, vol. 2 (1863).

Bluntschli, Johann Caspar: Deutsches Privatrecht, vol. 2 (1854).

Böttcher, Hans Viktor: Die Freie Stadt Danzig. Wege und Umwege in die europäische Zukunft (1995).

Bovensiepen, Rudolf: Leibrente, in: Fritz Stier-Somlo and Alexander Elster (eds.), Handwörterbuch der Rechtswissenschaft, vol. 3 (1928), 944–947.

Brämer, Hermann / *Brämer*, Karl: Das Versicherungswesen (1894).

Braumüller, Peter: Versicherungsaufsichtsrecht (1999).

Braun, Heinrich: Geschichte der Lebensversicherung und der Lebensversicherungstechnik (2nd edn., 1963) (cited as: Geschichte).

– Urkunden und Materialien zur Geschichte der Lebensversicherung und der Lebensversicherungstechnik (1937) (cited as: Urkunden und Materialien).

Brockhaus Enzyklopädie, vol. 26, vol. 30 (21st edn., 2006).

Brockhaus Enzyklopädie online (accessed on 12 June 2017).

Bruck, Ernst: Das Privatversicherungsrecht (1930).

– Reichsgesetz über den Versicherungsvertrag (7th edn., 1932).

Buchholz, Werner: Das schwedische Pommern vom Westfälischen Frieden bis zum Wiener Kongreß, in: idem (ed.), Deutsche Geschichte im Osten Europas, vol. 9 (1999), 237–304.

Buchka, Hermann von: Die Lehre von der Stellvertretung bei Eingehung von Verträgen (1852).

Burger, Dirk: Der Einfluß der wirtschaftlichen, sozialen und politischen Entwicklungen auf die Entfaltung der Versicherungsaufsicht im neunzehnten und zwanzigsten Jahrhundert. Eine Betrachtung für den Bereich der Individualversicherung (1988).

Büsch, Johann Georg: Abhandlung von dem Geldumlauf in anhaltender Rücksicht auf Staatswirtschaft und Handlung, vol. 2 (2nd edn., 1800).

Claproth, Justus: Rechtswissenschaft von richtiger und vorsichtiger Eingehung der Verträge und Contract, vol. 2 (4th edn., 1798).

Clark, George: The Nine Years War, in: J. S. Bromley (ed.), The New Cambridge Modern History, vol. 6 (1970), 223–253.

Coing, Helmut: Europäisches Privatrecht, vol. 1 (1985), vol. 2 (1989).

Crome, Carl: System des Deutschen Bürgerlichen Rechts, vol. 2/2 (1902).

Cyon, C.: Tontinen und Lebens-Versicherungen. Ein Beitrag zur Kritik der Tontinen Versicherungen der Amerikanischen Gesellschaften (2nd edn., 1892).

Danz, Wilhelm August Friederich: Handbuch des heutigen deutschen Privatrechts. Nach dem Systeme des Herrn Hofraths Runde, vol. 2 (Stuttgart 1797).

Das Bürgerliche Gesetzbuch mit besonderer Berücksichtigung der Rechtsprechung des Reichsgerichts (Kommentar von Reichsgerichtsräten), vol. 2/2 (9th edn., 1939).

Deeters, Walter: Kleine Geschichte Ostfrieslands (1985).

Delbrel, Sophie: Tontines in France from the Ancien Régime to the Third Republic, in: Phillip Hellwege (ed.), The Past, Present, and Future of Tontines. A Seventeenth Century Financial Product and the Development of Life Insurance (2018), 109–120.

Demps, Laurenz: Der Berliner Dom (1999).

Dernburg, Heinrich: Das Obligationenrecht Preußens und des Reichs (3rd edn., 1882).

– Die Schuldverhältnisse nach dem Recht des Deutschen Reiches und Preußens, vol. 2 (4th edn., 1915).

Directie van de Algemeene Maatschappij van Levensverzekering en Lijfrente (ed.): Bouwstoffen voor de geschiedenis van de levensverzerkingen en lijfrenten in Nederland (1897).

Dölemeyer, Barbara: Die Hugenotten (2006).

Du Pasquier, L. Gustav: Die Entwicklung der Tontinen bis auf die Gegenwart, (1910) 46 Zeitschrift für Schweizerische Statistik 484–513.

– Leonhard Eulers Verdienste um das Versicherungswesen, (1909) 54 Vierteljahresschrift der naturforschenden Gesellschaft in Zürich 217–243.

Dülmen, Richard van: Die Gesellschaft der Aufklärer. Zur bürgerlichen Emanzipation und aufklärerischen Kultur in Deutschland (1986).

Eccius, Max Ernst: Der Leibrentenvertrag des Bürgerlichen Gesetzbuchs, (1901) 45 Beiträge zur Erläuterung des deutschen Rechts 11–28.

Eckard, Dietrich Gotthard: Geheime Juristische Briefe, zwischen Zweyen Rechts-Gelehrten, bey dero Leben über Practische Controversien (25th Collection, Leipzig 1733).

Endemann, Friedrich: Lehrbuch des Bürgerlichen Rechts, vol. 1 (6th edn., 1899).

– Lehrbuch des Bürgerlichen Rechts, vol. 1 (8th edn., 1903).

Estor, Johann Georg: Teutsche rechtsgelahrheit anderer teil (Marburg 1758).

Euler, Martin: Allgemeine Wechselencyclopädie oder theoretisch-praktische Einleitung in die Wechselwissenschaften (4th edn., 1806).

Falck, Niels Nikolaus: Handbuch des Schleswig-Holsteinischen Privatrechts, vol. 3/2 (1838).

Fielder, Walter: Die Geschichte des Versicherungswesens der Reichsstadt Nürnberg (1958).

Fischer, Otto: Lehrbuch des preußischen Privatrechts (1887).

Fleischmann, Peter: Johann Wolfgang von Goethe erkundigt sich und vermittelt vier Interessenten für eine ganz neuartige Form der Leibrente, in: Norenberc – Nürnberg.

1050 bis 1806. Eine Ausstellung des Staatsarchivs Nürnberg zur Geschichte der Reichsstadt (2000), 146.

Florencourt, Carl Chassot de: Abhandlungen aus der juristischen und politischen Rechenkunst (Altenburg 1781).

Foltz, Max: Geschichte des Danziger Stadthaushalts (1912).

Forman, Jonathan Barry / *Sabin*, Michael J.: Tontines in the western world today, in: Phillip Hellwege (ed.), The Past, Present, and Future of Tontines. A Seventeenth Century Financial Product and the Development of Life Insurance (2018), 329–341.

Förster, Franz: Theorie und Praxis des heutigen gemeinen preußischen Privatrechts auf der Grundlage des gemeinen deutschen Rechts, vol. 2 (3rd edn., 1873).

Fortunati, Maura: Tontines in Italy, in: Phillip Hellwege (ed.), The Past, Present, and Future of Tontines. A Seventeenth Century Financial Product and the Development of Life Insurance (2018), 203–227.

Frank, Gustav: Geschichte der Protestantischen Theologie, vol. 3 (1875).

Freude, Felix: Die Kaiserlich Franciscische Akademie der freien Künste und Wissenschaften in Augsburg (1909).

Fuchs, Arne: Die Gefahrsperson im Versicherungsrecht (1974).

Fürstenwerth, Frank von / *Weiß*, Alfons: Versicherungs-Alphabet (10th edn., 2001).

Fuß, Nicolas: Éclaircissemens sur les Établissemens publics en faveur tant des veuves que des morts avec la déscription d'une nouvelle espece de Tontine ... calculés sous la direction de Monsieur Léonard Euler (St. Petersbourg 1776).

– Entwurf einer allgemeinen Leihe-Bank (St. Petersburg 1776).

– Erläuterungen über die öffentlichen Anstalten zum Besten sowohl der Witwen als Sterbefälle nebst der Beschreibung einer neuen Art von Tontine (Altenburg 1782).

Gallais-Hamonno, Georges / *Rietsch*, Christian: Financial Engineering in the 17th and 18th Centuries – Tontines in England, France, and Ireland, in: Phillip Hellwege (ed.), The Past, Present, and Future of Tontines. A Seventeenth Century Financial Product and the Development of Life Insurance (2018), 49–77.

Gareis, Carl: Die Verträge zu Gunsten Dritter. Historisch und dogmatisch dargestellt (1873).

Gelderblom, Oscar / *Jonker*, Joost: With a view to hold: The emergence of institutional investors on the Amsterdam securities market during the seventeenth and eighteenth centuries, in: Jeremy Atack and Larry Neal (eds.), The Origins and Development of Financial Markets and Institutions. From the Seventeenth Century to the Present (2009), 71–98.

Gengler, Heinrich Gottfried Philipp: Das Deutsche Privatrecht in seinen Grundzügen für Studierende erörtert (4th edn., 1892).

Gerber, Carl Friedrich Wilhelm von / *Cosack*, Konrad: System des Deutschen Privatrechts (17th edn., 1895).

Gesner, Johann Albrecht: Selecta physico-oeconomica (Stuttgart 1752).

Gierke, Julius von: Versicherungsrecht unter Ausschluß der Sozialversicherung, vol. 1 (1937).

Gierke, Otto von: Deutsches Privatrecht, vol. 3 (1917).

Glück, Christian Friedrich: Ausführliche Erläuterung der Pandecten nach Hellfeld, vol. 17/1 (1815).

Göckel, Rudolph Christian: Dissertatio inauguralis de montibus pietatis, vulgo von Leyh-Häusern, Pfand- oder Anlehn-Aembtern (Altdorf 1722).

Göde, Christian August Gottlieb: Ius Germanicum Privatum (Göttingen 1806).

Goldmann, Eduard / *Lilienthal*, Leo: Das Bürgerliche Gesetzbuch systematisch dargestellt, vol. 1 (2nd edn., 1903).

Gretschel, Karl Christian Kanis: Geschichte des Sächsischen Volkes und Staates, vol. 3 (1853).

Gretzschel, Matthias: Kleine Hamburger Stadtgeschichte (2008).

Groß, Reiner: Geschichte Sachsens (2001).

Große, Robert Walter: Wirtschaft und Versicherung (1928).

Gründler, Carl August: Polemik des germanischen Rechts, Land- und Lehnrechts, vol. 2 (1833).

Grünsteudel, Günther et al. (eds.): Augsburger Stadtlexikon (2nd edn., 1998).

Gutjahr, Alfred Andreas: Das Eindringen amerikanischer Lebens-Versicherungs-Gesellschaften in Deutschland (1920).

Haberstich, Johannes: Handbuch des Schweizerischen Obligationenrechts, vol. 2 (1885).

Hagen, Otto: Versicherungsrecht, in: Victor Ehrenberg, Handbuch des gesamten Handelsrechts, vol. 8/2 (1922).

Haidinger, Andreas: Das wohltätige und gemeinnützige Wien (1842).

Halberda, Jan: Tontines in Poland, in: idem (ed.), The Past, Present, and Future of Tontines. A Seventeenth Century Financial Product and the Development of Life Insurance (2018), 273–288.

Hanov, Michael Christoph: Quaestus Tontini Moralitatem Praeside, in: idem, Opuscula, vol. 1 (Halle 1761), 244–276.

Harpprecht, Christian Ferdinand: Jus contractus vitalitii in concursu creditorum (Tübingen 1754).

Harsdörffer, Georg Philipp: Der Grosse Schau-Platz Lust- und Lehrreicher Geschichte, vol. 2 (Hamburg 1651).

Heidel, Sonja: Die Regelung im VAG über Sicherungsfonds (2007).

Hellwege, Phillip: A Comparative Analysis from the Perspective of Legal History, in: idem (ed.), The Past, Present, and Future of Tontines. A Seventeenth Century Financial Product and the Development of Life Insurance (2018), 383–397.

– A Comparative History of Insurance Law in Europe, (2016) 56 American Journal of Legal History 66–75.

– Die historische Rechtsvergleichung und das europäische Versicherungsrecht, (2014) 131 Zeitschrift der Savigny-Stiftung für Rechtsgeschichte (Germanistische Abteilung) 226–265.

– Introduction, in: idem (ed.), A Comparative History of Insurance Law in Europe. A Research Agenda (2018), 9–26.

– Tontines in German-speaking Territories, in: idem (ed.), The Past, Present, and Future of Tontines. A Seventeenth Century Financial Product and the Development of Life Insurance (2018), 167–192.

Hellwege, Phillip (ed.): The Past, Present, and Future of Tontines. A Seventeenth Century Financial Product and the Development of Life Insurance (2018).

Hellwig, Konrad: Die Verträge auf Leistungen an Dritte (1899).

Heuvel, Christine van den: Osnabrück am Ende des Alten Reichs und in hannoverscher Zeit, in: Gerd Steinwascher (ed.), Geschichte der Stadt Osnabrück (2006), 313–444.

Hiersemenzel, Carl Christian Eduard: Vergleichende Uebersicht des heutigen Römischen und Preußischen gemeinen Privatrechts, vol. 2 (1855).

Hillebrand, Julius Hubert: Lehrbuch des heutigen deutschen Privatrechts (2nd edn., 1864).

Holzschuher, Rudolph Freiherr von: Theorie und Casuistik des gemeinen Zivilrechts, vol. 3 (3rd edn., 1864).

Honsell, Heinrich (ed.): Berliner Kommentar zum Versicherungsvertragsgesetz (1999).

Honsell, Heinrich et al. (eds.), Bundesgesetz über den Versicherungsvertrag (2001).

Hübner, Johann (ed.): Curieuses und reales Natur-Kunst-Berg-Gewerck- und Handlungs-Lexicon (6th edn., Leipzig 1731).

Illescas, Rafael: Tontines in Spain, in: Phillip Hellwege (ed.), The Past, Present, and Future of Tontines. A Seventeenth Century Financial Product and the Development of Life Insurance (2018), 229–237.

Jakob, Ludwig Heinrich von: Grundsätze der National-Ökonomie oder Theorie des National-Reihthums (3rd edn., 1825).

Jung, Johann Heinrich: Die Grundlehre der Staatswirtschaft, ein Elementarbuch für Regentensöhne und alle, die sich dem Dienst des Staats und der Gelehrsamkeit widmen wollen (Marburg 1792).

– Lehrbuch der Finanz-Wissenschaft (Leipzig 1789).

Jung, Ludwig: Ueber rechtliche Natur und zweckmässige Benutzung der Preußischen Renten-Versicherungs-Anstalt zu Berlin (2nd edn., 1840).

Justi, Johann Heinrich Gottlob von: Leben und Character des Königl. Pohlnischen und Churfürstl. Sächsisch. Premier-Ministre Grafens von Brühl in vertraulichen Briefen entworfen (1760).

– Staatswirthschaft oder Systematische Abhandlung alle Oekonomischen und Cameral-Wissenschaften, vol. 2 (2nd edn., Leipzig 1758).

– System des Finanzwesens (Halle 1766).

Kaestner, Abraham: De contractu vitalitio (Leipzig 1744).

Karup, Wilhelm: Theoretisches Handbuch der Lebensversicherung (new edn., 1874).

Kaser, Max: Das römische Privatrecht, vol. 1 (2nd edn., 1971), vol. 2 (2nd edn., 1975).

Kaulbach, Detlef et al. (ed.): Versicherungsaufsichtsgesetz (5th edn., 2012).

Klaber, Herz: Anweisung zur leichten Berechnung der zusammengesetzten Interessen, Jahrrenten, Leib- oder Lebensrenten, Tontinen (1832).

Klessmann, Eckart: Geschichte der Stadt Hamburg (2002).

Klingenburg, Karl-Heinz: Der Berliner Dom. Bauten, Ideen und Projekte vom 15. Jahrhundert bis zu Gegenwart (1992).

Koch, Christian Friedrich: Recht der Forderungen nach Gemeinem und nach Preußischem Rechte, vol. 3 (2nd edn., 1859).

Koch, Johann Thomas: Geschichte des Lotteriewesens in Bayern (1908).

Koch, Peter: Der Versicherungsgedanke bei Goethe und in seinem Umfeld. Ein Beitrag zum 250. Geburtstag des Dichters und Geheimen Rates, in: Verlag Versicherungswirtschaft (ed.), Beiträge zur Geschichte des deutschen Versicherungswesens, vol. 2 (2005), 78–82, 80.

– Geschichte der Versicherungswissenschaft in Deutschland (1998).

– Zum Tontinengeschäft in versicherungshistorischer Sicht, in: Verlag Versicherungswirtschaft (ed.), Beiträge zur Geschichte des deutschen Versicherungswesens, vol. 2 (2005), 27–30.

Koch, Peter / *Weiss*, Wieland: Gabler. Versicherungslexikon, vol. 3 (1996).

Koenige, Heinrich / *Petersen*, Adolf: Gesetz über die privaten Versicherungsunternehmungen (3rd edn., 1928).

Kölschbach, Joachim et al. (eds.): Prölss. Versicherungsaufsichtsgesetz (12th edn., 2005).

Kopitzsch, Franklin: Die Hamburgische Gesellschaft zur Beförderung der Künste und nützlichen Gewerbe (Patriotische Gesellschaft von 1765) im Zeitalter der Aufklärung, in: Rudolf Vierhaus (ed.), Deutsche patriotische und gemeinnützige Gesellschaften (1980), 71–118.

Kopitzsch, Franklin / *Tilgner*, Daniel (eds.): Hamburg Lexikon (1998).

Korn, Alfred: Handbuch des Zivilrechts (1908).

Korn, Christoph Heinrich et al. (eds.): Neueste Geschichte der Welt, auf das Jahr 1775, vol. 6 (Ulm 1777).

Korchagina, Tamara: The Russian experience with tontine insurance, in: idem (ed.), The Past, Present, and Future of Tontines. A Seventeenth Century Financial Product and the Development of Life Insurance (2018), 297–304.

Krainz, Josef: System des österreichischen allgemeinen Privatrechts, vol. 2 (4th edn., 1907).

Kriegk, Otto: Die Geschichte des Biergeldes in der Kurmark Brandenburg (1915).

Kritter, Johann Augustin: Abhandlung von Tontinen, in welchen einem jeden Interessenten die von Jahren zu Jahren wachsende Rente vorherbestimmt, und mit einer gewissen Geldsumme versprochen wird, (1786) Leipziger Magazin für reine und angewandte Mathematik 501–531.

– Anmerkungen zu dem Nürnbergischen im vorigen Jahre bekannt gemachten Plan einer Leibrenten-Gesellschaft oder Tontine worinn kein einziges Mitglied etwas verlieren kann, viele aber erstaunliche Gewinste bekommen sollen, (1779) Gothaisches Magazin der Künste und Wissenschaft 370–384.

– Aufklärung der Berechnungen der Wittwen- und Todtencassen für diejenigen, die sich in der Buchstabenrechnung nicht geübt haben, (1781) 2 Göttingisches Magazin der Wissenschaft und Literatur 390–416.

Krug, Leopold: Abriß der Staatsökonomie oder Staatswirtschaftslehre (1808).

Krünitz, Johann Georg (ed.): Oekonomisch-technologische Encyclopädie, vol. 71 (Berlin 1796), 'Leib-Renten, Jahr-Renten und Tontinen', 1–426.

Kübel, Franz Philipp von: Das einseitige Versprechen als Grund der Verpflichtung zur Erfüllung, in: Werner Schubert (ed.), Die Vorlagen der Redaktoren für die erste Kommission zur Ausarbeitung des Entwurfs eines Bürgerlichen Gesetzbuches (1980), 1171–1203.

Kullick, Christian: „Der herrschende Geist der Thorheit". Die Frankfurter Lotterienormen des 18. Jahrhunderts und ihre Durchsetzung (2018).

Kürble, Gunter: Der Exodus der amerikanischen Lebensversicherer aus Deutschland – die Tontine und die Vorgeschichte des Jahres 1894, (1990) 79 Zeitschrift für die gesamte Versicherungswissenschaft 581–623.

Kurz, Albert: Rechtsfreund für den Kanton Bern, ein populäres Lehrbuch des bernischen Privatrechts (2nd edn., 1858).

Langheid, Theo / *Wandt*, Manfred (eds.): Münchener Kommentar zum Versicherungsvertragsgesetz, vol. 2 (2nd edn., 2017), vol. 3 (2nd edn., 2017).

Laspeyres, Étienne: Geschichte der volkswirthschaftlichen Anschauungen der Niederländer und ihrer Literatur zur Zeit der Republik (1863).

Lehner, Peter Ulrich: Zur Entstehung des Versicherungswesens. Versuch einer gesellschaftlichen Begründung, in: Wolfgang Rohrbach (ed.), Versicherungsgeschichte in Österreich, vol. 1 (1988), 1–44.

Lehr, Julius / *Heckel*, Max von: Tontinen, in: Johannes Conrad et al. (eds.), Handwörterbuch der Staatswissenschaften, vol. 7 (2nd edn., 1901), 125–129.

Leib, Johann George: Wie ein Regent Land und Leute verbessern / des Landes Gewerbe und Nahrung erheben / seine Gefälle und Einkommen sonder Ruin derer Unterthanen billigmäßiger Weise vermehren / und sich dadurch in Macht und Ansehen setzen könne, vol. 4 (Leipzig 1708).

Leske, Franz: Vergleichende Darstellung des Bürgerlichen Gesetzbuches für das Deutsche Reich und des Preußischen Allgemeinen Landrechts, vol. 1 (1st and 2nd edn., 1900).

Linck, Heinrich: De redditu vitalitio, vulgò Von Leib-Renten (Altdorf 1682).

Liscow, Christian Ludwig: Ein Beitrag zur Literatur- und Kulturgeschichte des achtzehnten Jahrhunderts (1844).

Littrow, Joseph Johann von: Ueber Lebensversicherungen und andere Versorgungsanstalten (1832).

Loew, Peter Oliver: Danzig. Biographie einer Stadt (2011).

Lohse, J. / *Boutin*, H. / *Coqui*, F. Heinrich: Wie ist ein Fortbestand der Hamburgischen allgemeinen Versorgungs-Tontine zu sichern? (1832).

Lotz, Johann Friedrich Eusebius: Handbuch der Staatswirthschaftslehre, vol. 3 (1822).

Lueder, August Ferdinand: Ueber Nationalindustrie und Staatswirthschaft, vol. 3 (1804).

Lux, Sebastian Patrick: Die Lebensversicherung nach der VVG-Reform (2015).

MacLeod, John: Tontines in England and Scotland, in: Phillip Hellwege (ed.), The Past, Present, and Future of Tontines. A Seventeenth Century Financial Product and the Development of Life Insurance (2018), 143–151.

Malchus, Karl August von: Handbuch der Finanzwissenschaft und Finanzverwaltung, vol. 1 (1830).

Mancke, Walther: Amerikanische Geldauswanderungs-Agenturen (undated).

Manes, Alfred: Versicherungswesen. System der Versicherungswirtschaft, vol. 3 (5th edn., 1932).

Marperger, Paul Jacob: Montes Pietatis (Leipzig 1715).

– Montes Pietatis (2nd edn. with notes by Johann Heinrich Gottlob von Justi, Leipzig 1760).

Maurenbrecher, Romeo: Lehrbuch des gesammten heutigen gemeinen deutschen Privatrechtes, vol. 2 (2nd edn., 1855).

McKeever, Kent: The Evolution of the Tontine in North America, in: Phillip Hellwege (ed.), The Past, Present, and Future of Tontines. A Seventeenth Century Financial Product and the Development of Life Insurance (2018), 239–257.

– Tontines in Portugal – Nicholas Bourey's paleo-tontine of 1641, in: Phillip Hellwege (ed.), The Past, Present, and Future of Tontines. A Seventeenth Century Financial Product and the Development of Life Insurance (2018), 193–201.

Mensi, Franz Freiherr von: Die Finanzen Oesterreichs von 1701 bis 1740 (1890).

Michelsen, Johann Andreas Christian: Anleitung zur juristischen, politischen und öconomischen Rechenkunst, vol. 2 (Halle 1784).

Milevsky, Moshe A.: King William's Tontine: Why the Retirement Annuity of the Future Should Resemble Its Past (2015).

– What Can Tontine Design of the Future Learn from Its Past?, in: Phillip Hellwege (ed.), The Past, Present, and Future of Tontines. A Seventeenth Century Financial Product and the Development of Life Insurance (2018), 307–316.

Mittermaier, Carl Joseph Anton: Grundsätze des gemeinen deutschen Privatrechts, vol. 2 (6th edn., 1843).

Mohl, Robert von: Die Polizei-Wissenschaft nach den Grundsätzen des Rechtsstaates, vol. 2 (2nd edn., 1844).

– Erörterungen über die allgemeine Rentenanstalt in Stuttgart (1838).

Molnar von Müllersheim, Joseph: Betrachtungen über die mit der ersten österreichischen Sparkasse vereinigte allgemeine Versorgungsanstalt, aus ihrem würdigsten und folgenreichsten Gesichtspunkte als moralisches Wohltätigkeits-Institut (1827).

Motive zu dem Entwurfe eines Bürgerlichen Gesetzbuches für das Deutsche Reich, vol. 2 (1896).

Müller, Ulrich: Die Entwicklung der direkten Stellvertretung und des Vertrages zugunsten Dritter (1969).

Müller-Erzbach, Rudolf: Deutsches Handelsrecht (2nd and 3rd edn., 1928).

Murmellius, Johannes: Mammona oder Schlüssel deß Reichthumbs (Strasbourg 1623).

Nasser, Marcelo: Tontines in Latin America, in: Phillip Hellwege (ed.), The Past, Present, and Future of Tontines. A Seventeenth Century Financial Product and the Development of Life Insurance (2018), 259–272.

Nebel, Rolf / *Honsell*, Heinrich et al. (eds.): Bundesgesetz über den Versicherungsvertrag (2001).

Nebenius, Friedrich: Der öffentliche Credit, vol. 1 (2nd edn., 1829).

Nicolai, Ludwig Christian: Dissertatio inauguralis iuridica de contractu vitalitio, quo annui reditus ad dies vitae comparantur (Strasbourg 1738).

Nordwestdeutsche Klassenlotterie, Lotterie-Direktion, Hamburg (ed.), 350 Jahres Staatslotterie. 1612 – Hamburg – 1962 (1962/63).

Oberholzer, Hans-Martin: Zur Rechts- und Gründungsgeschichte der Privatversicherung (1992).

Oeltermann, J.: Kurze und allgemeine faßliche Darstellung der Hauptgrundsätze und Berechnungen bey Wittwen-Waisen-Leibrenten- auch Sterbepfennings-Cassen, Tontinen und ähnlichen Instituten (1805).

Oertmann, Paul: Das Recht der Schuldverhältnisse (1899).

Ogris, Werner: Der mittelalterliche Leibrentenvertrag. Ein Beitrag zur Geschichte des deutschen Privatrechts (1961).

– Tonti, Tontine, in: Adalbert Erler et al. (eds.), Handwörterbuch zur Deutschen Rechtsgeschichte, vol. 5 (1998), 276–277 (cited as: HRG V).

Ortloff, Friedrich: Grundzüge eines Systems des Teutschen Privatrechts mit Einschluß des Lehnrechts (1828).

Pearson, Robin: The Socio-Economic Setting for Developing Tontines from the 17th to the 19th Centuries, in: Phillip Hellwege (ed.), The Past, Present, and Future of Tontines. A Seventeenth Century Financial Product and the Development of Life Insurance (2018), 79–105.

Perlitz, Uwe: Das Geld-, Bank- und Versicherungswesen in Köln 1700–1815 (1976).

Phillips, Georg: Grundsätze des gemeinen deutschen Privatrechts mit Einschluß des Lehnrechts, vol. 1 (3rd edn., 1846).

Pöhls, Meno: Das Recht der Actiengesellschaften (1842).

Posner, Ernst (ed.): Die Behördenorganisation und die allgemeine Staatsverwaltung Preußens im 18. Jahrhundert, vol. 13 (1932).

Prölss, Erich R. / *Martin*, Anton: Versicherungsvertragsgesetz (30th edn., 2018).

Rhotert, Johannes: Ein Tontinenprojekt des Osnabrücker Rates von 1768 mit einem Rückblick auf einige andere Magistrats-Verordnungen aus dem 18. Jahrhundert, (1908) 33 Mitteilungen des Vereins für Geschichte und Landeskunde von Osnabrück 325–330.

Riebesell, Paul: Tontine, in: Alfred Manes (ed.), Versicherungslexikon (3rd edn., 1930), 1571–1573.

Rietsch, Christian / *Gallais-Hamonno*, Georges: Lorenzo Tonti, in: Phillip Hellwege (ed.), The Past, Present, and Future of Tontines. A Seventeenth Century Financial Product and the Development of Life Insurance (2018), 19–47.

Röder, Philipp Ludwig Hermann: Geographie und Statistik Wirtembergs (Laybach in Krain 1787).

Roelli, Hans / *Jaeger*, Carl: Kommentar zum Schweizerischen Bundesgesetz über den Versicherungsvertrag, vol. 3 (1933).

Roller, Christian Nikolaus: Versuch einer Geschichte der Kaiserlichen und Reichsfreyen Stadt Bremen, vol. 4 (1803).

Roloff, Marita: Die Entwicklung der Lebensversicherung in Österreich zwischen 1873 und 1936, in: Wolfgang Rohrbach (ed.), Versicherungsgeschichte Österreichs, vol. 2 (1988), 283–608.

Rößig, Karl Gottlob: Erste Grundsätze des deutschen Privatrechts (Leipzig 1797).

Rückert, Ludwig: Der Leibrentenvertrag (1857).

Runde, Justus Friedrich: Grundsätze des allgemeinen deutschen Privatrechts (Göttingen 1791).

Sames, Arno: Zwischen Kirche und Staat. Das Merseburger Domkapitel seit der Abtretung des Stifts durch Sachsen an Preußen 1815, in: Holger Kunde et al. (eds.), Zwischen Kathedrale und Welt. 1000 Jahre Domkapitel Merseburg (2005), 133–150.

Say, Jean Baptiste: Darstellung der Nationalökonomie oder der Staatswirthschaft, vol. 2 (3rd edn., 1819).

Scherer, Martin Georg Viktor: Recht der Schuldverhältnisse des Bürgerlichen Gesetzbuches für das Deutsche Reich (1899).

Scheuermann, Reimund: Einflüsse der historischen Rechtsschule auf die oberstrichterliche gemeinrechtliche Zivilrechtspraxis bis zum Jahre 1861 (1972).

Schirmer, Uwe: Die Verfassung des Hochstifts Merseburg vom Ende des 15. bis zur Mitte des 17. Jahrhunderts, in: Holger Kunde et al. (eds.), Zwischen Kathedrale und Welt. 1000 Jahre Domkapitel Merseburg (2005), 121–132.

Schlüter, Roland: Calvinismus am Mittelrhein. Reformierte Kirchenzucht in der Grafschaft Wied-Neuwied 1648–1806 (2009).

Schmidt, Otto Eduard: Minister Graf Brühl und Karl Heinrich von Heinecken. Briefe und Akten, Charakteristiken und Darstellungen zur sächsischen Geschichte (1733–1763) (1921).

Schmidt, Reimer: Versicherungsalphabet (8th edn., 1991).

– (ed.): Prölss. Versicherungsaufsichtsgesetz (11th edn., 1997).

Schmitt-Lermann, Hans: Der Versicherungsgedanke im deutschen Geistesleben des Barock und der Aufklärung (1954).

Schmoeckel, Mathias et al. (eds.): Historisch-kritischer Kommentar zum BGB, vol. 2/2 (2007).

Schmoller, Gustav von / *Hintze*, Otto (eds.): Die Behördenorganisation und die allgemeine Staatsverwaltung Preußens im 18. Jahrhundert, vol. 10 (1910).

Schneidt, Joseph Maria: Thesaurus Iuris Franconici (Würzburg 1789).

Schnyder, Anton K. / *Heierli*, Christian: Insurance Regulation, in: Jürgen Basedow et al. (eds.), The Max Planck Encyclopedia of European Private Law, vol. 1 (2012), 921–926.

Schoeps, Hans-Joachim: Preußen. Geschichte eines Staates (1995).

Schöpfer, Gerald: Sozialer Schutz im 16.–18. Jahrhundert (1976).

Schug, Albert: Der Versicherungsgedanke und seine historischen Grundlagen (2011).

Schumka, Alexander: Die Oberlausitz zwischen Prager Frieden und Wiener Kongreß (1635–1815), in: Joachim Bahlcke (ed.), Geschichte der Oberlausitz. Herrschaft, Gesellschaft und Kultur vom Mittelalter bis zum Ende des 20. Jahrhunderts (2001), 143–179.

Schwintowski, Hans-Peter / *Brömmelmeyer*, Christoph (eds.): Praxiskommentar zum Versicherungsvertragsrecht (3rd edn., 2017).

Scott, H.M.: Prussia's emergence as a European great power, in: Philip D. Dwyer (ed.) The Rise of Prussia. 1700–1830 (2000), 151–176.

Sepp, Karl: Der Leibrentenvertrag nach dem Bürgerlichen Gesetzbuch. Eine civilistische Studie (1905).

– Die Einheitlichkeit der Leibrente und ihrer Wirkungen (1903).

Seyberth, Philipp Heinrich: De reditu annuo praesertim vitali tontina et fiscis viduarum (Frankfurt and Leipzig, 1768).

Simon, Thomas: Merkantilismus und Kamerlismus. Zur Tragfähigkeit des Merkantilismusbegriffs und seiner Abgrenzung zum deutschen 'Kameralismus', in: Moritz Isenmann (ed.), Merkantilismus. Wiederaufnahme einer Debatte (2014), 65–82.

Sintenis, Carl Friedrich Ferdinand: Anleitung zum Studium des Bürgerlichen Gesetzbuches für das Königreich Sachsen (1864).

Sirks, Boudewijn: Tontines in the Dutch Republic and the early Kingdom (1670–1869), in: Phillip Hellwege (ed.), The Past, Present, and Future of Tontines. A Seventeenth Century Financial Product and the Development of Life Insurance (2018), 121–141.

Soden, Friedrich Julius Heinrich von: Die National-Oekonomie. Ein philosophischer Versuch über die Quellen des National-Reichthums, und über die Mittel zu dessen Beförderung, vol. 3 (1815).

– Lehrbuch der Nazional-Oekonomie (1810).

Soergel, Theodor (ed.): Bürgerliches Gesetzbuch nebst Einführungsgesetz, vol. 1 (3rd edn., 1926).

Sonnenfels, Joseph von: Grundsätze der Polizey, Handlung, und Finanzwissenschaft, vol. 2 (3rd ed., Wien 1771).

Sonnleithner, Ignaz Edlen von: Statuten und Reglement der mit der ersten Oesterreichischen Spar-Casse vereinigten Versorgungs-Anstalt, für die Unterthanen des Oesterreichischen Kaiserstaates, mit Erläuterungen (3rd edn., 1831).

Starck, Johann August von: Ueber den Zweck des Freymaurerordens (2nd edn., 1781).

Staudinger, Julius von: Die Rechtslehre vom Lebensversicherungsvertrag (1858).

Handausgabe des Bürgerlichen Gesetzbuchs auf Grund von J. v. Staudingers Kommentar (3rd edn., 1931).

J. v. Staudingers Kommentar zum Bürgerlichen Gesetzbuch und dem Einführungsgesetze, §§ 741–822 (12th edn., 1986).

– §§ 741–764 (new edn., 1996).

– §§ 741–764 (new edn., 2001).

– §§ 741–764 (new edn., 2008).

– §§ 741–764 (new edn., 2015).

– vol. 2/3 (9th edn., 1929).

– vol. 2/3 (10th edn., 1939).

– vol. 2/4 (10th and 11th edn., 1975).

Stobbe, Otto: Beiträge zur Geschichte des deutschen Rechts (1865).

– Handbuch des deutschen Privatrechts, vol. 3 (2nd edn., 1885).

Stoltenberg: Zwei Schreiben an die Direction der Hamburgischen Versorgungs-Tontine (1832).

Strohal, Emil (ed.), Planck's Kommentar zum Bürgerlichen Gesetzbuch mit Einführungsgesetz, vol. 2/2 (4th edn., 1928).

Struben, David Georg: Rechtliche Bedenken, vol. 4 (Hannover 1772).

Struensee, Carl August von: Abhandlungen über wichtige Gegenstände der Staatswirthschaft, vol. 1 (1800).

Stubenrauch, Moritz von: Commentar zum österreichischen allgemeinen bürgerlichen Gesetzbuch, vol. 2 (6th edn., 1894).

Süßmilch, Johann Peter: Die göttliche Ordnung in den Veränderungen des menschlichen Geschlechts, vol. 2 (2nd edn., Berlin 1762).

Sunnqvist, Martin: Tontines in Scandinavia, in: Phillip Hellwege (ed.), The Past, Present, and Future of Tontines. A Seventeenth Century Financial Product and the Development of Life Insurance (2018), 153–166.

Taussig, A.: Die Versprechungen der 'New-York' und der 'Equitable' (1885).

Tigges, Michael: Geschichte und Entwicklung der Versicherungsaufsicht (1985).

Tőkey, Balázs: Tontines in Hungary, in: Phillip Hellwege (ed.), The Past, Present, and Future of Tontines. A Seventeenth Century Financial Product and the Development of Life Insurance (2018), 289–296.

Troßbach, Werner: Der Schatten der Aufklärung. Bauern, Bürger und Illuminaten in der Grafschaft Wied-Neuwied (1991).

Ventzke, Marcus: Das Herzogtum Sachsen-Weimar-Eisenach 1775–1783. Ein Modellfall aufgeklärter Herrschaft? (2004).

Voet, Johannes: Commentarius ad Pandectas (1698).

Vogel, Emil Ferdinand: Geschichte der denkwürdigsten Erfindungen von der ältesten bis auf die neueste Zeit, vol. 3 (1843).

Vogenauer, Stefan: Contracts in Favour of a Third Party, in: Jürgen Basedow et al. (eds.), The Max Planck Encyclopedia of European Private Law, vol. 1 (2012), 385–388.

Wächter, Carl Georg von: Pandekten, vol. 2 (1881).

Wagenvoort, Herman: Tontines, Een onderzoek naar de geschiedenis van de lijfrenten bij wijze van tontine in de contracten van overleving in de Republiek der Verenigde Nederlanden (1961).

Wagner, Fred: Gabler. Versicherungslexikon (2011).

Waldeck, Philipp Gottfried Ludwig Wilhelm: Controversen-Entscheidungen des gemeinschaftlichen Ober-Appellationsgerichts des Herzogthums Braunschweig und der Fürstenthümer Waldeck, Pyrmont, Lippe, und Schaumburg-Lippe zu Wolfenbüttel, vol. 1 (1827).

Walter, Ferdinand: System des gemeinen deutschen Privatrechts (1855).

Wandel, Eckhard: Banken und Versicherungen im 19. und 20. Jahrhundert (1998).

Warneyer, Otto: Kommentar zum Bürgerlichen Gesetzbuch für das Deutsche Reich, vol. 1 (2nd edn., 1930).

Warschauer, Otto: Lotteriestudien (1912).

Weinert. Jan-Hendrik: Tontines in Europe Today, in: Phillip Hellwege (ed.), The Past, Present, and Future of Tontines. A Seventeenth Century Financial Product and the Development of Life Insurance (2018), 317–327.

Weishaar, Jakob Friedrich: Handbuch des Würtembergischen Privatrechts, vol. 3 (1833).

Wesenberg, Gerhard: Verträge zugunsten Dritter (1949).

Wiarda, Tileman Dothias: Ostfriesische Geschichte, vol. 8 (Aurich 1798).

Wienfort, Monika: Geschichte Preußens (2008).

Wiese, Gustav L.: Die Tontinen-Versicherung der 'Equitable' Lebens-Versicherungs-Gesellschaft in New-York (1892).

– Treu und Glauben der Equitable Lebensversicherungs-Gesellschaft New-York im Lichte der Wahrheit (1892).

Wild, Albert: Die Leibrenten-, Lebensversicherungs- und Renten-Anstalten. Eine theoretische und praktische Anleitung (1862).

Willenberg, Samuel Friedrich: Dissertatio juridica de vitalitio (Danzig 1701).

Winiwarter, Joseph: Das Oesterreichische bürgerliche Recht, vol. 4 (2nd edn., 1844).

Winter, Gerrit: Versicherungsaufsichtsrecht. Kritische Betrachtungen (2007).

Wolgast, Eike: Hochstift und Reformation. Studien zur Geschichte der Reichskirche zwischen 1517 und 1648 (1995).

Wood, Henry Trueman: A History of the Royal Society of Arts (1913).

Wortner, Manfred: Wandlungen der Lebensversicherung. Eine rechtliche und demographische Untersuchung (1972).

Wyler, Julius: Die Tontinen in Frankreich (1916).

Zedler, Johann Heinrich (ed.): Grosses vollständiges Universal-Lexicon aller Wissenschaften und Künste, vol. 44 (Leipzig 1745).

Zedtwitz, Clemens von: Die rechtsgeschichtliche Entwicklung der Versicherung (1999).

Zeller, G.: French Diplomacy and Foreign Policy in their European Setting, in: F.L. Carsten (ed.), The New Cambridge Modern History, vol. 5 (1969), 198–221.

Zetzsche, Dirk A.: Prinzip der kollektiven Vermögensanlage (2015).

Ziegler, Rudolph Heinrich: Dissertatio Juridica de Emtione Vitalitii (Erfurt 1708).

Zimmermann: Sendschreiben an die verehrliche Direction der Hamburgischen Versorgungs-Tontine und die dabei Interssirten Actionaire (1832).

Zimmermann, Reinhard: The Law of Obligations. Roman Foundations of the Civilian Tradition (1996).

Zincke, Georg Heinrich (ed.): Leipziger Sammlungen von wirthschafftlichen Policey-, Cammer- und Finantz-Sachen, vol. 18 (1744).

Index